The Dinosaur Project

The Dinosaur Project

The Story of the Greatest
Dinosaur Expedition Ever Mounted

Wayne Grady

THE EX TERRA FOUNDATION

EDMONTON

MACFARLANE WALTER & ROSS

TORONTO

Macfarlane Walter & Ross
37A Hazelton Avenue
Toronto, Canada M5R 2E3

The Ex Terra Foundation, a non-profit organization based in Edmonton, Alberta, Canada, is the sponsor and
coordinator of The Dinosaur Project, a joint scientific venture between Canada and China. Three of these
countries' most prestigious scientific institutions, the Canadian Museum of Nature, Ottawa, The Royal
Tyrrell Museum of Palaeontology, Drumheller, Alberta, and the Institute of Vertebrate Paleontology and
Paleoanthropology, Beijing, China, are scientific partners in The Dinosaur Project. Chief paleontologists of
the project are: Dr. Philip Currie of the RTMP, Dr. Dale Russell of the CMN, and Prof. Dong Zhiming of the
IVPP. The governments of Canada and Alberta have provided ongoing support and seed monies for both the
scientific and public programs of The Dinosaur Project including *The Dinosaur Project*. The assistance of the
above and all those who have helped is most gratefully acknowledged.

CANADIAN CATALOGUING IN PUBLICATION DATA
Grady, Wayne
        The dinosaur project : the story of the greatest
dinosaur hunt ever mounted

Includes index.
ISBN 0-921912-46-3

1. Dinosaurs - Alberta.   2. Dinosaurs - Canada,
Northern.   3. Dinosaurs - Gobi desert (Mongolia
and China). I. Title

QE862.D5G73 1993   567.9'1   C93-094147-0

The publisher acknowledges the support of the Ontario Arts Council.

Printed and bound in Canada

For Merilyn, again

CONTENTS

ACKNOWLEDGMENTS

MANY PEOPLE AND INSTITUTIONS HELPED ME DURING THE THREE YEARS IT took to research and write this book, too many to thank individually. But I do want to mention those who were especially generous, who gave me their time and their patience when there was little of either to spare, who favored me with their friendship, and who understood the importance of getting it right.

At the Ex Terra Foundation, Glenn Rollans and John Acorn made me feel confident that the task was possible, and I was possibly right for it. Mike Todor is a fine photographer and a great traveling companion. Linda Strong-Watson went over the manuscript as if it were a microsite, and proved there is always something new to be found. She also lent me her geo hammer in the Gobi Desert, and I still have it. Brian Noble and Kevin Taft both helped me to see several sides of a very complex and fascinating story.

Phil Currie, Don Brinkman, and Dave Eberth, of the Royal Tyrrell Museum of Paleontology, spent many hours thinking out loud for my benefit, a privilege for which I am extremely grateful. Dale Russell, of the Canadian Museum of Nature, showed me how science can move from wonder to knowledge and back to wonder again, a very valuable lesson. Kieran Shepherd taught me not to go prospecting in the desert with a bag of salted peanuts and no water bottle, and to laugh when you do. And Clayton Kennedy can come to get his *bai-jo* back any time.

In China, my conversations and field trips with Dong Zhiming and Zhao Xijin of the Institute of Vertebrate Paleontology and Paleoanthropology were enjoyable and informative. Chang Meeman and Qui Zhanxiang were also very helpful. And I especially want to thank Li Rong and Peng Jianghua for inviting me to their homes. Closer to home, I wish to express my gratitude to Betty Corson, who took my first draft and gently but firmly steered me toward a better second, and to Wendy Thomas, who helped produce an even better third (or was it fourth?). And especially to Jan Walter, who somehow managed to stay calm and supportive through all of them.

Finally, I want to gratefully acknowledge the support of the Canada Council, which gave me the time to put the finishing touches to a long and exhilarating project.

THE WOMAN ON THE PING-PONG TABLE HAS SHORT, GRAY HAIR AND WEARS A blue Adidas track suit and black cloth shoes with white plastic soles. She is giving lessons in the ancient Chinese art of Chi Gong, standing on the table with her eyes closed, swaying back and forth, her knees slightly bent and her arms held out chest high with her palms turned down in the classic Standing-on-Stake position. As she weaves, she speaks to the crowd gathered around her in a voice that is both soothing and commanding. "Concentrate on your breathing," she tells them. "Imagine you are breathing through your navel." The people in the crowd — elderly Han Chinese in blue Mao jackets, middle-aged workers in white nylon blouses, adolescents in tan Red Army uniforms or white dress shirts tucked into loose trousers, young Mongolian children in running shoes and blue jeans, all of whom live here in Urad Houqi, a remote village in Inner Mongolia — obediently raise their arms, bend their knees, close their eyes, and think about breathing. The woman on the Ping-Pong table tells them to relax, to spread their fingers and keep their arms parallel to the ground, to breathe very, very slowly, to be intensely aware of their *dan tian*, the point on their abdomen exactly five centimeters below the navel. They must learn to "listen to the *dan tian*, think about the *dan tian*, pay attention to the *dan tian*." The *dan tian* is the center of their bodies' electromagnetic energy — their *chi* — and controlling the *chi* is the way to promote health and prevent disease.

Soon everyone in the room is swaying back and forth, the children faster and less precisely than the adults. In a few minutes, loud sobs are heard from here and

there in the crowd, deep, soul-wrenching sighs, as though from people releasing
emotions that have built up inside them for generations. Long, low moans. Short,
staccato barks. The swaying intensifies; some seem to be rolling about uncon-
trollably, about to capsize. The woman's voice continues to soothe and command.
Suddenly a young man, wearing a baggy white shirt tucked into shiny black pants,
throws his head back and begins to crow like a rooster, shouting exultantly and
tossing his long hair again and again. He begins to strut about the room, eyes
squeezed shut, arms stiff as oars, crowing. The others peer at him through half-
opened lids, then close their eyes again to contemplate their *dan tian*.

The Canadians in the crowd are also standing with closed eyes, bent knees,
and raised arms. Phil Currie's 190-cm frame towers over the heads of the Chinese.
His eyes are closed. Don Brinkman's eyes are closed, his head bowed. He seems
to be asleep on his feet. Dave Eberth's eyes are closed so tightly that his forehead
is creased; he is not asleep. The woman on the Ping-Pong table opens her eyes
and glances over at him from time to time. Mike Todor is not even pretending to
be asleep; his eyes are wide open and his hands have slipped down to about waist
height. He is staring at the young man who is crowing. I am watching everyone:
the woman on the Ping-Pong table, the crowing rooster, the other Canadians, the
small children who somehow manage to concentrate on their *dan tian* while
pulling at each other's socks. What is it, I wonder, that brings this unlikely combination of people together to this distant corner of the Gobi Desert?

Phil's blond head seems to glow in the dim light that filters in through the
gymnasium's dusty windows, and I remember he once told me that he thought
of paleontology as a huge, dark building with only a few windows lit up, and that
all he could do as a paleontologist was walk around outside it, peering in through
the lighted windows to try to get some idea of the layout of the rooms. Standing
here now, it occurs to me that that is not a bad analogy for this book. Here we are
in July 1990; this is one lit window. Peek through another and we see Phil Currie,
aged eleven, curled up in his parents' living room in Port Credit, Ontario, reading
a thin book by Roy Chapman Andrews called *All About Dinosaurs*. Another window shows Roy Chapman Andrews himself, leading the American Museum of
Natural History Expedition into Mongolia, brushing sand off a fossilized bone in
the Gobi Desert in 1926, and his chief paleontologist Walter Granger shouting

exuberantly, "Roy, the stuff is here!" A fourth window opens on a vast Cretaceous plain in what is now Alberta, cut by a shallow inland sea along whose flat, sandy shore is strung out, as if in perpetual migration, a herd of vaguely familiar animals — *Centrosaurus*. A fifth shows a scene 90 million years older, a huge chunk of land — what will eventually be mainland China — drifting away from a larger landmass known as Laurasia to become the isolated breeding ground for dinosaurs that might or might not have been the ancestors of the centrosaurs. All of these scenes, giving into vast stretches of time and covering huge masses of space, come together to form a tentative sketch of what will be known to history as the Dinosaur Project.

ITS UNOFFICIAL NAME IS THE CANADA-CHINA DINOSAUR PROJECT, A UNIQUE COOP-erative program involving the scientific communities of two of the richest fossil-bearing countries in the world. Every year for five years, Canadian paleontologists traveled to the remoter regions of China to hunt for dinosaurs, and in return, Chinese scientists came to Alberta and the Canadian Arctic to do likewise. It was the most extensive, comprehensive field expedition in the history of paleontology — larger than the Andrews expeditions, larger than the Sino-Soviet Expedition of 1959-60. The administrative effort alone was staggering. Field camps accommodated as many as fifty scientists, students, technicians, drivers, cooks, photographers, film makers, and writers, whose combined contribution to the world's store of dinosaur lore, of dinosaur material, will take decades to sort out and quantify. The results of their work will mark a new stage in the advance of our knowledge of life on this planet.

Although the first scientists didn't actually take to the field until 1986, the Project was begun in 1980 (that is, if we forget about Laurasia and the centrosaurs for the moment) in Edmonton, the year the Alberta government set up the Paleontological Museum and Research Institute, a fancy name for a director, technicians, and a part-time communications coordinator whose job it was to come up with a location for a new paleontological museum that was to become the Royal Tyrrell Museum. One member of the new group was a young paleontologist who had been a curator at the Provincial Museum — Phil Currie. The communications coordinator was Brian Noble, an anthropologist and a man of great vision and

After talking to Phil Currie, Brian Noble formed the Ex Terra Foundation in 1982 to set up a scientific exchange between Canada and China: "I saw it as a sort of Dinosaurs for Peace."

energy who had worked with Phil in Dinosaur Provincial Park as a naturalist and who then went to the Provincial Museum as a publicist. The institute operated out of an office on the third floor of Edmonton's Boardwalk Building, above a large shopping concourse and food emporium that now contains, among other things, an Alberta gem store that sells jewelry made from fossilized marine creatures of the Triassic Period and a restaurant that specializes in beer and ribs.

One day Brian and Phil fell into a discussion about dreams. If Phil could have unlimited access to funding and logistics, Brian asked him, if he could go anywhere in the world to hunt for dinosaurs, where would he go?

Phil's answer was immediate: "Mongolia."

All About Dinosaurs, Roy Chapman Andrews's action-packed account of his bone-hunting adventures in various remote regions of the globe — dinosaurs seem always to be found in remote regions — begins with the words, "Dinosaurs are the strangest animals that ever existed on this earth. They were the kind of creatures you might think of as inhabiting another planet, or the kind you might dream of in a bad nightmare." One of the remotest regions described by Andrews was the Gobi Desert: "As you can imagine," Andrews wrote, "a desert is the best place in which to find fossils. That is because it has little vegetation to cover the top of the ground. The greatest desert in Asia is the Gobi. It stretches east and west through the center of Mongolia for 2,000 miles. A thirsty land; a land of desolation! A gravel desert with only stunted sagebrush, clumps of wire-like grass, and thorny bushes! Gazelles, wild asses, and wolves ranged the marching sands. Mongols, some of whom had never seen a white man, were the only people." The

Phil Currie (top) became chief paleontologist at Alberta's Royal Tyrrell Museum (left) the same year the Dinosaur Project was launched: "I had two dreams come true at the same time," he says. One of the first scientists contacted by Noble was Dale Russell, curator of fossil vertebrates at the Canadian Museum of Nature in Ottawa and one of the foremost paleontologists in the world. Dale had prospected for dinosaurs on every continent but Asia, and he eagerly accepted.

marching sands. A thirsty land. The only people. The day after he finished reading *All About Dinosaurs*, Phil told his parents that he wanted to be a paleontologist. His parents thought he had said pathologist and gave their consent.

Fulfilling a childhood dream was perhaps reason enough to want to go to Mongolia, but Phil had strong paleontological incentives as well. In recent years — since China's isolationist policies began to thaw in the late 1970s — Mongolia had emerged as one of the world's richest sources of dinosaurs; unlike Canada or even the United States, Mongolia has the complete faunal record of the Age of the Dinosaurs, all 150,000 millenia of it, with exposures dating from the Early Triassic to the Late Cretaceous periods in geological history. Eighty-five different genera of dinosaurs — a quarter of all those known to science — have been found there, most of them in the past two decades. Descriptions of Mongolian fossils had been leaking out in various scientific publications, but as Phil told Brian, "No one has compared Mongolian dinosaurs with those from North America." Phil suspected that the animals were not only related, but possibly the same, and he wanted to find out. A new expedition into central Asia, he said, would be one of the most rewarding paleontological enterprises of the century. Bonehunters had been digging up parts of the Gobi where no Western scientist had ever set foot, not even Roy Chapman Andrews, and they were finding species of dinosaurs that no Western paleontologist had ever seen.

Brian mulled over Phil's answer off and on for two years while preparations for the new museum plodded ahead. Discussions about its location bogged down; from a practical point of view, the best place to put it was in Brooks, a small town near the entrance to Dinosaur Provincial Park (where most of the museum's dinosaurs would come from, and where most of the people interested in seeing dinosaurs would go), but there was political pressure to place it in Drumheller (an even smaller town whose population of 40,000 during the heyday of coal mining had dwindled to 7,000). Phil became less and less interested in the administration of the museum and more and more eager to find dinosaurs to put in it; a new director, David Baird, was brought in, and when Drumheller was chosen as the site, Baird moved there in 1982, and Phil moved with him. Brian opted to stay in Edmonton. For one thing, his wife Marna was still studying art at the University of Alberta. Casting about for a new project, he remembered Phil's desire to go to the Gobi. As an anthropologist, he was interested in examining the cultural links between Mongolia and the native peoples of North America, and Phil's paleontological aspirations fit nicely into his own preoccupations. He knew that Carl Sagan had organized a joint space program between the United States and the Soviet Union that had fostered a great deal of understanding and respect on both sides, and he thought that a similar venture might be possible in the fields of paleontology and anthropology, "a sort of Dinosaurs for Peace," as he says. After more talks with Phil, they came up with a plan for a foundation that would raise money to send both of them to Mongolia. They called it Ex Terra: "From the Earth."

In January 1983, Brian applied to the Canada Council for an Explorations Grant to look into the possibility of setting up a Canada-Mongolia scientific exchange. He was given $8,700. Later that year he also applied for and received $10,000 from Bill Byrne at the Alberta Ministry of Culture to work on a marketing plan for a traveling exhibit of any artifacts resulting from such an exchange.

U.S.S.R.

JUNGGAR
BASIN

XINJIANG

Ulaan
Baator •

MONGOLIA

INNER MONGOLIA

GOBI DESERT

ORDOS
BASIN

Hohhot

Beijing

JAPAN

INDIA

PEOPLE'S REPUBLIC
OF
CHINA

Shanghai

China and Mongolia

0   1000 km
0   500 mi.

N

Hong
Kong

He hired Glenn Rollans, a longtime friend and former director of the International Affairs Summer School in Canmore, Alberta, where 160 of the province's top high-school students gathered every year to hear lectures and attend seminars with experts from External Affairs, the United Nations, and the Canadian International Development Agency. As Glenn says, "I had a lot of experience running a good, solid program with no resources to speak of. It was great preparation for Ex Terra." His job at Ex Terra was to canvass every museum in the world large enough to mount an exhibition of dinosaur material from Alberta and central Asia and ask them to indicate their moral support of such a project in writing. With a rented IBM Selectric and an $80 printing budget, he put together 150 information packages, sent them to such places as the American Museum of Natural History, the British Museum, and "any place else that looked like it might have an interest in scientific displays." By the end of the year, forty museums had written back saying they would like to hear more.

All they needed then was a show of interest from Mongolia. The problem here was twofold: first, there was no such place as Mongolia. The country Roy Chapman Andrews had led his team of American scientists into sixty-five years earlier had been divided into Outer Mongolia and Inner Mongolia and was under the quite distinct control of the Soviet Union and China, respectively. The actual site the Andrews expedition had worked, called by them the Flaming Cliffs, was in a Cretaceous river valley that was now part of Outer Mongolia. Accordingly, Brian flew to Moscow, where he encountered the second problem. Relations between Moscow and Outer Mongolia were in one of their off-again phases. No one in Moscow would speak to him about anything to do with Outer Mongolia. Eventually, he contacted the Canadian ambassador, Geoffrey Pearson, who gave him the name of the director of the Outer Mongolian Museum in Ulaan Baator, the capital. Brian wrote a long letter outlining his project and soliciting a show of support from Mongolia, to which he received no reply at all.

Meanwhile, things at home had begun to cool down. The new museum opened in Drumheller and was named the Tyrrell Museum of Paleontology (now the Royal Tyrrell Museum of Paleontology), after Joseph Burr Tyrrell, one of the first geologists to explore the Alberta badlands. Phil was fully occupied with setting up the museum's field and laboratory schedules. Linda Strong-Watson, who had worked with Phil at the Provincial Museum, was now chief technician at the Tyrrell. David Baird, the Tyrrell's director, was somewhat skeptical of Ex Terra's ability to pull off such an extraordinarily complicated international coup and was reluctant to lend it much support. "I don't think this is the kind of thing a bunch of amateurs should be doing," he told Brian. "This is the Tyrrell's jurisdiction." And although Brian had elicited some early excitement from Dale Russell, chief paleontologist at the National Museum of Natural Sciences in Ottawa — "Mongolia is okay," Dale had told Brian, "but where I'd really like to go is Xinjiang: Brian, let's talk about sauropods" — Dale's boss, Chuck Gruchy, was impatient to get going and felt that Ex Terra wasn't moving fast enough. He also wanted to expand the project to include the Canadian Arctic, which was the National Museum's jurisdiction. "We began," Glenn says, "to feel very isolated."

Then, in April 1985, a ray of light appeared from a completely unexpected source. Brian received a call from an acquaintance, Edmonton businessman Erick

**Chang Meeman (left) was director of Beijing's Institute of Vertebrate
Paleontology and Paleoanthropology (IVPP) in 1985, when Brian Noble
approached her with his plans for the Dinosaur Project.**

Schmidt, who said he was going to China as part of an Alberta trade mission to
sell Canadian laser technology to the Chinese government and suggested that
while he was there he could contact scientists on Ex Terra's behalf. There might,
he said, be a chance of organizing something through Beijing rather than Moscow.
Brian agreed. He had already despaired of Outer Mongolia; perhaps there was
hope for Inner Mongolia.

The director of China's Institute of Vertebrate Paleontology and Paleoanthropology (IVPP) in Beijing at the time was Chang Meeman, a soft-spoken,
forthright, and far-seeing specialist in Permian fish who had been educated at
Oxford and had spent many years working in the West — she knew Dale Russell's
brother Donald, who was also a paleontologist and who had been working in
France — and she had a pretty shrewd idea about exactly what China could gain
from a scientific association with Western specialists. Schmidt visited her in May,
saying he came from a friend in Canada and would like to propose a joint project

to look for dinosaurs. The two talked for a while, and when Schmidt left, Meeman discussed the proposal with several of her colleagues. "We had had similar proposals from other countries," she says. "France, for example, and the Soviet Union. My colleagues had worked with Soviet anthropologists before, and it seemed to me they were not terrifically happy about the idea of working with them again. And France doesn't have many dinosaurs — their scientists have to go to North Africa. And the United States did not offer to let our scientists travel to their country. So we agreed that it would be more interesting to have a joint project with Canada."

The next day Schmidt telephoned Meeman to say that a Saudi Arabian sheik who had come to Beijing to meet with the Canadian trade delegation had offered to take Schmidt in his private aircraft to see the terra-cotta army in Xi'an. Would Meeman like to come along? They could talk on the plane. Acting uncharacteristically on the spur of the moment, Meeman said yes.

The plane — actually on loan from the Chinese Red Army — left Beijing at five o'clock the next morning. Schmidt and Meeman spent the better part of the three-hour flight discussing the proposed project in general terms; according to Meeman, the conversation had a vague, wouldn't-it-be-nice-if tone to it, but then, on the return trip, Schmidt printed out a memorandum of agreement on his portable computer and asked Meeman to sign it. Meeman was taken aback. "I told him it would be a bit difficult for me to sign it," she says. People don't just sign things in China. She would have to receive permission from the IVPP's parent organization, Academia Sinica, before committing her government to such a venture. "But Mr. Schmidt said it was just a joke paper," she says. "He said he wouldn't show it to anybody." By now, the whole venture had taken on a kind of fairy-tale aura — the pre-dawn flight to Xi'an, the ghostly majesty of the terra-cotta army, talk about an international agreement. "So I signed it," she says with a small smile, "and we asked the sheik's secretary to sign as a witness, just for fun. We told him that the sheik was very rich, maybe he would support the project, and we all laughed and went home."

A few months later, Meeman received a telephone call from the Academia Sinica. "They said they had something signed by me. They said it looked like some kind of agreement, and they asked me how I could have signed such a document.

I told them that Dr. Schmidt and I had just talked about the possibilities, that the paper was not a formal agreement, that it was just for fun. In the end," she says, after a pause, "the people from the Academy were very kind. They understood. So, we went on."

That August, while Meeman was in Japan attending a symposium on Indo-Pacific fish fossils, Brian flew to Tokyo to meet her in person. She wasn't expecting him, but when he tapped her on the shoulder after a lecture she agreed to go for a stroll with him in Owano Park. "I was absorbed in the fish business," she says, "and not very interested in dinosaurs, but he was insistent." They sat down on a park bench and talked through the lunch hour, and Meeman agreed to try to set up a meeting in Beijing. That meeting took place later in the year. Brian met Chang Ming Cheng, the former head of the IVPP and the man who had co-directed the Sino-Soviet Expedition. Chang Ming Cheng introduced him to Yu Chao, one of China's top young graduate students in paleontology. Yu Chao told Brian, "I would very much like to study dinosaurs with Dr. Philip Currie."

After that, things moved quickly. The following year, in May 1986, Sun Ailing, the IVPP's assistant director, and Dong Zhiming, head of dinosaur research, flew to Edmonton and signed a Memorandum of Understanding at the Provincial Museum. The Dinosaur Project — the first expedition of Western scientists into Central Asia in sixty years, and one of the largest ever — was official. What happened after that is the subject of this book.

THE WOMAN ON THE PING-PONG TABLE HAS EVIDENTLY DECIDED THAT DAVE Eberth's *chi* is not moving in sufficient quantities from his *dan tian* to his *zuqiao*, the next acupoint in the greater circuit, so she hops down from her perch and begins to thread toward him through the entranced crowd. As she moves she waves her arms gracefully in the air, pushing at it with her hands, gesturing toward the spines of people as she passes. Some of the people she gestures toward call out in alarm, some start laughing, others start to cry. Dave's eyes remain still tightly closed. When she reaches him, she begins to run her hands along his back, without quite touching him. Her hands wipe invisible water from his shoulders, from his arms, from his sides. With both hands, she grabs an intangible clump of matter from the air behind his neck and heaves it away from him. Dave remains unmoved, but the man standing beside him, who has been weaving back and forth in his sleep, suddenly falls backward like a plank, hits his head on the concrete floor with a dull thud, and lies perfectly still. Dave opens his eyes. The woman turns from him and makes a perfunctory gesture toward the man on the floor, who instantly sits up and begins to rub the back of his head. The ceremony is over. Throughout the room, the spell is broken. People begin to collect their coats and shoes and begin to leave.

Outside the gymnasium, in the bright, dusty courtyard where a dozen young men are playing pool on tables set out in the open air, I find myself standing beside the man who fell to the floor. I ask him what he had felt.

"Nothing," he said. "*Fa.*"

"What is *fa?*"

"*Fa*," he says, making the same gesture with his hands that the woman had made inside, "*fa* is a kind of pushing, a kind of dreaming." He looks at me. "You enter a different place."

Fa, I think, has brought us here.

CHAPTER 1

Taking Flight
Tang Zhilu's braincase and the dinosaur-bird theory

THE ALBERTA BADLANDS FOLLOW THE RIVER VALLEYS, LONG, DEEP TRENCHES CUT through the flesh of the earth. You drive across flat, fertile prairie until you come upon them, so suddenly that you barely have time to realize that the dark line ahead of you is a hole before the road plunges down a coulee and descends ninety meters to the bottom. At first you think you have entered some dead place, a nightmare landscape of giant hoodoos and gray, wrinkled buttes like ancient elephants sleeping in the sun, crumbling cliffs with mean, shriveled vegetation at their bases, and the merest trickle of brown water carving its desultory way between them.

Where the rivers bend, there are sand-and-gravel flood plains, and here the vegetation is thick and the air is cool. The size of the gravel suggests that at times the river must run high and fast, but in midsummer it seems to lie there waiting for someone to tilt the ground. At the water's edge, among the cottonwoods and tumbleweed and sage-brush and prickly-pear cactus, there are abandoned ranch buildings and the bleached skulls of dead cattle. Higher up, away from the river, in the hot canyons and coulees where the dinosaurs are found, there is not the slightest hint of wind or shade or coolness. There is furtive sound, but you feel like the only living, moving thing. "To approach the badlands," writes Alberta novelist Robert Kroetsch, "is to find a gap in the known and expected world."

During the last week in August 1986, Li Rong and Tang Zhilu, two Chinese paleontologists, were picking their way through the stretch of the Red Deer River badlands known as Dead Lodge Canyon, at the center of Dinosaur Provincial Park. It was hot and tiring work, with the temperature over 37 degrees Celsius by ten

**Sandstone bluffs in the Alberta badlands in Dinosaur Provincial Park,
laid down 75 million years ago and exposed during the last Ice Age,
have yielded more dinosaurs than any other Cretaceous site in the world.**

o'clock in the morning. It was also discouraging work. They knew they were walking through some of the richest exposures of fossil-bearing rock in North America. More dinosaur bones had been taken out of Dead Lodge Canyon than from any other comparable site in the world. The skeletons, buried here in sand, silt, and volcanic ash more than 70 million years ago, had been fossilized by the unimaginably slow action of water upon bone, minerals in the water gradually filling in the spaces and pores, millennia upon millennia, epoch after epoch, until the bone had become a perfect image of itself in stone that yet retained most of its original chemical material. The sand around it, meanwhile, had been compressed and hardened into sandstone, softer than the fossilized bone, and the volcanic ash had hardened into clay that turns into a thick gumbo when wet and crumbles into powder underfoot when dry. Wind and rain and river had eroded the sandstone and clay, turning them back into sand and dust, leaving the fossilized bone intact and, in some places, exposed. Despite the cactus and the sage-brush, the badlands are no desert. Dinosaur Provincial Park receives up to forty centimeters of rain a year, and the rain erodes the soft sandstone away from the cliff walls and valley floor, exposing new skeletons all the time. Paleontologists who have prospected the badlands for years keep coming back to see what new treasures the elements have exposed.

Li Rong and Tang Zhilu had been prospecting this same portion of the park since arriving in Alberta in late June. Their home was a small trailer at the park entrance, the usual accommodation for park staff, and in it they cooked their own food, did their own laundry, and at night wrote up their field notes and charted the next day's routes over the parched gray landscape that surrounded them.

It was the first season of the Dinosaur Project, the first time either Li Rong or Tang Zhilu had been out of China, and no one had a very clear idea of what to expect — except that they would find dinosaurs and learn a few things about Western paleontological techniques in the process. Peter May, the paleotechnician with the Tyrrell Museum in Drumheller who was running the dinosaur program in the park in June, recalls that for the first few months "things weren't that organized. We were trying to understand what they wanted us to teach them, what they wanted to look at." Neither spoke a word of English. Their sponsor in Beijing allowed them the equivalent of one Canadian dollar a day for expenses, the same amount they would have received in China, and the Tyrrell Museum was paying for their food. Peter would drive them down to Brooks to buy groceries and guide them through the bewildering array of packages in the town's supermarket. He took them to a rodeo in Patricia and introduced them to the Patricia Hotel, whose western-style restaurant, called the Steak Pit, featured a huge barbecue in the corner on which guests could cook their own beef or buffalo steaks.

Also with Peter, they had collected a horned *Centrosaurus* skull, complete with the identifying neck frill, and the six-meter trunk of a fossil tree for display in the park's field station. But since the end of June, they had found little else worth keeping: a few fragments of fossilized turtle shell, scraps of dinosaur bone, some *Albertosaurus* teeth. They had studied preparation techniques in the field station's small laboratory, and by August, when Linda Strong-Watson, the Tyrrell's head technician, took over from Peter, they had settled into a routine of lab work and prospecting without much hope of finding anything big. It was August 23, and they were scheduled to return to China on the twenty-sixth. They were caught in a state of ambiguity familiar to scientists, the feeling that things were winding down and there hadn't been a major find, tempered with the knowledge that major finds are often made on the last day of the field season.

Tang Zhilu is tall, well over 180 cm, with dark features and straight black hair. He is the principal technician with the Institute of Vertebrate Paleontology and Paleoanthropology (IVPP) in Beijing, having joined the institute in 1975 while still a geology student at the University of Beijing. In China, university students find jobs or are assigned to them before they graduate and then go to postgraduate school to train for them. After graduating in 1979, Tang Zhilu became a full-time research assistant at the IVPP and spent two years in south-central China, in the Middle Jurassic beds of the Sichuan Basin. It, too, was a dinosaur-rich area; over the years, more than a hundred skeletons had been dug out of the ground there, including ten specimens of the long-necked sauropod *Shunosaurus*, a new species of the armor-plated stegosaur, as well as a number of fossil fishes, amphibians, and flying reptiles, or pterosaurs.

Tang Zhilu works slowly and methodically, like a fine carpenter. He savors the color of rock — different colored stones talk to him about the different kinds of dinosaurs they conceal. He especially likes green sandstone, because in China it is often associated with the great dinosaurs — the sandstone in Sichuan is green. But there is no green sandstone in Dinosaur Park. After green sandstone he likes red sandstone, where the hooded *Protoceratops* are found. None of that here, either. The park is gray, with shades of brown and red and even black, sandy deposits laid down in the Cretaceous by fast-moving streams as they emptied into shallow embayments of a huge interior sea. This gray sandstone, however, contains most of the same dinosaur families — even some of the same genera — found in the red sandstone of Inner Mongolia. Tang finds this puzzling. One of the reasons he is here — in fact, one of the aims of the Dinosaur Project — is to determine why this should be so.

Li Rong is the head of vertebrate paleontology at the Inner Mongolian Museum in Hohhot, the capital city of Inner Mongolia. Many of China's best dinosaur localities are in Inner Mongolia, and Li Rong is one of the few people who knows where they are. He is a walker. Despite his preference for wearing ordi-

The IVPP's chief technician, Tang Zhilu (left), spent two years in China's Sichuan Basin, an area almost as rich in fossils as Alberta's badlands, before joining the Dinosaur Project. Li Rong, head of vertebrate paleontology at the Inner Mongolian Museum in Hohhot, is an expert at finding Inner Mongolia's most abundant dinosaur localities. He is best known for finding China's largest dinosaur trackway, at Chabusumu, in the Ordos Basin.

nary street shoes and pressed trousers in the field, he has walked hundreds of kilometers across the Gobi Desert, collecting dinosaur bones for his museum. Two years before, in 1984, while prospecting in the Ordos Basin, he had been told by some local shepherds about a valley paved with bird footprints near Chabusumu, and he had walked there. What he discovered were dinosaur footprints, one thousand of them, covering an area forty-three kilometers long and thirteen kilometers wide. It turned out to be China's largest dinosaur trackway site. Some of the prints were the size of elephant tracks; others were less than two and a half centimeters across. Li Rong walked the entire area and mapped every single footprint — a process that involved measuring the height, width, and depth of every imprint as well as the distance between them. It took him all summer. The next year he and two assistants returned to the valley and removed a slab of rock containing two dozen prints, and beneath it they found layers of fossil fish and crocodile bones. He brought them and the slab back to Hohhot.

It is an axiom of paleontology that dinosaur bones are found in the most inhospitable places on earth, so neither Li Rong nor Tang Zhilu were complaining about the heat. They drank a lot of water. At noon, when they stopped for lunch, they drank a lot more water. Before long, Tang Zhilu stood up and walked around the point of a cliff to relieve himself. It is another axiom that no paleontologist ever stops prospecting. Whether clambering over an outcrop or simply taking a stroll, your eyes flick over the ground around your feet, always ready for that telltale off-white flash that sends a signal to your brain: *bone!* So as Tang Zhilu stood up against the sandstone cliff, his eyes scanned the exposure, swept the debris at the bottom of the coulee, and sifted the loose sand accumulating at his feet.

And then he saw it. Partly washed out of the side of the cliff about thirty centimeters from the ground, the coffee-colored curve of bone that promised to extend farther into the rock face. Quickly, he retrieved his field pack, took out his awl, his paintbrush, his plastic bottle of Glyptal — a mixture of electrically insulating glue and acetone that coats the bone to protect it from the elements — and his geological hammer, and went to work. For half an hour he carefully scratched away at the soft matrix with the awl and brushed away the grains of sand, stopping every so often to daub the newly exposed bone with Glyptal. The sandstone was easy to work, and in a few minutes he had exposed enough bone to realize that there was more embedded in the cliff.

As the surface of bone grew, so did his excitement. To the untrained eye the gnarled, knobby object he was uncovering looked like the inside of a large walnut, but Tang Zhilu recognized it as part of a skull — one of the most important of all paleontological finds, since the skull contains half of an animal's anatomical information. Tang suspected that this one might be bird: it had only one occipital condyle, the upper half of the universal joint that connects the back of the skull to the vertebral column. Mammals and amphibians have two condyles; crocodiles, dinosaurs, and birds have one — but this skull, he thought, was much too small to be crocodile. It *might* be dinosaur, but the size and shape seemed closer to bird. He scraped away.

When he had removed enough of the surrounding matrix to ensure that the skull was not accompanied by any more of the skeleton, he undercut around it and, with the pointed end of his hammer, broke it out of its little cave. The result-

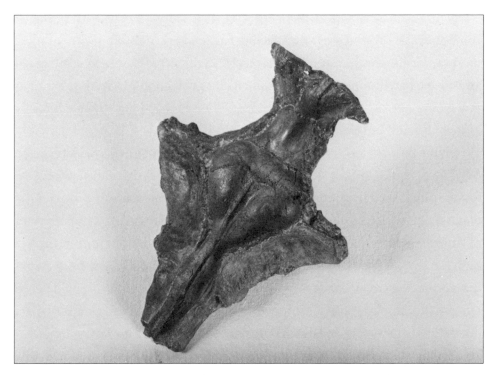

**This braincase, from the dinosaur *Troodon formosus*,
discovered by Tang Zhilu, has enough bird-like features to clinch the century-old
debate about whether or not birds are descended from dinosaurs.**

ing block was about the size and shape of a brick. He put it in his field pack, and that evening, when he returned to the field station, he showed it to two of his Canadian colleagues, Linda Strong-Watson and Kevin Aulenback.

Kevin was one of the first technicians Linda had hired to prepare specimens for the new Tyrrell Museum. Young, enthusiastic, with a shock of brown hair and round wire-rimmed glasses, Kevin is the kind of instinctual amateur whose wild guesses occasionally lead to deeper understandings. His fascination with bones began when he started taking owl pellets apart at the age of seven. By the time he was twelve, he had an extensive collection of mammal skeletons in his bedroom. "My mother used to get mad at me for boiling cougar skulls on the kitchen stove," he says. His knowledge of skeletal anatomy is precise and scientific; he can look at a tiny white bone the size of a pinhead and tell you it is a meadow vole's third metatarsal. This ability had impressed Linda at the Provincial Museum of Alberta when Kevin applied for a summer job there while still an undergraduate at the

Northern Alberta Institute of Technology. Linda sat him down with a fragmented rhinoceros jaw on which her own technicians had been working without much headway for six months. Kevin had never seen a rhinoceros jaw before, but in half an hour he had fit nine new pieces onto it. He got the job. He worked with Phil in the dinosaur lab, assembling skeletons. When Phil and the others left for the Tyrrell Museum in Drumheller, Kevin went with them.

In the field station's preparation lab, Kevin examined Tang's discovery carefully. What he saw did not look like a conventional skull — it had no jaw or teeth, for one thing — but he recognized it nonetheless as a braincase, the interior part of the skull that houses the brain. He also knew it was important. The park is full of large dinosaurs, the most common being a type of hadrosaur, one of the herbivorous reptiles about the size of six large horses. So finding bone from an animal smaller than a Shetland pony was a significant event. But Kevin could not yet tell whether this braincase belonged to a dinosaur-sized bird or a bird-sized dinosaur. There was still too much sandstone in and around it — more brick than bone — and so Kevin began to "fine-prep" it quickly so he and Linda could identify it from the stack of illustrations back at the museum in Drumheller. Phil was due back from the Arctic in two days, and Tang Zhilu was returning to China the day after that. Kevin wanted to have the mystery cleared up before then.

Over the next two days, Kevin cleaned off the sandstone, grain by grain, using a dental prod, a compressed-air hose, and a dissecting microscope. The inside of a braincase is a delicate, lace-like labyrinth, and removing the rock that encases it without damaging the filigree of bone is a slow, nerve-racking process. But as Kevin worked, his instincts told him that what was emerging under his scope was not bird but dinosaur. It was enough *like* a bird, however, to make positive identification difficult. He could not wait to show it to Phil.

West Meets East

TANG ZHILU'S DISCOVERY CAME AT THE END OF THE FIRST SUMMER OF THE Dinosaur Project. Work had begun in May, when three Canadians — Phil Currie, Dale Russell, and Brian Noble — flew to China to scout out sites in Xinjiang (pronounced Shin-jang and formerly spelled Sinkiang). Xinjiang's official name is

Xinjiang-Uigyr Autonomous Region and, situated in the extreme northwest, it is known as the gateway to China. Marco Polo entered China through Xinjiang in the thirteenth century, and in the 1930s the Soviet Union eyed the province as the weakest link in the country's 9,600-km border. It turned out to be one of those sparsely populated, vast territories that are at the same time indefensible and impenetrable. The Chinese discovered that ten centuries ago.

Geographically, China is a lot like Canada. The two countries are about the same size: Canada is nearly 10 million square kilometers; China, since the loss of Outer Mongolia, is about 9.6 million. In both countries, the bulk of the population is in the east and south; the west is a series of oil-rich, flat, arid grasslands and mountainous regions; and the north is a sparsely populated territory of starkly beautiful but somewhat terrifying proportions. Although China's population, at 1.3 billion (22 percent of earth's total) is fifty times that of Canada's, the population density in the Gobi Desert — which stretches across the northern roof of the country and occupies about one-sixth of its total area — is less than one person for every two and a half square kilometers, about the same as Canada's Northwest Territories. Mongols and Inuit look startlingly alike and are, in fact, distantly related. The Gobi is China's Arctic.

The Canadian team flew first to Beijing and spent a day or two meeting with IVPP people. Then, accompanied by the IVPP's eminent dinosaur specialist, Dong Zhiming, they boarded a Soviet Tupolev jet liner on Saturday, May 3, and flew to the ancient city of Urumqi, the most inland city in the world. Located on the vanished trade route between Europe and the Orient, Urumqi (pronounced Oo-room-chee), since the discovery of oil in Xinjiang, has become an industrial center. Nestled somewhat incongruously in the foothills of the Tien Shan, or Heavenly Mountains, it is a sort of Chinese Calgary. Its name in Uigyr means "green water," and its 1 million citizens live along poplar-lined boulevards split by open canals that cool and humidify the dry air blown over them from the Taklamakan Desert to the south. Taklamakan in Uigyr means "you enter and never return." Apart from Uigyr, there are twelve other nationalities in Xinjiang, including Kazakh, Tartar, Kirghiz, and Mongol. The Han Chinese, exiled to remote regions of China by Mao Zedong during the famines of the 1960s, comprise less than 5 percent of Xinjiang's population, though they dominate the province's government.

The "Dinosaur People," as the IVPP group was called, were met at the airport by Professor Teng Tingkang, the regional director of Academia Sinica, and the vice-director, a Mr. Gemade, one of Xinjiang's three thousand Tartars. They went to Academia Sinica's Urumqi headquarters, which doubles as a sort of hotel, and the next afternoon, after a day of sightseeing and shopping in Urumqi, the group set off in a Toyota Land Cruiser for Jimsar, an oil town of ten thousand people about 128 km due east of the capital, on the edge of the Junggar Basin.

Xinjiang-Uigyr Autonomous Region is a cluster of deep, dish-shaped depressions separated by great folded mountains, like unglazed bowls set on a high, flat table. The Tien Shan Mountains, forty kilometers to the south of Jimsar, soar more than 5,500 m above sea level, and yet the town itself is barely 915 m, and the Turpan Basin, to the southeast, drains into Lake Aidinghu, the lowest lake in the world at 142 m below sea level. Jimsar is an ancient settlement on the northern Silk Road, built during the Tang Dynasty — it was already four hundred years old when Marco Polo passed through it on his way to Cathay in 1282 — but the boom in oil and coal exploration since the establishment of the People's Republic in 1949 has plunged it into a perpetual state of construction, with new high-rise office towers and hotels going up everywhere. Phil thought of it as "a hotel town."

Although Jimsarians have seen plenty of Russian and French oil engineers in recent years, Phil, Dale, and Brian were the first Westerners to stay at the hotel. The landlord ate with them in a private room; they were served squid and sea cucumber with lots of garlic and boiled mutton. They were joined by Yan Hangyuan, a regional agricultural scientist who kept emptying Phil's beer glass against the restaurant wall and filling it up with Coke. Outside, they were followed everywhere by crowds of curious locals who were fascinated by Phil's height, blond hair, and blue eyes. They trailed him to the bath house and watched through the windows as he showered in the dark.

The next morning, after a breakfast of sweet cake and hot milk, the group left Jimsar and drove east for an hour and a half, passing through desert farmland irrigated with melting snow from the Tien Shan Mountains. After the village of Qitai (Chee-tie), they turned north along a freshly paved oil road toward Jiangjunmiao, a lonely spot in the Junggar badlands where a shrine to a twelfth-century general once stood. They had entered the Gurbantunggut Desert, a western extension of the Gobi, composed of vast sand dunes covered with coarse grass and dotted with oil rigs, yurts, and herds of incurious, semi-wild camels. The jeep went through an army checkpoint, after which the road deteriorated into clay and gravel, and Dong Zhiming pointed out some abandoned adobe houses backed by red ridges of Late Jurassic sandstone — the Shishugou Formation — in which he had found two dinosaur specimens in 1984. They stopped, but Dale noted that the site was "not wonderful for bone," although there were a great many fossilized logs lying about: the basin, although desert now, had been green and fertile 150 million years ago. One of the logs had turned to pure green-white agate and measured twenty-two meters long and nearly a meter across. They spent the night in a truck station called Hongliugou, a kind of motel tucked under a ridge of folded Carboniferous hills drilled through with diamond and gold mines, and the next day they clambered up the Jurassic and Cretaceous beds surrounding Jiangjunmiao. "Found a few bones, but mostly wood," Phil wrote in his field book. That evening they returned to Jimsar.

In their room, Dale and Dong Zhiming talked until one-thirty in the morning about the Project. Although the apparent lack of bone was a concern, they knew that they were in rich dinosaur country: the Junggar Basin had already yielded an extraordinary array of dinosaurs in exposures representing the entire range of dinosaur-bearing rock, from the Triassic to the Cretaceous. The lower beds had contained the primitive, ox-sized therapsid *Lystrosaurus*, a mammal-like reptile older than the dinosaurs; middle formations such as the Shishugou and Wucaiwan had contained a carnosaur — referred to unofficially as "Jiangjunmiaosaurus" — and a sauropod that showed intriguing similarities to the North American *Camarasaurus*, one of the long-necked, long-tailed herbivores that weighed about ten tonnes and measured nearly twelve meters from snout to tailtip. The upper beds of the Tugulu Group had yielded a pterosaur with a wing span of nearly three meters, and the fragmentary remains of a new species of the advanced stegosaur, *Wuerhosaurus*. As they talked, Dale and Dong Zhiming discussed the best place to establish a single field camp that would be convenient to as many of the Junggar's widely distributed and largely untapped riches as possible.

Both Dale and Dong Zhiming exhibit an exuberant approach to paleontology; they love to take vast amounts of information and mold it into patterns of under-

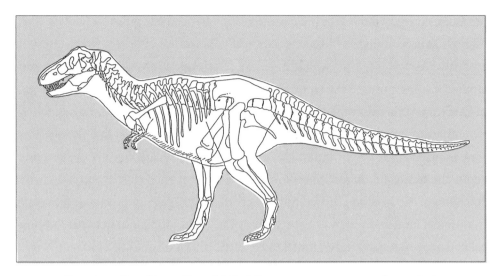

For a long time it was thought that *Tyrannosaurus rex* was descended from earlier large carnivores, such as *Allosaurus*. Evidence unearthed by Dinosaur Project member Tang Zhilu, however, suggests that *T. rex* may in fact have evolved from much smaller dinosaurs, such as *Troodon*.

standing. According to Dale, science is "a way of thinking; it's how we move from what we think we don't know to what we think we know."

Dale is a tall, lanky, intense man who exudes energy as a dynamo exudes a magnetic field. Born in San Francisco in 1937, he grew up on a farm in northeastern Oregon. His brother Donald, who is ten years older than Dale, went to Oregon State College (now Oregon State University) in Eugene and used to send his geology textbooks home for Dale, who was still in grade school at the time. Dale fell in love with the dinosaurs in them. When it was his turn to go to college, he took a Bachelor of Arts with a double major in geology and biology at the University of Oregon, also in Eugene. He now knows that he grew up several kilometers from an island of the central Pacific Ocean that was pushed up into central Oregon sometime during the Jurassic Period. In the 1950s, however, geology was little more than a handmaiden to the oil industry. Dale got his paleontology, he says, "working for Dr. J. Arnold Shotwell of the Museum of Natural History at the university, collecting Neogene mammals from the eastern part of the state." Plate tectonics — the theory that the continents actually float on the earth's molten core — was not widely accepted until the 1960s. Even in Berkeley, where he went to get his Masters, biogeography and drifting continental plates were subjects for students to argue about over beer in the grad pub; bringing them up in class, says Dale, "did you no good at all."

In 1964 Dale traveled east, to Columbia University in New York City, to study under one of the most celebrated paleontologists of the day. Edwin H. Colbert was curator and chairman of the Department of Vertebrate Paleontology at the American Museum of Natural History. Dale worked with him on mosasaurs, Late Cretaceous marine lizards remotely related to the modern Komodo Dragon. Mosasaurs were fierce predators, so successful that their skeletons make up nearly one-quarter of all known vertebrate specimens collected from marine chalk deposits. The following year he moved to Canada to work in Ottawa's National Museum of Natural Sciences (now the Canadian Museum of Nature).

Apart from discovering, describing, and even naming more than a dozen new species of dinosaurs, Dale has worked with the Herzberg Institute of Astrophysics in Ottawa on extraterrestrial theories of dinosaur extinction. Four years before the Dinosaur Project was created, he traveled to the NASA Ames Research Center in Moffett Field, California. There he studied the evolution of the central nervous system, which became one of his primary interests. He has written that, if present environmental conditions persist and "imminent human extermination is avoided" for another 900 million years, "our brain would exceed its present volume by a factor of about 6.25," and that "creatures of human or superior intelligence may rapidly colonize transiently favorable planetary environments." He did not place any bets on our chances of surviving that long, but he brought a battery of knowledge to bear on what we would be like if we did.

Dale is a devout Roman Catholic, and much of his thinking is deeply influenced by his faith in an orderly and directed universe. The world and its creatures, he believes, were created with a purpose, they conform to a pattern, and it is a scientist's job to discover what that pattern is. One of his personal heroes is Pierre Teilhard de Chardin, the French anthropologist and Jesuit who went to China in 1922 to search for the origin of human life, and who wrote, in *The Phenomenon of Man* (1955), that "evolution is an ascent towards consciousness," and that human intelligence is the apotheosis of the evolutionary process.

Dong Zhiming's background is no less varied. He, too, studied the Old Geology and, like Dale, had much of his intellectual foundations built for him by

Since joining the IVPP in 1960, Dong Zhiming has discovered and named more than twenty new dinosaur species and is now one of China's leading dinosaur specialists.

Teilhard de Chardin, who left the IVPP library scores of books on paleontology, most of them in French, many of them his own works, and prospected in the Ordos Basin of the Gobi Desert with Dong Zhiming's first teacher, Yang Zhong-jian (better known in the West as C.C. Young).

Dong Zhiming is a benign Buddha: short, stocky, with dark hair and sharp, black eyes around which deeply furrowed lines appear when he squints into the sun, or booms out his great laugh, which he does often. Although his English is not extensive, he is gregarious and witty and always makes himself understood. He joined the IVPP in 1960 after studying biology at the University of Shanghai, which in those days was a progressive center of learning with more ties to the West than the universities in Beijing. He survived the Cultural Revolution by doing his work at the IVPP and keeping his head down. His favorite word in English is "dangerous," which he uses to mean anything from "difficult" to "curious." He first prospected this part of the Junggar Basin in 1962, but most of his work has been done in Sichuan and Zigong, in the south, where he discovered one of the largest dinosaur bonebeds in China. Since 1973 he has named nineteen dinosaurs, including the sauropod *Bellusaurus*, the carnivorous *Tugulusaurus*, and his specialty, the stegosaurs *Huayangosaurus* and *Wuerhosaurus*.

The morning after Dale and Dong Zhiming's late-night discussion, the group drove north again into the heart of the Junggar Basin, stopping for lunch at an oil-drilling camp belonging to the Xinjiang Petroleum Company. After securing two rooms for the night, they struck north again, then turned sharply and headed east across the desert. Here, as everywhere, the gravel was scarred by the tracks of oil rigs and seismic trucks. They passed four gazelles, small, brown, and so swift they easily kept pace with the jeep going eighty kilometers an hour, then cut crazily across its path and vanished over a low dune. A dusty fifty-six kilometers later they stopped to examine a Lower Cretaceous outcrop and found a satisfying amount of bone: pterosaurs, crocodiles, and sauropods. Heartened, they climbed back into the jeep and drove to a place Dong Zhiming called Dinosaur Valley — Middle Jurassic redbeds overlain by the Lower Cretaceous strata from the Tugulu Group. They found more bone, including the skeleton of a baby sauropod and, on the same level, a brachyopod, possibly a *Sinobrachyops*, a primitive amphibian hitherto known only in eastern China. The rock was soft and white and easy to work. Dale called it "the richest and most interesting site we've seen so far."

By nine-thirty that night they were back in the oil camp, talking excitedly about their plans to return to the Junggar the following summer. They would set up camp at the one spot that was closest to all the promising localities they had visited in the past five days but that had not yet been fully explored by the Chinese: Jiangjunmiao.

Paper Chase

With the decision about next year's localities made, it remained only to return to Beijing to work out the fine points of the Scientific Agreement. The group returned to Urumqi on the evening of May 10, spent two days touring the local sights — including the Geological Museum of Xinjiang, where they examined the museum's wealth of Permian fish fossils and, on the second floor, a panel depicting the economic benefits of geology — then flew back to the Chinese capital on May 13.

After Urumqi, Beijing seemed to flow like a perpetual-motion machine. Its wide, arrow-straight streets ran between regimental rows of sycamores and silver poplars and were filled with taxis and trucks and more than 6 million bicycles, all of which seemed to move as effortlessly as water along a millrace, even during rush hour. The trees roared with cicadas, and the sidewalks beneath them were not so much for walking as for gathering, talking, eating, playing cards, even sleeping. There were people everywhere: old men in blue or gray Mao jackets on

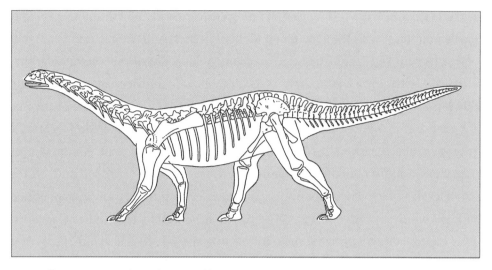

Bellusaurus **is a relatively small (five meters, five hundred kilograms) sauropod, known only from three specimens found in the Middle Jurassic beds of the Junggar Basin in Xinjiang. Their small size probably means they were juveniles, but it is not yet known of what larger species.**

benches and low concrete walls, their bamboo bird cages hanging from the lower branches and their trouser legs pulled up over their knees; young mothers with their children in wicker bicycle seats, sacks of potatoes slung across the crossbar; vendors in their market stalls, selling racks of cooked and raw meat — including dogs and cats — piles of bruised peaches and mountains of in-season, weirdly familiar vegetables — tomatoes, huge cabbages, string beans — transported daily on the flat-bottomed bicycle trucks that clogged the alleys between the austere Soviet-style apartment buildings.

The IVPP offices were housed in a vast, dark, gloomy complex in the north-central part of the city, across from the Beijing Zoo. It was really a compound of buildings; the main office faced an outer courtyard protected from the street by a swinging gate and a guardhouse, with a row of poplars on the right and a long, low garage on the left. A rear courtyard, reached by passing through the main office building, was a muddy square formed on two sides by low-rise apartment buildings for current and retired IVPP employees, and a kind of warehouse and workshop area along the fourth side, where many fossil displays were stored and mounted.

Like other government institutions in China, the IVPP is required to pay much of its own way — even the Red Army owns many of China's hotels, including the Da Du, where the Canadians were staying. The IVPP sold eggs from two thousand chickens that fortunately are not kept on the premises. It did, however, run an auto repair shop located in the garage below Chang Meeman's second-floor office; consequently she kept her windows closed. In the sun-dappled courtyard, the high-pitched whine from the cicadas in the poplar trees drowned out the sound of banging metal from the garage. There was no traffic noise at all: the compound might have been in the stillest countryside.

The Dinosaur People spent the next ten days discussing ways to put their dreams on paper. They were joined by one of the IVPP's other paleontologists, Zhao Xijin, a neat, dapper man in his fifties with thinning black hair and a wide smile. Zhao Xijin studied paleontology in Moscow and returned to China during the 1950s to work as an oil geologist in the Gobi Desert. Like Dong Zhiming, he worked with C.C. Young — the two named the family, Mamenchisauridae, to which China's largest dinosaur belongs. Since then he had made sauropods his specialty; in 1986, he was preparing the first descriptions of no fewer than six new genera of them.

Most of the discussions took place in Dong Zhiming's office on the ground floor, next to the bicycle-clogged foyer and looking out on the outer courtyard. The tall windows were so grimy that only a wan light penetrated the room. The air danced with dust. The office was a charnel house for three decades of bone collecting. The limbs and scapulae of a huge, Jurassic sauropod lay on the cement floor just inside the door. Tables strewn with bits of fossil lined the walls. Tall, wooden specimen cabinets divided the room in half, their drawers filled with shoeboxes of bones; metal lockers lining the inner wall contained more boxes of uncatalogued specimens, bits of skull and pelvis; unidentified leg bones; piles of phalanges and ribs. On a work table beside Dong Zhiming's desk, the vertebrae of a small theropod were lined up like pieces from a jigsaw puzzle of a snake. The skull and neck of a baby *Protoceratops*, mounted in a tray of red sandstone, shared a gunmetal side table with a dust-covered Smith-Corona typewriter.

Chuck Gruchy, then assistant director of the National Museum of Science, arrived in Beijing on the nineteenth to participate in the discussions. The wording of the Scientific Agreement was debated at great length; there were the usual problems in translating a general idea into a specific document. Eventually, the agreement was typed up by Phil and Dale on Dong Zhiming's dusty typewriter. It authorized field work in China to continue for the next three years and specified that "all specimens collected or subsequently used for research and exhibition will remain the property of the country of origin." Twelve Canadian and twenty-two Chinese scientists and technicians would be involved. Expenses would be borne by Ex Terra and its Canadian museum partners; all the logistics in China, from food and lodging to travel permits, excavation permits, transit permits, exit permits, and drivers — private ownership of vehicles is almost unknown in China, and only members of the Chinese Drivers Union can drive government vehicles — would be handled by the IVPP. Sun Ailing and Chang Meeman estimated that a year's field work in Xinjiang would cost about 340,000 yuan, or $80,000 Canadian. The Canadian partners would provide two-thirds of that, and the IVPP one-third.

The agreement was signed on May 23, 1986, and the Canadians returned home. A little over a month later, the first group of Chinese scientists — Dong Zhiming, Zhao Xijin, Yu Chao, Li Rong, and Tang Zhilu — stepped off a Canadian Airlines plane in Edmonton.

Arctic Migrations

ON TUESDAY, JULY 1, 1986 — CANADA DAY — FOUR CANADIAN MEMBERS OF THE Dinosaur Project boarded another Canadian Airlines plane in Ottawa. Dale Russell, his field assistant Clayton Kennedy, Chuck Gruchy, and Rick Day, another National Museum technician, were headed for Resolute Bay, a kind of way station on the southern tip of Cornwallis Island in the Canadian Arctic. The flight left early in the morning, but by midnight Dale and his colleagues were getting off their plane back in Ottawa. Heavy fog over Resolute had forced the aircraft to turn back at Frobisher Bay. They didn't get into Resolute until late afternoon on July 4.

On the fifth, thick fog once again blew in from the pack ice surrounding Cornwallis Island, and by mid-afternoon it was so dense that all incoming flights for the day were canceled. At five o'clock, however, the ceiling lifted briefly, and a Pacific Western Airlines flight from Edmonton managed to squeak in for a landing. On it were Phil Currie, Dong Zhiming, and Yu Chao, who were joining the National Museum team to hunt for dinosaurs on Axel Heiberg Island, about 480 km north of Resolute. Then the fog closed in again, and the two teams hunkered down to wait in the Resolute "hotel" run by the Polar Continental Shelf Project, the vital logistical arm of the Department of Energy, Mines and Resources without which few scientists travel north of the 70th parallel.

Dale had been working in the far north for many years. In fact, the Canadian Arctic was to the National Museum what Dinosaur Provincial Park had become to the Tyrrell Museum: a kind of private game preserve for pale-

Zhao Xijin studied paleontology with the great C.C. Young in the 1950s; together they named the Mamenchisauridae, a family of dinosaurs that would play an important role in the Dinosaur Project.

ontological research. Dale had been prospecting for fossils that he could coordinate with what he already knew about dinosaur patterns elsewhere, but so far he had been unable to find anything but fossils of marine vertebrates: plesiosaurs, mosasaurs, and the like. This time he had picked a promising spot on Axel Heiberg where he could reasonably expect to find dinosaur material, and he welcomed the assistance of the other members of the Dinosaur Project in his search.

He was not the first explorer to hunt for fossil material in the far north. In 1852, members of the Belcher Search Expedition, a rescue mission sent to the Arctic to look for the lost Franklin Expedition of 1845, had reported finding ichthyosaur vertebrae on Exmouth Island, in what is now known as Belcher Channel. The following year, on Cameron Island, the same explorers found another vertebra that at first was thought to be that of a dinosaur and was later named *Arctosaurus*. It would have been the first dinosaur ever found in Canada had not subsequent studies shown it to be not a dinosaur but a trilophosaur, one of the reptilian herbivores that flourished from the Arctic to the equator more than 225 million years ago and then suddenly vanished during the mass extinctions that marked the end of the Triassic Period.

Since the middle of the last century, virtually all the vertebrate fossil material found in the Arctic has belonged to marine animals found in marine environments all over the world. This is not surprising, since the Arctic has been a very watery place since the birth of the North American continent. The Arctic islands were formed by silt deposits from huge, Mississippi-sized rivers that flowed into the shallow Arctic Basin. The islands, then, were terrestrial habitats at least during the Late Cretaceous, and Dale was convinced that dinosaur material would eventually be found on some of them.

In fact, the theory that was beginning to take shape was that a series of dinosaur migrations must have occurred between the Asian and North American land masses at various times throughout the Age of Reptiles. Similarities between the dinosaurs of China and North America, especially during the Late Cretaceous, were hard to explain any other way. For example, American paleontologists working on the North Slope of Alaska in the late 1970s had turned up troodontid teeth and bones, tyrannosaurid teeth, a possible *Lambeosaurus,* and several ceratopsians. The list was strikingly familiar to the Canadians, since it could have been a list of dinosaurs found along the Red Deer River in Alberta. And it was known that the same families of dinosaurs were found in China. How to explain such a similarity if not by means of migration routes between the two continents, mass movements of dinosaurs across land bridges connecting North America and Asia through the Arctic? There are such hypothetical land bridges. The Bering Peninsula is thought to be a remnant of one of them — the Bering Strait, through which Pacific waters flow north into the Arctic Ocean, is still less than fifteen meters deep in places. "Beringia" is the name given to the last known Bering land bridge, which sank 12,000 to 24,000 years ago and across which the first human beings to inhabit North America are thought to have dispersed from northern Asia: dinosaurs could easily have done likewise on some previous Beringia at various times throughout the Mesozoic.

A second land bridge is thought to have connected the eastern Arctic to northern Asia through Greenland and Spitzbergen Island. *Iguanodon* footprints have been

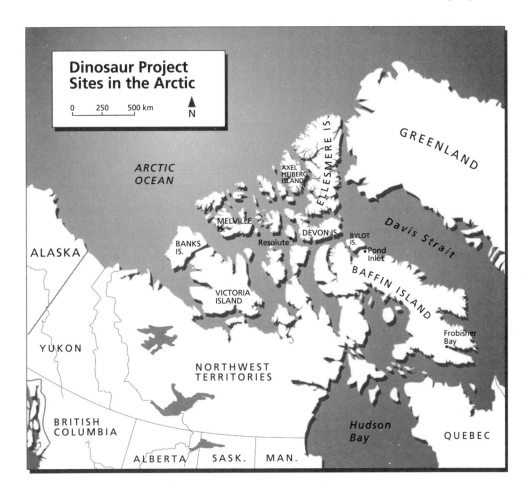

Dinosaur Project Sites in the Arctic

0   250   500 km

N

ARCTIC OCEAN

GREENLAND

ELLESMERE IS.

AXEL HEIBERG ISLAND

MELVILLE IS.

DEVON IS.

BANKS IS.

Resolute

BYLOT IS.

Pond Inlet

Davis Strait

BAFFIN ISLAND

ALASKA

VICTORIA ISLAND

Frobisher Bay

YUKON

NORTHWEST TERRITORIES

BRITISH COLUMBIA

Hudson Bay

QUEBEC

ALBERTA   SASK.   MAN.

found on Spitzbergen. If dinosaur material were found in the Yukon and Alaska, perhaps more could be found in the Late Cretaceous exposures in the eastern Arctic.

Dale identified two likely places to look; Axel Heiberg Island and Ellesmere Island, the most northerly land masses in the Canadian Arctic, both contain exposures of the Isachsen Formation, a Lower Cretaceous rock formation that stretches right across the Arctic, measuring one and a half kilometers thick near Greenland and tapering to a bare ninety meters at the western end of the Arctic Ocean. Its sediment sources were fluvial deposits from a series of great rivers that flowed into the Arctic from the southern highlands across vast flood plains where they picked up plant and animal debris as well as silt. Paleo-river mouths are good places to look for fossil material. Dinosaurs seem to have frequented places where there was plenty of fresh water and vegetation, and the wet sand associated with fluvial deposits favored the fossilization of their bones. Also, fast-moving rivers would pick up the skeletons of animals that died anywhere along their shores and carry them downstream, where they would collect at the delta as the water slowed down to enter the ocean. Furthermore, within the Isachsen there were seams of coal. Coal is petrified plant material, and its formation requires millions of years of the right climatic conditions: swamps, trees, dry spells, then swamp again, lots of trees, and so on. The right conditions for forming coal are also the right conditions for finding dinosaurs. "It all sounded wonderful," says Phil. "But the only way to test these things is to go there." So the Dinosaur Project team cooled their heels in Resolute, waiting for the fog to lift and the Polar Continental Shelf Project bosses to allow them to continue their journey to Axel Heiberg Island.

Finally the morning of July 8 came with a clear sky filled with fast-moving, puffy clouds, and word was given for the Twin-Engine Otter to be warmed up. The Project's gear was still stranded in Frobisher, but the Polar Shelf people lent the group a box and a half of provisions — everything from twenty-seven tins of salmon to four small rolls of toilet paper — and the plane took off. The weather was cold, and snow was threatening. At 30 degrees Celsius, a Twin Otter needs three hundred meters of runway to take off; at minus 30 degrees, it needs only eighty-two meters. That morning, the plane took off on sixty meters. A few hours later, it dropped the seven men at the first fly-in camp, on Sand Bay, a deep, narrow fjord cutting into Axel Heiberg above Skrugar Point, which looks out over Massey Sound in the southwestern sector of the island.

The first thing they did, after setting up their tents, was to go for a short prospecting trip. The southern end of Axel Heiberg is on the inner part of the Franklinian geosyncline, a wide belt of thickly folded sedimentary rocks consisting mainly of fossiliferous carbonates and shales that eventually swings east and connects with Ellesmere Island and Greenland, which were a single land mass during the Cretaceous. The Princess Margaret Range of mountains that forms the island's backbone is more or less permanently covered with ice and rises nearly 2,300 m above Sand Bay and the Dinosaur Project's tiny camp.

When the seven men went prospecting, they found one Arctic poppy, clusters of purple-flowering mosses, and beds of Arctic willows — "trees" that grow no higher than ten centimeters — that still had not leafed out. They also found

**Dinosaur Project members prospected for dinosaurs here on
Axel Heiberg Island in the Canadian Arctic in 1986, hoping to find evidence
of dinosaur migration to Arctic feeding grounds 70 million years ago.**

scattered bits of coal and fossil wood. But no bones.

The landscape was as bleak and majestic as anything they had ever seen. It was like traveling back in time to the Ice Ages. Its physiographic designation is "rock desert," but its interior is buried under nearly one and a half kilometers of ice. The tongues of the island's two vast inland glaciers, the White and the Thompson, advance to lick the shoreline and fill the bays with push moraines. Deep crevasses split open in the summer and squeeze shut again in winter, when the really cold weather comes. Occasional erratics, up-ended by the retreat and advance of the glaciers, stand like pagan statues along the gravel ridges. When the crew emerged from their tents on the morning of July 9, they found that ten centimeters of snow had fallen during the night, turning what had been gray into an eye-aching white. Then it began to rain. The next day the rain turned to pellet snow, and everyone stayed in camp; Chuck cooked a dinner of pork roast, with oatmeal and clotted cream for dessert. Spirits rose.

All the time they remained in radio contact with the Polar Shelf operation at Resolute, and with Jim Bassinger, a scientist with the University of Saskatchewan who had set up a camp on the northeastern corner of Axel Heiberg, at about 80 degrees north, where he and a small group of graduate students were studying the fossil forest he had found there the year before.

On July 11, Dale discovered the presence of "ophiomorpha all over." Ophiomorpha are fossilized shrimp holes; known as trace fossils, they look like petrified snakes or tree roots running down through the section, but are actually the filled-in holes left by shrimps or worms as they burrowed down into the mud at the bottom of lakes and shallow ocean floors. Their sizes and shapes are peculiar to the different creatures that made them and they can be identified accordingly. Although finding trace fossils in this location was interesting — evidence of anything but trees was welcome — it was also bad news as far as dinosaurs were concerned, since the kind of paleo-environment that supported shrimp — shallow, still, brackish swamp beds — was not the kind of habitat dinosaurs had frequented.

It was also becoming clear that thin and extremely carbonaceous streaks of black in the gray gravel were the wrong kind of coal deposits — they, too, indicated a brackish, near-shore environment, not a promising place to find dinosaurs.

Finding nothing but wood and trace fossils at Sand Bay, the group decided to split up in order to cover more ground. A helicopter was called in from Eureka, a weather station on nearby Ellesmere Island, and Dale and Dong Zhiming were moved to a fly-in camp several kilometers south of the bay, while Phil and Clayton Kennedy shifted farther inland. Chuck Gruchy, Yu Chao, and Rick Day stayed at the main camp to continue prospecting there. Still, no one found any dinosaur bones.

Dale found petrified cycad stumps measuring more than thirty centimeters in diameter and wood fragments that he calculated might have come from trunks up to twice that thickness, evidence of the Arctic's relatively balmy climate during the Lower Cretaceous. Rick found many impressions of fern leaves and took a series of fossil pollen samples. Dale also discovered more plesiosaurs and began to notice some interesting differences between the proportion of plesiosaurs to mosasaurs in the Arctic compared to that found farther south. In the Arctic, plesiosaurs dominated, whereas in Kansas mosasaurs outnumbered plesiosaurs. From such evidence — the size and kind of trees, the nature of their pollen, and the location and type of marine animals found — a better appreciation of the Arctic paleo-habitat was beginning to emerge. "Under the mild arctic climate," Dale later wrote, "a luxuriant blanket of cone-bearing trees followed the plain down from the southern highlands. Additional varieties of trees blended into the patchwork of forest rings which continued across the broad lowlands to a shallow northern sea. Cycad-like plants were less common, preferring relatively warm, well-drained sites. Many different kinds of ferns grew on sandbars and riverbanks. Others sprouted within dank moss moors and hung like garlands from the crowns of bleached, decaying trunks in shaded areas behind the advancing forest fronts." To his picture of "this archaic boreal Eden," he added that a dinosaur trackway had been found in the fossil muds of Alaska and in Spitzbergen, but that so far none had turned up in the Canadian Arctic. "It will be found," he predicted.

By July 17, when everyone had reconvened at the Sand Bay camp, Dale estimated that the seven men had spent a combined total of 305 hours prospecting the area without finding a single trace of dinosaur bone. During discussions over dinner, they decided to set up a second camp on the eastern edge of Eureka Sound. Phil, Dale, and Dong Zhiming, meanwhile, would go farther north to join Jim Bassinger in the fossil forest, and then all of them would accompany Bassinger's group to survey the Fosheim Peninsula on Ellesmere Island.

On the Fosheim, which Phil describes as "the banana belt of the Arctic," the grassy plains had the majestic Sawtooth Mountains as a backdrop. Although the Sound was choked with ice, there was no snow on the plateau, and the temperature soared above 10 degrees Celsius. Except for the mosquitoes, they felt themselves in paradise.

The Isachsen Formation on Ellesmere Island gives way to the Kanguk, the sandstone of which is whiter in color with a bit of green showing through on its north-sloping anticline. Working with Bassinger's group, they found more wood and leaf fossils, and Dong Zhiming got another plesiosaur about eighty meters south of the camp. But no dinosaurs. On July 23, Dale reported finding "scraps of bone" about four and a half kilometers from camp, and the next day Phil found something called *Inoceramus lundbreckensis* — a gigantic clam shell nearly 180 cm in diameter — also known from Kansas but never before found so far north. Exciting, but still not what they were looking for. On July 25, everyone was back in Eureka, where the weather was cooler, there were no mosquitoes, and they were able to wash their clothes for the first time in three weeks. Two days later the seven men were back in Resolute, and on their way home.

Phil had one of the "scraps of bone" in his pocket. It was dark gray, about the size of a roll of pennies, and it was the only thing resembling dinosaur bone they had found in three weeks of cold, wet prospecting. When he arrived at the Tyrrell Museum and examined the specimen carefully in his lab, he saw that it had growth rings and a distinct grain. "It was a piece of palm tree," he says. "So in the end we had nothing."

Tired and discouraged, he filed his bit of palm tree and headed down to Dinosaur Park to see how the rest of the Dinosaur Project had fared during his absence. It had been a disappointing first year. The trip to China had been culturally interesting, but they had found no new fossils in Xinjiang. The Chinese scientists in Alberta had established personal relations with the Canadians, but they, too, had found nothing exciting from a scientific point of view. And now nearly a month in the Arctic had failed to corroborate Phil and Dale's conviction that the far north held the next great fossil bonanza. As soon as Phil arrived at the field station, however, Kevin Aulenback handed him Tang Zhilu's braincase. Phil took one look at it and immediately his spirits soared.

"I just went through the roof," he says. "I realized at once what it was." He was holding the braincase of *Troodon formosus*, a small, swift, bipedal dinosaur of the Late Cretaceous. Phil had seen very few like it: C.H. Sternberg had found a partial *Troodon* skull in 1917; Dale Russell and John Acorn had found two more in the 1960s and 1970s; and in 1982, Linda Strong-Watson had found a *Troodon* braincase in the park. But this one was much more complete, more astonishingly beautiful, than anything he had ever encountered before. Here was the raw material he needed for advancing his research into the arcane connection between ancient dinosaurs and modern birds.

Dinosaurs Are Alive and Well and Living as Birds

WHEN PHIL EXAMINED THE BRAINCASE CAREFULLY BACK AT THE TYRRELL, HE FOUND that it was riddled with air passages. Both middle ears were large chambers that had been filled with air from the creature's throat. Air canals running over the top of the skull joined the chambers. The sinus system was also connected at the front of the skull to a balloon-like cavity, called a bulbous parasphenoid, greatly increasing the amount of air behind the eardrums. Phil and one of his graduate students, Brooks Britt, had been studying pneumatic sinuses and were coming up with some highly speculative theories about their function. Filling the ear canals with air, they reasoned, was a way to improve hearing by allowing the animal to pick up very low-frequency sounds. *Troodon* was a theropod — a predator — and some of its prey, perhaps the young of dome-headed hadrosaurs, for example, may have evolved resonators inside their skulls that emitted vibrations too low for ordinary predators to detect. With large, hollow skull bones, *Troodon* would have been able to pick up these sounds and hence be a more effective predator. Tang's braincase provided a fascinating glimpse into the relationship between animals that existed more than 75 million years ago.

It also provided something else: *Troodon* wasn't the only dinosaur to have these sinus passages. *Tyrannosaurus rex* had them, too. Before the discovery of Tang's braincase, it was assumed that all the small theropods were related to each other and called coelurosaurians, and all the big theropods were related to each other and called carnosaurs. The small predators *Troodon* and *Ornithomimus* belonged to one group; the huge theropods *Tyrannosaurus* and *Allosaurus* belonged to another. With the new evidence provided by the braincase, it seemed that *Troodon* is more closely related to *Tyrannosaurus* than to other coelurosaurians, and *Tyrannosaurus* may not be related to *Allosaurus* at all. "It may be," says Phil, "that all the Late Jurassic dinosaurs, like *Allosaurus*, just crashed, died out, instead of evolving into tyrannosaurs. And then the smaller, more sophisticated forms replaced them in the Cretaceous and evolved into *Tyrannosaurus*. So, thanks to the Dinosaur Project, we're beginning to develop a whole new perception of dinosaur relationships, about what was going on between them."

Finally, the *Troodon* braincase told Phil something else. The only other animals besides troodontids and tyrannosaurids to have such pneumatic systems in their skulls are modern: crocodiles and birds. It has long been known that crocodiles and dinosaurs are indirectly related by common ancestry, although crocodiles are not the direct descendants of dinosaurs. They are, rather, distant cousins. And until recently it has been assumed that at some point in the past, birds branched off from the common ancestors of dinosaurs and crocodiles. It now appears that that assumption has been wrong: birds may be the direct descendants of dinosaurs.

The idea that some dinosaurs may have evolved into birds is not new. Since the turn of the century, dinosaur anatomists have divided all dinosaurs into two major groups, based on the structure of their pelvic girdles. As amphibians crawled out of the water to become land-based reptiles, their musculature underwent significant adaptations in order to support their body weight on land — particularly in the limbs and the places where the limbs attached to the trunk, that is, at the shoulders and hips. The iliac bone in the pelvis strengthened its connection to the spine by the addition of one vertebra in animals that walked on all fours, and by several vertebrae in animals that became bipedal. Two distinct types of pelvic girdles thus emerged, and paleontologists place dinosaurs in two orders depending upon whether they had the lizard-like pelvic structure (Saurischia), or the bird-like structure (Ornithischia). Pelvic structure was mainly a classification tool, however, and was not meant to suggest that because some dinosaurs had hips like birds they were necessarily related to them. Indeed, the bird-hipped Ornithischians — stegosaurs, ankylosaurs, ceratopsians — were in almost every other way the least bird-like dinosaurs of all. They were herbivorous, walked on all fours, and were heavily armored. The dinosaurs that rose up on two legs, developed bird-like claws and beaks, and ate meat were from the Saurischian order, though not all Saurischians followed suit.

Before Darwin, there were two predominant theories about creation and evolution. One held that the earth and its creatures had been created by God in much the same state as they existed today; some erosion had taken place on earth, caused for the most part by Noah's Flood, and some alteration had occurred in the beasts of the field, caused by interbreeding, but basically God had fixed all the forms forever. A giraffe was a giraffe was a giraffe. Species were immutable. Extinction was unthinkable.

The other hypothesis, devised by the French biologist Jean-Baptiste-Pierre-Antoine de Monet, Chevalier de Lamarck, was that species evolved very rapidly by a process of inherited characteristics. An offspring could inherit acquired characteristics from its parents, physical attributes that gave it a competitive edge over other species. In the case of giraffes, for example, one ancestral giraffe began to eat leaves from a tree instead of grass from the ground, so it began stretching its neck upward; its young were born with slightly longer necks; the young of that young had even longer necks; and so on until all giraffe necks became as long as they are today. But the idea that a cold-blooded, land-hugging reptile like a dinosaur could change itself, by means of inherited characteristics, into a warm-blooded, skylarking bird seemed to stretch Lamarckism too far. Developing a longer neck was one thing; developing a whole new body plan was something else entirely.

In *The Origin of Species*, published in November 1859 — three years after the discovery of *Troodon* — Darwin proposed a third alternative: that species evolved by means of natural selection. In other words, parents produced more offspring than the territory they inhabited could support, each offspring had a slightly different set of qualities, and the ones whose qualities were most suited to that particular habitat survived to pass their genes on to future generations, and those whose weren't, didn't. If an ur-giraffe, for example, lived in an area where the best food was to be had from tall trees and produced three young — one with a long neck, one with a medium-sized neck, and one with a short neck — then the long-necked one would live and the other two would die. That long-necked giraffe would produce a spectrum of offspring, and the ones with long necks would survive, and so on. Eventually, through countless generations, the genes that had accidentally given giraffes long necks would become so prevalent that eventually all giraffes would be born with long necks. When applied to dinosaurs, Darwin's theory meant that over thousands, perhaps millions, of years it was possible for a land-based, hairless species of reptile to evolve into a flying, feathered species of bird.

The problem was that for creatures like giant reptiles to evolve into tiny hummingbirds would require millions upon millions of generations, and the geological record as it was understood at the time showed that the earth simply had not existed long enough to allow for such gradual change. And where were the links in so long a chain of biological permutations? In order to prove that one species could become another species "by slowly and still existing causes, and not by miraculous acts of creation" as Darwin suggests, the fossil record would have to show a complete series of gradually changing animals, starting with one form and ending with another, with each intervening phase completely and scientifically accounted for.

Darwin admitted that such proof for his theory was lacking, but he blamed it on the scarcity of fossils, not on any weakness in his reasoning. He lamented, "Geological research though it has added numerous species to existing and extinct genera, and has made the intervals between some few groups less wide than they otherwise would have been, yet has done scarcely anything in breaking down the distinction between the species, by connecting them together by numerous, fine, intermediate varieties."

Two years after the publication of *Origin*, however, stonecutters working in a limestone quarry in Bavaria turned up something that went a long way toward taking up Darwin's challenge. It was the nearly complete skeleton of what looked like a dinosaur about the size of a large crow. It had dinosaur hands, feet, tail, and a dinosaur skull complete with dinosaur teeth. Etched into the rock around the entire skeleton, however, were the distinct impressions of feathers. Although very similar to the dinosaur *Compsognathus* in almost every respect (it had much longer fingers, not unlike those of a bat's), it had evidently possessed feathers and, presumably, the power of flight.

Britain's greatest paleozoologist, Thomas Henry Huxley — known as "Darwin's Bulldog" for his fierce defence of evolution — declared that *Archaeopteryx lithographica*, as the specimen was called (the generic name means "ancient wing," and the species name was derived from the fact that the Bavarian quarry was famous for providing limestone plates for lithographers), substantiated Darwin's theory of evolution, and in his next edition of *Origin*, Darwin gratefully acknowledged that "the wide interval between birds and reptiles has been shown by [Huxley] to be partially bridged over in the most unexpected manner, on the one hand by the ostrich and extinct *Archaeopteryx*, and on the other hand by the *Compsognathus*, one of the dinosaurians — that group which includes the most gigantic of all terrestrial reptiles."

The operative word in Darwin's acknowledgment is "partially." *Archaeopteryx* was only one link in a very long chain between dinosaurs and birds; other links were still hypothetical. Darwin's opponents — and even Darwin himself — realized that a more complete series was needed. "He who rejects these views on the nature of the geological record," he wrote, "will rightly reject my whole theory." Darwin insisted that evolution was a gradual process, a slow, continuous, character-by-character transition from species to species, and paleontologists began to despair of ever being able to unearth sufficient evidence to prove or disprove such a concept.

As a result, the paleontological community's response to Darwin's request for more data began to cool off. They accepted the general notion of evolution, but rejected its mechanism, natural selection. Based on their own findings, they felt that evolutionary change could be sudden, or progress in surges, with species developing rapidly and then staying relatively unchanged for millennia — a theory that is gaining new momentum today under the name "punctuated equilibrium." This theory helped to explain the gaps in the fossil record: gradual changes that took place over several million years would be bound to turn up in geological digs; sudden changes that occurred in a few thousand years could easily be missed.

In 1925, the German ornithologist Gerhard Heilmann published *The Origin of Birds*, in which he agreed with Huxley's list of characters shared by theropods and birds: bipedal bodies with short torsos, massive hips, long necks and long hind legs; ankle joints that concentrate movement on a single hinge; expansion of the upper hip bone, the ilium; hind feet in which the inner toe points backward; pubic bones turned backward; and holes in the vertebrae for air sacks that connect to the lungs. But he pointed out that birds could not possibly be descended from dinosaurs because dinosaurs lacked one of the essential requirements for flight: a wishbone.

The wishbone, or furcula, is a fusion of the two collarbones, an improvement that gives them the strength to resist the stress of flapping wings during take-off. Ancestors of the dinosaurs had them, but dinosaurs had apparently lost them, and it is a tenet of evolution that once a character evolves out, it is gone forever. Horses cannot redevelop toes. *Archaeopteryx* had a wishbone, which meant it could not have been related to dinosaurs in any sense that mattered. To say that dinosaurs and birds were descended from a common ancestor, concluded Heilmann, was like saying that human beings are related to ants because they both have their origins in the Precambrian soup. It is far more likely, Heilmann maintained, that birds were more recently descended from thecodonts.

That belief is still held by some scientists today. In the early 1970s, two researchers at the University of Kansas, Larry Martin and Ken Wextall, published a paper listing thirty-five characteristics that birds and crocodiles shared that were

The discovery, in 1861, of this *Archaeopteryx*, a dinosaur surrounded by distinct feather impressions, provided an early link in the chain connecting dinosaurs to birds.

not found in dinosaurs. This list purported to prove Heilmann's contention that birds and crocodiles are more closely linked than birds and dinosaurs. Their paper reopened the long-slumbering debate. Other paleontologists — Phil Currie among them — began to think about it. "The list was a pretty powerful statement of relationship," says Phil. "It sort of begged to be whittled away at." Over the next few years, the whittlers not only got the list down to two, but had gone on to add 125 characteristics shared only by dinosaurs and birds and not found in crocodiles — such as bipedal gait; lower hind legs longer than upper hind legs; the strong, S-curved neck; details of the front part of the skull and hip joints; larger knee crests; and a reduced outer toe. Except for two items on Martin and Wextall's original list, the case for a close dinosaur-bird connection was made.

One of those last remaining elements on Martin and Wextall's list was the sophisticated pneumatic system of the middle ear. Crocs have it, birds have it, and now, thanks to Tang Zhilu's braincase, we know that small dinosaurs had it, too (no one has ever suggested that birds evolved from *Tyrannosaurus*).

"The relationship between dinosaurs and birds," says Phil, "is an open-and-shut case."

The Dinosaur Project had got off to a very good start, after all.

CHAPTER 2

Dragon Bones
The Dinosaur Project and the new paleontology

IN LATE JULY 1912, THREE PROFESSIONAL AMERICAN BONEHUNTERS CROSSED INTO
Canada at Coutts, Alberta, at the Montana border, and made their way by train
to Lethbridge, which one of them later described as a "pretty town, with a beautiful park that promises to be a beauty spot some day in the near future." They could
see the Canadian Rockies looming up in the west. From Lethbridge, they continued north to Calgary, where they had a rowboat made. Then they boarded the train
again, this time heading northeast to the town of Acme, where they disembarked,
rowboat and all, hired a horse and wagon, and made their way through Rosebud
to Drumheller, "a small town at that time, with a couple of stores." They set up
camp about a kilometer upstream from the town and the next day began prospecting for dinosaurs. Almost immediately, they were rewarded. "We soon began to
find great numbers of loose bones," wrote their leader, "piled up as jetsam and
flotsam of the sea."

The leader was Charles Hazelius Sternberg, whose reputation as a fossil
hunter was such that he had just been appointed Head Collector and Preparator
of Vertebrate Fossils by the Geological Survey of Canada. He had been born in
upstate New York in 1850, the son of a Lutheran minister, and by the time he
moved with his family to Kansas when he was seventeen, he was already a dedicated amateur paleontologist, specializing in Tertiary mammals and plants. He
received his first payment against expenses — $300 — from the great Philadel-
phian paleontologist Edward Drinker Cope himself, in 1876, and had gone on to
collect fossils for Cope for the rest of his career — until, that is, he became employed

by the Canadian government.

From Cope, Sternberg had learned cutthroat bone hunting. Cope and his arch rival, Othniel Charles Marsh, professor of paleontology at Yale University, had been engaged in what have been called "the bone wars" throughout the 1870s and 1880s. It was a fierce scientific rivalry that entailed some of the most underhanded shenanigans in the history of science, but it also amassed stupendous collections of fossils. Both Cope and Marsh were men of means, and it was well-known in the field that any significant fossil could be turned into instant cash by communicating the find to one (or better, both) of these learned collectors.

Sternberg had met Cope in 1871,

Charles Hazelius Sternberg (1850-1943) was known as the world's greatest bonehunter when he came to the Alberta badlands in 1912. In his four years with the Geological Survey of Canada, he and his sons formed the basis of the National Museum's important dinosaur collection.

when the paleontologist traveled to Kansas to poach fossils in territory that had been claimed the previous year by Marsh. From his base camp in Fort Wallace, Cope and his seven assistants, one of whom was Sternberg, explored the shallow badlands in the western part of the state. One of their first finds was a twenty-three-meter fossil of a marine serpent, which was named *Liodon dyspelor* Cope, and before the summer was out, the team had collected thirty-seven species, many of them previously unknown, including turtles, a pterosaur, and a giant fish of which the head alone was as large as a cow's.

Another famous American bonehunter had already visited Alberta's badlands. Barnum Brown had staked out the territory in 1910, floating down the Red Deer River on a flat-bottomed barge with the president of the American Museum of Natural History, Henry Fairfield Osborn. Brown's finds were duly shipped back to the American Museum in New York, to the growing dismay of the people of Alberta, who thought Canadian fossils should remain in Canada. The Geological

**Using dynamite, picks, and shovels, the Sternbergs spent months removing
tonnes of overburden from this theropod quarry in the Alberta
badlands in 1913. They then removed tonnes more to make a road to
the site, so they could hoist the specimen onto a horse-drawn wagon.**

Survey was consequently urged to place a qualified representative in the field, and
it had hired Charles Sternberg to fill that role.

Sternberg's boss at the GSC was Lawrence M. Lambe, a former army officer
who had joined the GSC as an artist and had spent several summers, from 1897
onwards, in the Alberta badlands, collecting, describing, drawing, and interpret-
ing dinosaur fossils. Lambe was a careful and meticulous worker and made many
lasting contributions to paleontology. One of the most valuable of them, apart from
hiring Sternberg, was his demonstration that the dinosaurs found along the Red
Deer River were older than those from other Cretaceous formations in Arizona
and Wyoming.

Charles Hazelius Sternberg's assistants were his two sons, Charles and Levi,
and before the end of their first day of prospecting near Drumheller they found
"our first dinosaurian bone of a *Trachodon*," one of the duck-billed, herbivorous
dinosaurs known as hadrosaurs. Hadrosaurs were extremely common even then.

They were the first dinosaurs ever discovered in North America; in 1856, a single tooth had been discovered by an army map-making crew working in the Judith River badlands of Montana, in strata that was thought to be more or less the same geological age as Alberta. The tooth was sent to Joseph Leidy, who named it *Trachodon*, meaning "rough tooth." Later material found in the Lance Formation in South Dakota and Wyoming was named *Anatosaurus*, or "duck lizard," because of its peculiar flat-lipped features and webbed feet, which made it look like a cross between Bullwinkle and Daffy Duck. In 1858, a colleague of Leidy's at the Academy of Natural Sciences in Philadelphia discovered some fossilized bones in a rock quarry

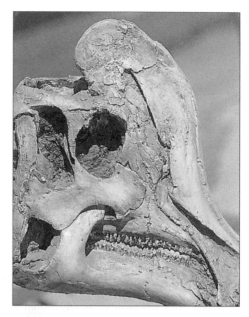

Corythosaurus casuarius, the duckbilled dinosaur discovered in the Alberta badlands in 1913 by Charles Sternberg: Dale Russell believes the huge crest acted as a resonator, enabling the animal to emit low-frequency sounds that would carry over great distances.

near Haddonfield, New Jersey; Leidy declared them to be dinosaur bones and named them *Hadrosaurus*, or "big lizard," from the Greek *hadros*, meaning stout.

Duckbills are the most abundant of the Alberta dinosaurs, making up nearly 60 percent of all dinosaur fossils so far discovered there. Descended from iguanodontids — in fact, the division between the Early and Late Cretaceous periods is often defined as the time when hadrosaurs replaced iguanodontids in the fossil record — hadrosaurs differ from their ancestors in several important ways. They are longer, for one thing. The iguanodonts were big — Dale Russell describes an *Iguanodon bernissartensis* cow as "measuring eight meters in length and weighing nearly four metric tonnes," and the flatheaded *Edmontosaurus* (as *Anatosaurus* is now called) could be two meters longer and more than a tonne heavier.

Three Asian hadrosaurs are among the largest known anywhere: the tube-headed lambeosaur *Barsboldia* and the flatheaded hadrosaur *Saurolophus*, both found in Mongolia, were twelve meters long and weighed ten tonnes, and the largest known hadrosaur, the *Shantungosaurus* from eastern China, was nearly fifteen meters long and weighed about twelve and a half tonnes when alive. Unlike most hadrosaurs, *Shantungosaurus* walked on its hind legs, somewhat like a *Tyrannosaurus*, although it evidently went down on all fours to graze. Each of its hind feet had three toes, each toe hoofed like the foot of a horse and splayed out to support the animal's tremendous weight.

Iguanodonts too were similar to hadrosaurs, but they had bird-like three-toed feet with flat claws. Hadrosaurs had more teeth than iguanodonts, arranged in compact dental "batteries" or "magazines." "There are three rows of teeth in the cutting surface and magazines below containing two thousand teeth in all," Sternberg wrote. "As fast as one tooth is worn out it is shed and another takes its place. Further, they are so arranged that only alternate teeth can drop out at a time."

Returning to Alberta in the summer of 1913, the Sternbergs decided to take a page out of Barnum Brown's book and travel deeper into the badlands using the Red Deer River as a highway. They built a flat-bottomed scow that was three and a half meters by eight and a half meters, and on its plank deck they pitched two tents — one for cooking and the other for sleeping. This they towed by means of a motor boat, and in sixteen hours they traveled the 128 km downriver to Steveville, at the north end of Dead Lodge Canyon in what is now the heart of Dinosaur Provincial Park, and began prospecting even while the water heated up for coffee.

They were looking for complete skeletons of big dinosaurs. The first dinosaur fossils ever found in western Canada — a mere handful of bones and teeth from Saskatchewan — had been discovered in 1873 by George Mercer Dawson, a geologist with the North American Boundary Commission. Dawson sent them to Cope in Philadelphia for analysis, and Cope identified them as fragments of hadrosaur bones, turtle shells, and some gar fish scales. Nothing new (to Cope) and nothing very exciting. The great museums of the day were interested in huge, crowd-drawing displays — *Brontosaurus* skeletons stretching twenty-four meters from skull to tailtip — rather than in bits and pieces from microsites such as Dawson had found in western Canada.

One of Dawson's assistants on the Boundary Survey, though, made a more significant contribution to Canadian paleontology: Joseph Burr Tyrrell, a native Ontarian who first traveled with Dawson to Alberta in 1883 to help map Alberta.

The Sternbergs' flat-bottomed scow anchored about five kilometers below Steveville, on the Red Deer River, in 1913. They were the first to prospect in Dead Lodge Canyon, now the center of Dinosaur Provincial Park and the area that has yielded the most dinosaurs.

A year later, leading a survey field party in the badlands — Tyrrell's territory was an 18,210-hectare chunk of Alberta, roughly the area between the present sites of Calgary and Edmonton, with Drumheller more or less at its center — the young geologist made a startling discovery. "I was climbing up a steep face about four hundred feet high," he later recalled. "I stuck my head around a point and there was this skull, leering at me, sticking right out of the ground. It gave me a fright." Obviously, what he had found was no gar scale or crocodile tooth: when the skull was sent to Cope — no doubt at Dawson's suggestion, since there was no one in Canada qualified to look at it — Cope identified it as belonging to a large carnivorous dinosaur, which he named *Dryptosaurus sarcophagus*. In 1905, Osborn named a new genus for this species: *Albertosaurus sarcophagus*, an early cousin of *Tyrannosaurus rex*.

Tyrrell's large dinosaur sparked a flurry of interest in Canadian specimens, especially at the Geological Survey in Ottawa. When the Sternbergs arrived in Dead

Joseph Burr Tyrrell (1858-1957), after whom the Royal Tyrrell Museum of Paleontology is named, found the first large dinosaur in Alberta in 1884, while looking for coal. It was later named *Albertosaurus*, a relative of *Tyrannosaurus rex*.

Lodge Canyon almost thirty years later, in the summer of 1913, they were looking for big skeletons, and they found them. They discovered a *Corythosaurus* skeleton, one of the large crested hadrosaurs that looks as if it is wearing an old-fashioned football helmet. On another outing, Charles and Charlie literally stumbled upon an *Albertosaurus* skeleton, one "that promised to be the most perfect one known to science at that time." Unfortunately, it was entombed in a high, narrow ridge, and Charlie and an assistant, Jack McGee, spent six laborious weeks removing the tonnes of overburden that lay above the bones, then carefully chiseling the skeleton from the cliff face. A roadbed was carved into the side of the ridge so that a cart and horse could be brought up to the quarry. Each bone had to be shellacked, wrapped in Japanese rice paper, and then encased in plaster-soaked burlap to be readied for removal. Blocks of stone containing dozens of bones were carved whole from the cliff and hoisted by means of a block-and-tackle mounted on a tripod onto the wagon. The ridge was so narrow, writes Sternberg, "that if the horses had balked or a wheel had slipped, they would have been dashed to pieces in the gorge below." When they got the blocks back to Ottawa, Charlie spent eight months removing the bones from them with awls, small knives, chisels, and dental picks.

But the results justified the effort. The *Albertosaurus* skull was ninety centimeters long, its thirteen-centimeter teeth were double-edged and serrated, and Charles imagined it with flashing eyes and a forked tongue descending on a hapless hadrosaur. "His entire body, from the front of the jaw to the end of the tail, was twenty-nine feet in length. His powerful hind limbs, on which the entire body

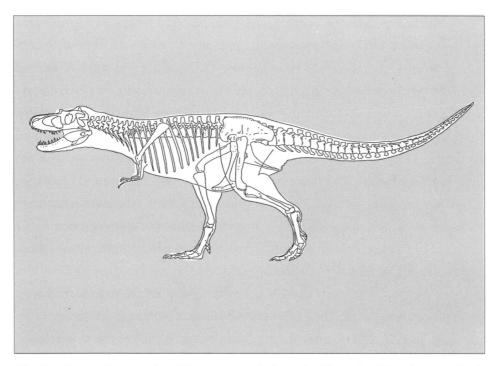

The Sternbergs discovered an *Albertosaurus* skeleton in Alberta in 1913 "that promised to be the most perfect one known to science." *Albertosaurus* stood up to five meters tall, weighed a thousand kilograms, and was a swift and powerful predator; specimens have also been found in the United States and possibly Mexico.

was balanced, were ten and a half feet in length. He had three great claw-armed toes, and one not so large, raised from the ground like the spur of a rooster. We were unable to imagine to what use they could have been put."

The Greatest Animal Show on Earth

As it happened, the Sternbergs had set up their camp less than one and a half kilometers from that of Barnum Brown. Like the Sternbergs, Brown was from Kansas; he had been born on Abraham Lincoln's birthday and was named after the circus magnate, P.T. Barnum. Also like the Sternbergs, he had spent the early part of his bone-hunting career in the Cretaceous formations of Wyoming and Montana. He began collecting for the American Museum of Natural History in 1897, and at his death in 1963 he had supplied that museum with the largest display of Cretaceous dinosaurs in the world.

Brown had an uncanny instinct for fossils; he could move into a quarry that had been worked over countless times and still come up with a major find. "Brown is the most amazing collector I've ever known," Osborn once said to Roy Chapman Andrews. "He must be able to smell fossils." It was Brown who, in 1902, discovered the world's first *Tyrannosaurus rex* in the Hell Creek Formation of southern Montana; two years later, in the Kirtland Formation in New Mexico, he unearthed the skull of a hitherto-unknown duckbill, which he named *Kritosaurus navajovius*; other kritosaur species have since been found in Alberta. He came to Canada in 1910 at the invitation of John Wegener, from Drumheller, who had found fossil bones on his ranch in the badlands. Brown knew of the colossal bone fields described by George Dawson, Joseph Tyrrell, and Lawrence Lambe, and he must also have known of another Canadian bonehunter, Thomas Chesmer Weston, who had gone west in the summer of 1888 as a member of the GSC and who had been the first man to penetrate the badlands by floating down the Red Deer on a flat-bottomed boat. In this manner Weston had discovered one of the richest fossil beds then known — precisely at the point near Dead Lodge Canyon where both Brown and the Sternbergs set up their camps in 1913.

The Sternbergs' field work that year was highly successful. Almost immediately, Charles H. found two more or less complete skeletons of a new duckbill, which Lambe named *Stephanosaurus marginatus*, or "the crowned lizard from Steveville." Barnum Brown, however, who had found a better skeleton nearby, had already named his *Corythosaurus casuarius* because, as Sternberg writes admiringly, "the crested head resembled a Cassowary," a large, ostrich-like bird found in New Guinea and Australia. *Corythosaurus* being the older name is the one that has stuck, although the subfamily is called Lambeosaurinae and includes *Lambeosaurus*, named in honor of Lawrence Lambe. Today, articulated skeletons of lambeosaurs outnumber those of flatheaded hadrosaurs in Dinosaur Provincial Park by two to one, making them probably the most common dinosaur in North America. The crest or "coxcomb" that adorns the top of a lambeosaur's head is thought to have functioned as a sound resonator, enabling the animal to communicate with other members of its species, either for individual identification or as a mating call. "The hollow crests emitted low-frequency sounds that would have carried well over great distances," writes Dale Russell. "In *Corythosaurus* 'males'

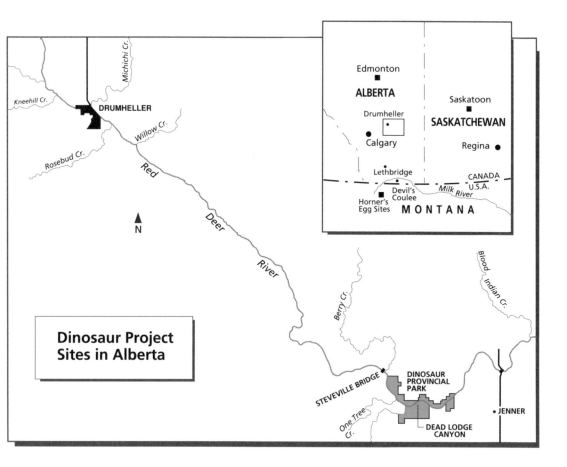

the rounded crests are larger and more inflated than those of 'females,' while *Lambeosaurus* 'males' bear a backwardly projecting rod that is absent in 'females.' The crests were not formed in hatchlings and began to develop when the juveniles attained a length of between one-third and one-half that of an adult. They thus very likely aided males and females in recognizing each other, the signal being acoustic in corythosaurs and visual in lambeosaurs." Russell places the designations "male" and "female" in quotes because it is difficult to identify gender confidently from skeletal remains alone.

Lambe was delighted with the Sternbergs' 1913 finds. Their field work for that summer, he wrote in his summary, "reveals in striking manner the wonderful variety of the dinosaurian life of the period. The field collection...includes members of the *Ceratops* (horned dinosaurs, quadrupedal, plant eaters), *Trachodontidae* (duck-billed dinosaurs, plant eaters), *Theropoda* (flesh eaters), and *Stegosauridae* (heavily armored plant eaters). *Plesiosaurs*, crocodiles, turtles, amphibians, and fishes are abundantly represented, and some mammalian remains were also found." These were the bones (except for the stegosaurid specimen which had been misidentified) that, when shipped back east, would form the basis of the great fossil collections of the National Museum of Science in Ottawa (now the Canadian Museum of Nature) and the Royal Ontario Museum in Toronto. Many of them are on display in both those institutions; many more are still in storage, still encased in the soft Alberta sandstone exactly as they were carved out by the Sternbergs more than seventy-five years ago. As Phil Currie has observed in another context, science is slow.

How Old Is Earth?

DURING THE EIGHTY YEARS SINCE THE STERNBERGS INITIATED THE GREAT Canadian Dinosaur Rush, major theoretical changes have taken place in our view of earth's history. For one thing, our concept of the length of that history has increased by a factor of forty. At the beginning of this century, when the Sternbergs were digging into the sandstones of Wyoming and Alberta, they had only a vague idea of how old that sandstone was. Sternberg wrote in amazement that he was witnessing for the first time evidence of life that had been hidden "for 3 million years or more." The beginning of the Cretaceous Period he placed at about 5 million years ago. Today, we know that it lasted 75 million years and ended 65 million years ago. Such a dramatic increase in our estimate of the age of earth has had a tremendous impact on the natural sciences: it has made Darwin possible.

The chief objection to Darwin's theory of gradual evolution had been that the earth was not old enough to allow for it. Creationists followed Archbishop James Ussher of Ireland, who in 1654 had claimed, based on genealogical evidence in the Bible — he counted up the ages listed in the "begatitudes" — that earth had been created on October 26, 4004 B.C., at nine o'clock in the morning. Ussher's arithmetic went out of serious contention with the publication in 1795 of *Theory of the Earth*, by James Hutton, the Scottish physician-turned-farmer often cited as "the father of modern geology." By a careful study of rocks and landforms, stream beds and cobblestones, Hutton deduced that all aspects of earth's crust had been produced by unimaginably slow forces that were still active in the present, and that therefore an enormous amount of time was required to create a continent out of an ocean floor, or a fertile plain out of a mountain. Hutton gave geologists their first dark inkling of what John McPhee has called "deep time." "The result of our physical enquiry," wrote Hutton, "is that we find no vestige of a beginning, no prospect of an end."

Sixty years later, geologists rejected Hutton's unsettling estimate of an infinite sweep of time and revised earth's age downward to conceivability — a few millions of years— but they agreed with Hutton's "principle of uniformity," which held that the processes of nature were constant. This belief was still around as late as 1865, when Lord Kelvin mathematically calculated the age of earth at between 20 million and 40 million years, based on estimates of cooling rates and the current temperature of earth's core (which he determined by assessing the difference between the temperature at the surface and that at the bottom of a mine shaft, and multiplying by earth's radius). His calculations depended entirely upon the supposition that the rate of cooling in earth's mantle has been constant since creation. Similarly, in 1899, Irish geologist John Joly came up with an earth age of 80 to 90 million years by calculating the amount of salt washed into the oceans each year, and dividing that figure into the estimated total amount of salt contained in the seven seas. By the turn of the century, there were almost as many estimates of the age of the planet as there were geologists on it; they averaged out to about 100 million years.

The problem with all of these calculations was that they were based on the assumption that changes on earth took place at a constant rate, an assumption that was untenable even at the time, given such unpredictable but nonetheless natural occurrences as, for example, volcanoes, which can add a thousand meters of rock to the earth's surface in a relatively short time. Too many of the factors involved — sedimentation rates for different kinds of rock, the actual thickness of the crust, extinction and proliferation of species — vary so much and so randomly that even relatively simple equations become unsolvable. And many of those variables had not even been discovered yet. Lord Kelvin's cooling constant for rock, for example, was formed decades before the discovery of the heating properties of uranium, which have an extraordinary effect on terrestrial temperatures.

It was not until 1906, when a radio-chemist at Yale University named B.B. Boltwood began pondering one of uranium's other properties — radioactive decay — that the implications of "deep time" really began to sink in. Boltwood noted that as uranium decayed, it turned into lead and did so at a constant rate, called its half-life. In a series of different uranium-bearing rocks arranged according to the amount of lead contained in each, those with the most lead invariably came from the oldest geological formations. Calculating the length of time it took uranium to turn into lead provided a reliable estimate of how old those formations were. The mathematics involved were not much more complicated than Lord Kelvin's (or even Ussher's), but the variables were better known.

Calculations by Boltwood and, later, Yale geologist Joseph Barrell determined that the oldest rock formations known at the time were about 1.8 billion years old. The oldest fossil-bearing rocks — in other words, the oldest records of life on earth — went back nearly 500 million years. This revision caused a great upheaval in the way people had to think about the planet and life on it — including their own. It also renewed interest in Darwin's account of how species evolved: 500 million years seemed plenty of time for one species to change into another.

The uranium-lead method had a flaw, however: there is more than one kind of uranium, and each kind decays at a different rate into a different kind of lead. Uranium-235, for example, decays to lead-207 six times faster than uranium-238 decays to lead-206. It also became clear that at least some lead — called primordial lead — had been present at the formation of the planet and so had to be excluded from the calculation. And as if that were not enough, it was even found that at least one kind of lead — lead-208 — didn't come from uranium at all, but from thorium-232. Not until mass spectrometers were perfected in the late 1930s were scientists able to distinguish between all these different isotopes, and not until 1956 was the existence of other decay series brought into play. The uranium-lead and thorium-lead series could be checked for accuracy against a whole range of similar radioactive progressions: rubidium-87 to strontium-87; potassium-40 to argon-40.

The result is an approximate age for earth of 4.6 billion years. No rock that old has ever been found — the oldest so far is in southern Greenland and was formed 3.76 billion years ago — but that is nonetheless the accepted age of the planet.

Of those 4600 million years, the Age of Reptiles spans only 180 million, or less than 4 percent of it. Still, the dinosaurs were incredibly successful. *Homo habilis*, the species of hominid from which we sapiens are believed to have descended, lived 3.5 million years ago. Compare earth's history to a pair of outstretched arms, as McPhee does in *Basin and Range*, and human history is wiped out by the paring of a fingernail on one hand; cut off the finger at the middle knuckle and the dinosaurs disappear as well.

Geologists divide those 4600 million years into eras, periods, and ages in much the same way we divide a year into months, days, and hours. The oldest (and longest) era, called the Precambrian, stretches from the dark backward and abysm of Time, when no life was (except for gray-green bacteria), to about 570 million years ago, when the first multicellular beings began stirring in the oceans. American paleontologist Stephen Jay Gould believes that like all the eras on the Geological Scale (with the exception, so far, of the one we are in now), the Precambrian may have ended with a mass extinction that wiped out nearly all life on earth and ushered in the Paleozoic Era, "paleo" meaning ancient and "zoic" meaning life. The first period in the Paleozoic, the Cambrian, is distinguished by the "Cambrian explosion," a sudden proliferation of life from the few multicellular organisms that survived the crash to a vast and complex array of body plans — the Burgess Shale fauna — such as earth has not seen since.

The last period of the Paleozoic Era was the Permian, which came to a sudden end 225 million years ago; again, a catastrophe of unimaginable proportions, the Permian/Triassic Extinctions, marked the boundary between two eras, with 96 percent of all species being eradicated by we know not what. The event ended the dominance of the amphibians and opened ecological niches that were filled by the great reptiles. As a measure of the extent of the catastrophe, consider that after it the world sea level dropped 310 meters. No wonder reptiles, which could lay their eggs on dry land, took over from amphibians, which still needed to return to water to reproduce.

The Paleozoic Era was followed by the Mesozoic ("middle life"), which is divided into the three periods that make up the Age of Reptiles: the Triassic, the Jurassic, and the Cretaceous. These are named either after the geographical areas in which the rocks that typify them were first studied — rocks from the Jurassic

Period, for example, were first identified in the Jura mountains of Switzerland —
or for attributes of the rocks themselves. "Cretaceous" comes from the Latin word
for chalk, *creta*, since the period was first associated with the white cliffs of Dover,
in southern England. (Although chalk, a form of limestone, was the first rock identified from the Cretaceous, the sandstones of China and North America are more
typical of the period.) Triassic refers to the three divisions of stone from Germany
that were first identified in it: the Bunt Sandstein; the Muschelkalk (mussel limestone, after the shells from which it is made); and the Keuper (white and brown
sandstone).

Formation of the Badlands

CRETACEOUS ALBERTA, THE HOME OF THE HUGE CARNOSAURS *ALBERTOSAURUS*
and *Tyrannosaurus rex*, the smaller theropods, *Troodon* and *Dromaeosaurus*, and
their prey, the hadrosaurs and ceratopsians, was a low, swampy shoreline on the
edge of the Western Interior Seaway, a huge body of salt water stretching down
the center of what is now North America from the Arctic Ocean to the Gulf of
Mexico. The low shoreline was a thin corridor between the seaway and the foothills
of the mountains to the west. At the end of the Late Cretaceous, the Rocky
Mountains had just begun to form, a result of the collision between the Pacific
and North American plates. As the young orogenous zone was pushed up, the layers of sediment on top of it were loosened, and rain-fed rivers gushing out of the
new mountains washed the soil off to either side: in the west, the sediments spread
out along the ocean floor to form the Pacific continental shelf; to the east, they created a vast alluvial plain between the mountains and the seaway. Fast-running,
silt-laden rivers cut through the alluvial plain, forming deep river channels and
vast deltas where the rivers spilled into the seaway, growing ever larger as the
shoreline retreated to the east.

Eventually this alluvial plain became a 480-km-wide corridor resembling the
present-day deltaic shorelines of the southern United States. In a remarkable,
trance-like passage in *Hunting Dinosaurs*, Sternberg describes this habitat as "a
low country but little above sea level, great flats near the sea covered with high
swamp grass, rushes and moss, through which meander sluggish streams,

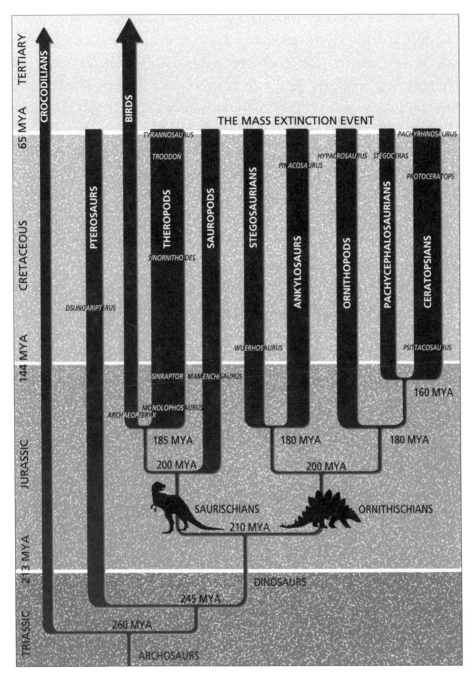

THE MASS EXTINCTION EVENT

CROCODILIANS

BIRDS

PTEROSAURS

THEROPODS

SAUROPODS

STEGOSAURIANS

ANKYLOSAURS

ORNITHOPODS

PACHYCEPHALOSAURIANS

CERATOPSIANS

TYRANNOSAURUS

TROODON

PINACOSAURUS

HYPACROSAURUS *STEGOCERAS*

PACHYRHINOSAURUS

PROTOCERATOPS

SINORNITHODES

DSUNGARIPTERUS

WUERHOSAURUS

PSITTACOSAURUS

SINRAPTOR *MAMENCHISAURUS*

MONOLOPHOSAURUS

ARCHAEOPTERYX

160 MYA

185 MYA   180 MYA   180 MYA

200 MYA   200 MYA

SAURISCHIANS   ORNITHISCHIANS

210 MYA

DINOSAURS

245 MYA

260 MYA

ARCHOSAURS

TERTIARY

65 MYA

CRETACEOUS

144 MYA

JURASSIC

213 MYA

TRIASSIC

The Age of the Reptiles comprised three geological Periods: the Triassic, Jurassic, and Cretaceous. Alberta's badlands cover about 10 million years of the Cretaceous; China has exposures from all three Periods. During the Dinosaur Project's five field seasons, dinosaurs from all main groups were found.

lagoons, and bayous, often widening out into lakes of considerable size, all receiving the high and low tides of the nearby ocean. On the rising land the giant redwoods cast their shadows across the silent streams. They grow in fairy circles with the parent tree in the center often, or in case she has dropped out, a hollow circle is formed. Palms, sycamores, figs, magnolias and many other trees that now adorn our forests, thrived along the Cretaceous everglades."

As they do today, those everglades provided a perfect environment for all sorts of terrestrial, freshwater, and marine life. Many kinds of large dinosaurs roamed the corridor in the Late Cretaceous, most of them duckbills or tubeheads — *Corythosaurus, Lambeosaurus, Kritosaurus, Prosaurolophus*. But there were also the horned dinosaurs, like *Centrosaurus* and *Chasmosaurus*, and the armored ankylosaur *Euoplocephalus*. The Late Cretaceous was a warm and humid time; fossilized pollen and spore samples found in Dinosaur Provincial Park indicate that in the lowlands cypress trees were common, "as were plants allied to the modern parasitic mistletoes, cycads, tree ferns, and the often-herbaceous lilies," writes Dale Russell in *An Odyssey in Time*. "Other interesting plants included bushy podocarps (bonze pines), katsura trees, and members of the cashew-poison ivy family." Petrified cypress logs sixty centimeters in diameter and more than fifteen meters long have been found wedged into ancient sandbars, and "one stump has been found that belonged to a pineapple-like 'cycad' (bennettitalean) which grew so abundantly during the older part of the dinosaurian era." Analysis of the growth rings of these petrified trunks suggests that they lived through alternating wet and dry periods. On the higher ground, deciduous trees flourished, and the flatlands between the low river marshes probably resembled African savannahs. All in all, seventy-five different plant species have been identified in the Judith River Formation in Dinosaur Park alone. Dinosaurs were so numerous on the flatlands, writes Russell, that "the region was probably littered with broken branches and received a rain of dung amounting to 500 metric tonnes per square kilometer per year. Footprints and trails criss-crossed flatlands that in many areas would have been strongly reminiscent of nothing lovelier than a barnyard."

After the Cretaceous, the Interior Seaway dried up and disappeared, so that the two halves of the continent eventually became one. But sediments continued to wash down from the western mountains, and over the next 50 million years or so the Cretaceous deposits were buried under many meters of more recent material. Then came the Ice Ages, when glaciers more than a kilometer thick covered much of North America. During the most recent period of glacial advance, the Wisconsin, which ended about 11,000 years ago (if it ended at all — some say we are still in it), so much of the earth's fresh water was tied up in glaciers that the world sea level was seventy-six meters lower than it is today. As the glaciers melted, much of that water collected in vast inland lakes before bursting through their gravel and ice barriers in a mad rush for the sea. Many such lakes covered the central plains of North America. The biggest was Glacial Lake Agassiz in the east, 400 km wide and more than 1,100 km long — the largest freshwater lake that ever existed on this continent. It occupied most of what is now western Ontario, Manitoba, Saskatchewan, North Dakota, and Minnesota and was fed by streams running westward from the Appalachian and Laurentian highlands. Its main outlet was the Glacial River Warren, which cut south and east until it joined the present-day Mississippi channel.

One of Glacial Lake Agassiz's western counterparts was Glacial Lake Bassano, a huge body of fresh meltwater trapped between the Rockies in the west and the retreating face of the glacier in the northeast. Glacial deposits formed a natural dam and, when this dam burst, the floodwaters roared out with tremendous force. Blocked from their preglacial east-flowing riverbeds by the glacier itself, the meltwaters ran south along the ice edge, carving through the soft sandstone and till to form the Red Deer Valley. Dinosaur Provincial Park is at about the southern extreme of the glacier; here the water found an ancient preglacial channel running almost due east, which it followed until it joined the South Saskatchewan River at what is now the Alberta-Saskatchewan border.

The torrent of water draining out of Glacial Lake Bassano carved a riverbed 80 m across and more than 135 m deep, cutting down through 75 million years of sediment and exposing layers of the earth that had not seen sunlight since the Age of Reptiles. Along the chasm, encased in the sandstone, mudstone, and volcanic ash, lay the fossilized bones of the dinosaurs. As the lake bed emptied, the torrent slowed to a meandering trickle at the bottom of a scoured ditch. Over the next 10,000 years a few tenacious evergreens fought for rootholds in the canyon's dendritic clays, and the erosion begun by the draining of Glacial Lake Bassano was continued by steady rains and huge snowfalls.

The Sternbergs returned to Alberta every summer for three more years. In 1916, however, war preparations in Ottawa began to sap funding from dinosaur projects, and after the famous fire on Parliament Hill that year the government moved its offices into the Victoria Memorial Museum while its own buildings were being rebuilt. The GSC was squeezed into the basement, where there was barely room for staff, never mind monthly intrusions of gigantic plaster-of-paris packages from Alberta. To all intents and purposes, the First Great Canadian Dinosaur Rush was over barely five years after it had begun.

Paleontology in China

ALBERTA'S BADLANDS CONTAIN ROCK EXPOSURES FROM THE LATE CRETACEOUS Period that are from 65 million to about 84 million years old. China, by way of contrast, has a fossil record covering the entire Mesozoic Era, from the Early Triassic to the Late Cretaceous, and beyond that into the Cenozoic Era, the Age of Mammals. Ironically, it was the presence of mammal fossils in China that first brought European paleontologists to that country, although it has been the dinosaurs that have brought them back.

The Chinese have been fossil bonehunters for thousands of years. They called them *Long Gu* (dragon's bones) and *Long Ya* (dragon's teeth) and ground them up into powder and drank them in tea as a cure-all for almost every ailment known to humankind, from dysentery to malaria. The oldest medical text in China, purportedly written by the mythological emperor Sheng Nung, prescribes *Long Ya* as a cure for spasms, epilepsy, madness, and convulsions in children. The historian Lei Hiao, who died in A.D. 477, advised those who searched for dragon bones to take only those of the highest quality: "Dragons' bones from Yen Chou, Tsang Chou and Tai Yen are the best. Those which are narrow with broad veins are from female dragons; those which are coarse, with narrow veins, are from the opposite sex. Those showing five colours are best; the white and yellow are medium quality and the black ones are worst. As a rule, it may be said that those in which the veins are longitudinal are impure, and those collected by women are useless."

Dragon bones were mined, like gold and diamonds, and because they fetched such high prices in China's apothecary shops, the whereabouts of the richest mines was a closely guarded secret. In 1899, a German scientist named K.A. Haberer traveled to China to study the natural history of its interior, but owing to the hostility to foreigners after the Boxer Uprising, his activities were restricted to the so-called treaty ports: Shanghai, Ningpo, Ichang, and Peking. There, Haberer was more or less obliged to collect fossils by buying them from apothecaries. In 1903, he shipped his collection to the famous paleontologist Max Schlosser, in Munich, who distinguished in it bones from no less than ninety different species of extinct mammals, including saber-toothed tigers, mastodons, camels, rhinoceri, and the three-toed proto-horse *Hipparion*. But only one specimen in the shipment created a stir in Europe: among the pile of paleo debris was a tooth, an upper molar, that was quite possibly human. Schlosser named it *Gigantopithecus*, because it was nearly three times the size of a modern molar, and casually mentioned in his monograph that, on the basis of that one tooth, China would be a good place to search for the origins of modern man.

Since Darwin's *The Descent of Man*, published in 1871, the idea that human beings were descended from apes had gained general acceptance: in fact, Huxley had shown in 1863 that in most visible characteristics man differed less from the anthropoid apes than those apes differed from the lower primates. And there was more evidence for the theory than there was for the dinosaur-bird connection: Gibraltar Man had been found in 1848, Neanderthal Man in 1856, and Java Man (*Pithecanthropus erectus*, now called *Homo erectus*), the oldest hominid fossil then known, had been found in 1892 by the brilliant but erratic Dutch anatomist Eugène Dubois. By the beginning of this century, the question concerning the descent of human beings from apes was not whether it had happened, but where and when.

There were two theories: man must have originated either in Africa, where gorillas and chimpanzees still lived and where both *Homo erectus* and the later Cro-Magnon Man seemed to have come from, or in southeast Asia, where the orang-utan was found. The discovery of Java Man and *Gigantopithecus* — both older than Neanderthal Man by at least a million years — had placed Asia in the lead in the race to be paleontology's Garden of Eden. But Africa was still a hot contender, since ancient migration routes into Europe and Asia had been determined by anthropologists to have led into the north through present-day Ethiopia.

The identification of Asia as the home of humankind sat well with the scientific racism of the day: Europeans did not want to think of themselves as the descendants, however remote, of black Africans. In 1915, Henry Fairfield Osborn of the American Museum admitted that human evolution took place outside of Europe: "The sudden appearance in Europe at least 25,000 years ago of a human race with a high order of brain power and ability was not a leap forward, but the effect of a long process of evolution elsewhere." But he assured his readers that anthropological evidence showing that early European cultures had come out of Africa "does not mean that ... these Lower Paleolithic races were of negroid or Ethiopian affinity, because the Neanderthals show absolutely no negroid characters." Osborn hinted coyly that "when the prehistory of eastern Europe and of Asia has been investigated, we may obtain some light on this antecedent development."

Osborn followed up his conjecture the following year by approving an American Museum expedition to China, the stated purpose of which was to find evidence of early man. The expedition had been proposed by Roy Chapman Andrews, who was under no illusions about the purpose of it. "The main problem," Andrews wrote, "was to be a study of the geological history of central Asia; to find whether it had been the nursery of many of the dominant groups of animals, including the human race; and to reconstruct its past climate, vegetation and general physical condition, particularly in relation to the evolution of man." The Andrews expedition was not looking for dinosaurs; it was not even looking in dinosaur-aged rock. It was to concentrate on the last million years or so of earth history.

Andrews was not a paleontologist. He was a zoologist and an adventurer. Although the suggestion that film maker Steven Spielberg modeled his character Indiana Jones, the swashbuckling hero of *Raiders of the Lost Ark*, on the intrepid Andrews is probably not true — "Who's Andrews?" Spielberg is reported to have said when asked — the archetype fits well. Andrews was born in Beloit, Wisconsin, in 1884, and after college he joined the American Museum staff as a janitor in 1906. Twenty years later he was its director. Most of the intervening years were spent in the field: in 1908 he worked at a whaling station near Vancouver, British Columbia, studying cetacean behavior as the whalers sank their harpoons into them; during a trip to Japan he rediscovered the gray whale, long thought to have been extinct.

By the end of the First World War he was in Peking as an agent for U.S. Naval Intelligence. Altogether he spent eighteen field seasons in China; it was the time of the warlords, when the country was divided into a quiltwork of feifdoms, each controlled by a powerful local bandit. For Andrews it was a vestige of the American Wild West; he walked about carrying sidearms, he chased and was chased by gangs of marauders, he risked his life regularly in the name of science.

Apart from his love of adventure, his qualifications for the mission were solid: he was well enough known in New York City to be able to raise the necessary private capital for the expedition (the museum could not have afforded such a venture on its own), and he was smart enough to surround himself with people who were experts in their fields. For his chief scientist he chose Walter Granger, a paleontologist with an impressive background in fossil collecting, and sent him to Peking in 1921 to begin preparations for the trek into the Gobi the following year.

While in Peking, Granger found that a small group of foreign paleontologists was already there, working for the Chinese government, also looking for evidence of early man. They included Amadeus Grabau, founder of the Chinese Geological Survey and a professor at the University of Peking; Swedish geologist J. Gunnar Andersson, who had been with the Chinese Geological Survey since 1914; his assistant Otto Zdansky; and the Canadian anatomist Davidson Black, who was teaching at the Peking Union Medical College.

Black was on the trail of Peking Man. He and Andrews were the same age — Black was born in Toronto, Ontario, in 1884, the son of a Queen's Counsel lawyer who died when Black was two years old. A graduate of the University of Toronto School of Medicine, Black had become interested in paleontology in 1915 after reading *Climate and Evolution* by William D. Matthew, a Canadian paleontologist who was in New York working on fossils Cope had collected for the American Museum. Matthew's book, a study of the role of climate change in the dispersal of land vertebrates, cemented in Black's mind the importance of Asia as the possible ancestral home of man. When, in 1919, he was offered the post of professor of neurology and embryology at the Peking Union Medical College, one of the most advanced medical schools in the world, built (at a cost of $9.5 million) and solely funded by the Rockefeller Foundation, he had accepted immediately.

Within two years, Black had become as involved in the study of anthropolo-

For ten years (1921 to 1930), Roy Chapman Andrews led Central Asiatic Expeditions into Mongolia to search for the origins of *Homo sapiens*. He didn't find them, but he did collect the first specimens of dinosaurs that would later be the focus of the Dinosaur Project.

gy as he was in the teaching of neurology. Stories about Haberer and *Gigantopithecus* were still fresh among the learned circles in Peking, and when Andersson and Zdansky began excavating in a series of Pleistocene caves about fifty kilometers south of the city, in an area known as Chou K'ou Tien, or "Chicken Bone Hill," Black was easily able to follow their progress. The two geologists invited Walter Granger, who specialized in fossil mammals, down to Chou K'ou Tien to show them how to extract bone from limestone and to provide him with a taste of Chinese working conditions.

When Andrews arrived the following year, he was so impressed by Black that he invited him to join the American expedition as its chief anatomist — an invitation Black turned down, although he did agree to accompany Andrews as far north as Urga (now called Ulaan Baator), the capital of Outer Mongolia. The expedition left Peking in a horn-tooting motorcade on April 17. Two weeks later it reached Iren Dabasu — near present-day Erenhot, on the Chinese side of the border between Inner and Outer Mongolia — where Andrews set up camp to await permission to proceed into Soviet-influenced Outer Mongolia.

That evening, one of Andrews's geologists, Charles Berkey, found part of a fossil limb bone that Granger said could not be mammalian. "It might possibly be a bird," he told Andrews, "but it must have been some bird to have a leg-bone like that."

Later the same evening, Davidson Black found the rest of the limb bone while walking to his tent. Berkey and Granger put the two pieces together and immediately began to hunt for the place where the bone had come out of the rock. They found it at the top of a nearby outcrop and called Andrews to look. There was no doubt about it, they told Andrews: the bone was not mammalian, and it was not bird. It was dinosaur. "We are standing on Cretaceous strata of the upper part of the Age of Reptiles," said Berkey; "the first Cretaceous strata, and the first dinosaur ever discovered in Asia north of the Himalaya Mountains."

In fact, the first dinosaur discovery in China had taken place nearly ten years earlier in the province of Shantung, slightly south of Peking, where the Yellow River empties into the Yellow Sea, but still well north of the Himalayas. The find had been made by one of the Geological Survey's mining engineers, W. Behagel, and the bone was in the Geological Museum in Peking in 1921, when Gunnar

Andersson showed it to Walter Granger. Granger identified it as definitely dinosaur, probably sauropod, and possibly Cretaceous. A few years after Behagel's discovery, in 1914, a Russian paleontologist, A.N. Krystofovich, had found dinosaur bones on the banks of the Amur River, in the extreme north of Manchuria. The Russians were somewhat close-mouthed about their work, so Andrews may be excused for not knowing about it. But Granger definitely knew of the earlier find. Whether he told Andrews or not is unknown, but Andrews made no mention of it. For the next seven years Andrews returned to Mongolia to hunt for early man, without success. Instead, he gleaned support for Osborn's theory from the mammal and dinosaur material he found in abundance. "The dinosaur bone," he wrote, "was the first indication that the theory upon which we had organized the expedition might be true: that Asia is the mother of the life of Europe and America." For Andrews, the dinosaur bone he found *had* to be the first; otherwise the entire expedition was a failure.

When Black returned to Peking a few weeks later, he found that yet another foreigner had arrived in China to look for hominid fossils. This was Pierre Teilhard de Chardin, chief paleontologist with the Institut Catholique in Paris. For two years, another French Jesuit and naturalist, Father Emile Licent, had been finding evidence of Paleolithic (Old Stone Age) Man in cliffs on the western side of the Ordos Basin, in north-central China — pieces of quartz that seemed to have been shaped into cutting tools by human hands — and he had invited Teilhard de Chardin to help him find actual hominid fossils. The two men worked diligently, unearthing nearly half a tonne of stone fragments and bones from dozens of species of mammals, many of them obviously deposited there by prehistoric human hunters, and finally, in 1924, a tooth of one of the humans. Since *Gigantopithecus* is now known to be an ape, Teilhard and Licent were the first paleontologists to find evidence of early man in China.

Zdansky was the second. Still digging in Chou K'ou Tien in 1926, Zdansky found a molar and pre-molar of a hominid apparently much older than that found by the French priests in the Ordos. That year two scientific papers appeared, one in the journal *Nature* and another in *Science*, dating the teeth as Late Pliocene or possibly Early Pleistocene. The owner of the teeth was named *Sinanthropus pekinensis* — Peking Man. The author of both papers was Davidson Black.

Andrews was not alone on the trail of ancient man: others included Canadian anatomist Davidson Black (third from right); French paleontologist Teilhard de Chardin (second from right); and Black's colleague, George S. Barbour (far right). Two of China's top paleontologists were also working here at the Peking Man site: W.C. Pei (far left) and C.C. Young (fourth from left). The tall man standing at center is probably the famous British anthropologist Sir Grafton Elliot Smith.

"Whether it be of Late Tertiary or early Quaternary age," Black wrote of Peking Man, "the outstanding fact remains that for the first time on the Asiatic continent north of the Himalayas, archaic hominid fossil material has been recovered accompanied by complete and certain geological data. The actual presence of early man in eastern Asia is therefore now no longer a matter of conjecture."

It was also no longer a matter of much importance. For Black was too late. Or rather, Peking Man was. His place on the lowest rung of humankind's evolutionary ladder had already been usurped in February 1925, when Raymond A. Dart announced the discovery of a Late Pliocene hominid skull that was at least 2 million years old. The skull had been found near Taung, in South Africa; Dart named it *Australopithecus africanus*. Peking Man, in fact all of Asia, was out of the running.

Meanwhile, the American expedition forged on. From the point of view of human prehistory, the expedition was a complete bust. No ape-man, cave-man, or stone-age-man was ever found. From a more general paleological standpoint, however, Andrews and his team made some very important discoveries. After leaving Iren Dabasu in 1922 and entering Outer Mongolia, they followed an ancient caravan route to Shabarakh Usu, dubbed the Flaming Cliffs by Andrews because of the incredible range of colors striating the Late Cretaceous sandstone. There they found the first *Protoceratops*, an early horned dinosaur with a relatively small neck frill, distantly related to the North American *Triceratops*. They also found the first dinosaur eggs known to science, a sensational discovery that brought Osborn over from the United States. Perhaps he saw the eggs as symbolic substantiation for his theory about Asia: if China was not the cradle of life on earth, perhaps it was the nest.

Andrews continued to lead five expeditions into the Gobi, the last one in 1930. Chinese nationalism was growing particularly onerous to a man of Andrews's temperament. Scuffles with armed brigands in the Gobi had been one thing — the Chinese government had been as anxious to control the warlords as Andrews was. But China's internal politics underwent enormous upheavals throughout the period of the American expeditions. On May 4, 1919, students in Peking had rioted to protest what they saw as foreign — mainly Japanese — influence on Chinese affairs. The movement spread into a general rejection of all foreign control, and a resurgence of the anti-Western paranoia fostered during the Boxer Rebellion, and culminated in another violent outbreak in 1925, during which student rioters were shot and imprisoned. A nation-wide boycott of all British and Japanese trade ensued. Sun Yat-sen, China's leader since the 1911 revolution, appealed to the West for military aid to put down the student movement, was refused, and so turned to the Soviet Union. In response, two alternative political parties were set up: the Chinese Communist Party, established by Mao Zedong and Chou En-lai; and the Nationalist Party, or Kuomintang, led by Jiang Gaishek. The three-way civil war that ensued — four-way, if one counts continuing skirmishes with the warlords — lasted from 1926 to 1935, the year of Mao Zedong's famous Long March. Andrews spent 1931 and 1932 in Peking writing up his notes on the expedition's field work, then returned to the United States to become director of the American Museum.

Davidson Black stayed on in China. He had always been most eager to work with his Chinese colleagues and treated them as equals. Andrews stopped going to the Gobi in 1929 because the Chinese government forced him to take Chinese

**The Central Asiatic Expedition in the Nakou Pass, en route to Peking.
Andrews was the first to use motor vehicles on a scientific expedition,
but could do so only with caravans of camels to keep his motorcade
supplied with gasoline. Note the Great Wall rising in the background.**

scientists along (one of whom was C.C. Young). In 1929 Black received $80,000 from the Rockefeller Foundation to set up the Cenozoic Research Laboratory in Peking, and he gladly shared the directorship with the Chinese scientist V.K. Ting. Teilhard de Chardin was his official advisor on animal fossils, but C.C. Young was named assistant director and chief paleontologist. Black continued working in China until his death in 1934. The German paleontologist Franz Wedenreich replaced Black for a time, but when Mao Zedong pushed the Kuomintang off mainland China onto the island of Formosa and declared the People's Republic of China in 1949, the Cenozoic Research Laboratory was renamed the Laboratory of Vertebrate Paleontology (it became the IVPP in 1958), and C.C. Young was appointed its director.

Young — Dong Zhiming calls him "the father of Chinese vertebrate paleontology" — was born in 1897 and lived until 1979. He graduated from the University of Peking in 1923, which means he studied paleontology under Grabau, and he

A Polish expedition to Mongolia in 1971, seen here camped near the Altan Ula range, found a *Velociraptor* that was almost identical to the North American *Deinonychus*. Why different climates should have similar dinosaurs was one of the questions the Dinosaur Project set out to answer.

went to Munich to study under the great German paleontologist Friedrich von Huene. After receiving his Ph.D. in 1927, he returned to China to study fossil rodents collected at the Peking Man site; he also accompanied Teilhard de Chardin and Emile Licent into the Ordos. He traveled with Andrews to Inner Mongolia in 1930, but returned to direct the excavations at Chou K'ou Tien and remained there until 1931. Over the next forty years, he concentrated on dinosaur fossils, discovering and naming more than twenty different species, including one of the dinosaurs destined to play a major role in the Dinosaur Project: the huge sauropod *Mamenchisaurus*.

However, as in North America, the exciting years of discovery were over. In the early 1920s, when it was thought that China would turn out to be the birthplace of *Homo sapiens*, the world's attention was focused on the finds of the three groups of paleontological adventurers. After that, the little field work that took place did so behind a bamboo curtain, with very little information filtering through to the international scientific community. A series of expeditions from Soviet-bloc countries — Polish expeditions into Outer Mongolia during the late 1940s and from 1965 to 1971, and the foreshortened Sino-Soviet Expedition of 1959-60 — yielded tonnes of fossils, but none of it was made available to scientists in the West. Just as the Great Canadian Dinosaur Rush fizzled out during the First World War, so the first great dinosaur rush in China ended in 1930, when Roy Chapman Andrews pulled his team out of Central Asia. Not until the late 1970s, when China's political attitude toward the West began to thaw, did Western paleontologists begin to hear again about the fascinating abundance of Central Asia's fossil fauna. What they heard, and what they were finding in their own back yards, stimulated a new era in paleontological research. Even the idea of China as an ancestral home was revived. When members of the Dinosaur Project got their first look at the material coming out of the Gobi Desert, they began to suspect that what is now Asia might have been the birthplace of the dinosaurs. Perhaps, in a way entirely unsuspected by him, Osborn was right after all.

The New Paleontology

WHEN PHIL CURRIE MOVED TO EDMONTON IN 1976 TO WORK FOR THE PROVINCIAL Museum, he was still writing his doctoral thesis under Bob Carroll, at McGill. In Phil's words, Carroll was "one of the movers and shakers" in vertebrate evolution. Carroll's research had led him into new fields of paleontological theory; he was questioning assumptions about fossil reptiles that had been made for a century and a half. In his book *Vertebrate Paleontology and Evolution*, Carroll notes that until the early 1970s, paleontologists assumed that since dinosaurs closely resembled modern lizards and crocodiles anatomically, they must have been like them in other ways as well. "Since these modern reptiles have a low metabolic rate and limited capacity for sustained activity," Carroll writes, "it was long assumed that dinosaurs had a similarly sluggish way of life." That view and its related assumptions have been challenged only in the past two decades. Contemporary paleontologists have found "much evidence...to suggest that dinosaurs differed significantly from modern reptiles physiologically and may have more closely resembled modern mammals and birds."

The challenge came from paleontologists whose backgrounds were not in geology, the traditional prerequisite for a degree in paleontology, but in biology. Carroll is a professor of biology, and biology is the backbone of the new paleontology. The effect of the application of biology to paleontology has been likened to that of particle physics on astronomy: new worlds of thought have been opened up. Paleontologists no longer look at dinosaurs strictly as fossils; they are considering them as animals.

"We were a whole new school of kids coming up," says Phil, "working on brand new ideas and new ways of looking at things. As biologists, we were intensely interested in ecology, and no one had ever done that kind of work on dinosaurs before. Suddenly we began to wonder if we could learn something about dinosaur behavior by applying biological principles to paleontology."

Carroll's specialty was the group of Permian reptiles called eosuchians, or "early crocodiles" — small, lizard-like animals that may have given rise to the suborder Lepidosauria, which includes modern lizards and snakes, and to the Archosauromorpha. Phil's research was in aquatic eosuchians, which eventually led him to the ancestors of the Archosauria, the suborder that includes the dinosaurs.

At McGill, he studied material that had been found by field paleontologists, some of it as long ago as the nineteenth century. When he moved to the Provincial Museum, he became a field paleontologist himself. He and Linda excavated a *Gryposaurus* skeleton from the Milk River, and a partial *Edmontosaurus* from the Red Deer River. He soon turned his attention to Dinosaur Provincial Park, and what he found there upset much that had been known about dinosaurs in North America. As a rule, carnivores were thought to make up about 20 to 25 percent of North American dinosaurs, for example. Of the thirty-five species of dinosaurs found in Dinosaur Park, however, thirteen of them are carnivores, representing six different families of theropods. "Some of these families look as though they might be related," says Phil. As the new science director of the Tyrrell Museum, he initiated massive multidisciplinary field programs in the park "with the aim of testing things like dinosaur physiology." What he learned from the programs, however, told him more about dinosaur behavior than dinosaur anatomy: "We found ourselves getting down to the nitty-gritties."

Among the nitty-gritties was an interest in determining growth series within a species — how juveniles differ from adults, for example, or males from females. Baby dinosaurs are not simply miniature versions of adults; they change anatomically and physiologically as they mature, sometimes so much so that juveniles and adults of the same species have actually been mis-classified as different species. Phil's work led him to begin studying population structures — a highly speculative field that included theories about such things as the ratio of adults to juveniles, how herds moved, whether baby dinosaurs stayed together in groups and were cared for by adults or dispersed shortly after hatching.

Where earlier paleontologists had contented themselves with anatomical descriptions of individual dinosaurs, the new paleontologists were equally interested in how dinosaurs interacted with each other, with their environment, and with members of other species. They wondered about predator-prey dynamics. Did theropods hunt alone, like bears, or in packs, like wolves? Were herbivores solitary, like moose, or did they gather in herds, like buffalo? Did they lay their eggs in nests, like birds, or in holes in the ground, like turtles? Were they warm-blooded or cold-blooded? How intelligent were they?

These questions began to coalesce into new theories about dinosaur physiology, variation, speciation, extinction, and behavior. "It all started with the warm-blooded debate," says Phil. In the late 1960s, American paleontologist John Ostrom discovered a hitherto unknown small dinosaur, a theropod he named *Deinonychus*, in the Montana badlands. Small theropods at that time were little known; this one was a cousin of the mighty *Tyrannosaurus rex* — it was carnivorous and bipedal, with short forearms adapted to holding prey — but it weighed only about sixty-eight kilograms and was less than three meters long. Its distinguishing characteristic, in fact the attribute that gave it its name, was a huge, hooked, deadly looking claw on each hind foot, obviously used as defensive weapons as well as tools for killing prey. Ostrom hypothesized that in order to bring this hind-leg claw into position for attack or defense, *Deinonychus* must have been an agile, well-balanced, and swift animal — a far cry from the prevailing view of dinosaurs as sluggish, ponderous morons. "That slashing attack required highly accurate foot-eye coordination," Ostrom concluded, "and a keen sense of balance. Such agility and speed are not what we usually visualize in cold-blooded reptiles.

The image is more that of the large flightless birds like the ostrich." Thus, not only did *Deinonychus* revive the century-old theory of a possible connection between dinosaurs and birds; it also introduced an entirely new possibility: that some dinosaurs at least were warm-blooded.

One of Ostrom's colleagues at the Montana dig was a young graduate student named Robert Bakker. Excited by Ostrom's ideas about warm-bloodedness, Bakker spent the next decade and a half working out a whole new view of dinosaur physiology in which he posited that all Jurassic and Cretaceous dinosaurs, from the tiny *Compsognathus* to the huge sauropods, were warm-blooded. This generalization has been modified recently, but the broad outlines of it are intact. Phil concedes that *Tyrannosaurus* and the large sauropods were big enough to maintain constant body temperatures without being warm-blooded — "It's really kind of egotistical of human beings to think that dinosaurs would naturally want to be like us" — but today few paleontologists seriously doubt that the small dinosaurs, at least, were warm-blooded.

Deinonychus also opened the door to another theory about dinosaur behavior: herding. In the same quarry as *Deinonychus*, Ostrom found partial skeletons of a herbivorous dinosaur, *Tenontosaurus* — a six-meter, 450-kg monster, possibly a link between iguanodonts and the later hadrosaurs — and reasoned that the quadruped was the prey animal of the small theropods. He concluded that *Deinonychus* must have hunted in packs. Since then, evidence from a wide variety of sources — egg colonies, trackways, bonebeds — has proven beyond reasonable doubt that some of the larger herbivores also traveled in herds, and a scenario has developed in which packs of small, vicious predatory theropods followed huge herds of hadrosaurs and ceratopsians much as wolf packs track herds of caribou today.

This image led to a consideration of dinosaurs as migratory animals: obviously, herds of up to 10,000 animals, each weighing four tonnes and eating hundreds of kilograms in vegetation daily, could not stay in one spot for very long. Recently, biologists have begun to work out migratory patterns for the gigantic herds of buffalo that once dominated the Canadian and American prairie grasslands based on the natural crop rotation of prairie tallgrass and wheatgrass; paleontologists are working on similar migration patterns for dinosaurs.

At about the same time that North American paleontologists were working out these theories, reports began to appear in scientific journals about new dinosaur discoveries in China. Phil and Dale were aware that the large dinosaurs found by the Sternbergs in Alberta were also known in Asia; the large tyrannosaurids, the hadrosaurs, and some ceratopsians were common to both continents — different species, but the same families. So were the Late Jurassic sauropods; *Brachiosaurus* is known in both North America and Tanzania, "which leads one to think," Edwin Colbert wrote in 1965, "that these enormous dinosaurs migrated widely during the time of their dominance, pushing across intercontinental land bridges, possibly even moving along chains of connecting islands by swimming across sea channels between the lands." Colbert's hypothesis intrigued his former student, Dale Russell.

What fascinated Phil was his realization that even the new smaller dinosaurs being discovered in Alberta were similar to dinosaurs that had hitherto been known only in Asia. "Almost every family of dinosaur in Asia is also represented in North America," he says. The fact that the larger animals were found on both continents was not totally surprising; larger animals can move quickly and over great distances and are also not so dependent upon specific types of environment. Large carnivores eat meat — any meat. But the smaller, more specialized dinosaurs intrigued him. They needed particular kinds of environments to survive. And yet, *Saurornithoides* from Mongolia was very closely related to *Troodon* from North America, even though the paleo-environments of the two continents had been quite different. Why, then, were the two dinosaurs so similar?

A Polish expedition into Outer Mongolia in 1971 found dramatic confirmation of the similarities between animals from North America and Asia. Led by Dr. Zofia Kielan-Jaworowska of the Polish Institute of Paleobiology, the expedition uncovered the skeletons of two dinosaurs from the Late Cretaceous: a *Protoceratops* and a *Velociraptor*. The skeletons of the two animals — one a small herbivore and the other a small theropod — were clutched together in a deadly embrace, the large, sickle-like claw of the *Velociraptor* still embedded in the hollow where the *Protoceratops*'s exposed underbelly had been. From Kielan-Jaworowska's description of the scene (published in her account of the expedition, *Digging for Dinosaurs*), as well as from her scientific analysis of the fossils, it was apparent that *Deinonychus* and *Velociraptor* were almost the same dinosaur. How closely were they related? When *Saurornitholestes* turned up in Dinosaur Park, it, too, seemed almost identical to *Velociraptor*.

Similarly, ankylosaurids — armored, armadillo-like dinosaurs — are found on both continents. And many of the freshwater turtles from Alberta were also known in Mongolia. Reading about the similarities between these specimens was not enough; Phil wanted to see the actual bones, and he wanted to study the environments at first hand. "When we started turning up small, Asian stuff in Alberta," he says, "we knew we needed to go to China to find out just how similar they actually were."

In its first year of field work, the Dinosaur Project gave North American paleontologists an intriguing glimpse into the vast and diverse life of Mesozoic Asia. "It's like a huge building," says Phil, "with thousands of windows. But there are only about ten lights on at any one time. And we're trying to make some sense out of the whole building by peeking through the few windows that are available to us." Over the next four years, the Canadian and Chinese scientists would be trying to turn on a few more lights.

CHAPTER 3

Worlds Apart

Zhao Xijin's Mamenchisaurus *and continental drift*

IN EARLY JULY OF 1987, MORE THAN A MONTH BEFORE THE CANADIANS WERE scheduled to fly to China for the Dinosaur Project's first full field season, Clayton Kennedy flew to Edmonton. The Ex Terra Foundation had purchased a Sprung Instant Structure — a huge, specially designed tent spacious enough to house a circus — to serve as a mess tent and communal meeting area at the field camp in Xinjiang. Clayton had been seconded from the National Museum of Natural Sciences in Ottawa, where he was Dale Russell's chief technician, to learn how to assemble the tent and to look over other equipment purchased by Ex Terra for field operations in China.

The tent had already been sent to Beijing. It was ten meters wide and twelve meters long — a buff-colored umbrella bolted to aluminum arches that curved up to form a ceiling nine meters above the ground. Erecting it would require wrenches and scaffolding. Ex Terra had paid nearly $25,000 for it. To make it livable in the desert, Ex Terra had also bought four 10,000-BTU air conditioners and a 15-kilowatt generator. There was also a large chest freezer, two refrigerators, two jackhammers, and an air compressor (to run the jackhammers). These were packed into ten wooden crates, the largest of which was the size of a five-tonne truck box and weighed 2,100 kg. On July 28, Clayton drove down to Sprung headquarters — the Western Tent & Awning Company, just outside Calgary — and was shown how to erect a smaller version of the Ex Terra tent in an oilfield thirty minutes from the city; it took him a day and a half. It rained the whole time. When he walked around inside the structure for the first time, he felt as though he were inside a hot-air balloon.

He drove back to Edmonton on Friday, July 31, the beginning of the August 1 long weekend. The temperature was 30 degrees Celsius, and the air was hot and heavy; the sky in the west was black with storm clouds that rose up to fifteen kilometers and rumbled like angry giants. Clayton felt himself coming down with the 'flu. At three o'clock that afternoon, the tornado that had been building up in the southwest, over Red Deer, hit Edmonton with 483-km-an-hour winds that ripped houses apart and sent trucks and buses hurtling through the air. Dense clouds released hail pellets big enough to smash car windshields, and a cold, biting rain flooded sixty-six city streets and raised the level of the North Saskatchewan River fifty centimeters in four hours. The fury lasted only a short time, but when the wind died down twenty-six people were dead, three hundred were injured, and a thousand were left homeless. It was the worst natural disaster in Edmonton's history. When Clayton and Brian Noble flew to Vancouver and on to Beijing on Monday, August 3, they felt things could only get better.

In Beijing, they found a different kind of chaos. The crates had arrived ten days before and had already been sent on to Xinjiang, along with the Beijing jeep and three of the five Jeep Cherokees that Ex Terra had purchased in May with a $150,000 donation from the Donner Canadian Foundation. The jeeps were to be the expedition's main source of field transportation for the next four years. Because the airport customs shed had not been equipped with fork-lifts, the huge crates had had to be hoisted on to the back of a truck by hand — by IVPP hands — and the truck had been driven to the train station. Rather than hoist the crates off the truck, the drivers had simply driven the truck on to a flat-bed railway car, along with the jeeps. They then had to remain at the station to keep an eye on everything until the train left. The departure was delayed. They kept an eye on things for five days. They never left the station. They slept in the vehicles. Their wives and children brought them food. They used the station's toilets. They drank the station's water and got sick. Finally, when the train left, the drivers were able to move into one of the passenger cars. They sat on hard seats all the way to Urumqi — a fourteen-day trip, three weeks in all, counting the delay in Beijing and a four-day wait in Hami — a city of 250,000 about 480 km from Urumqi — while a washed-out bridge was repaired. They were still en route to Urumqi when Clayton and Brian landed in Beijing.

The two Canadians spent a week in the Chinese capital. It was Clayton's first time in China, and for him Beijing was an endlessly fascinating and infinitely mysterious city. In Ottawa he had taken a few lessons in Chinese to prepare himself for the trip, but in Beijing he was still barely able to make himself understood. He had studied *pinyin,* which is the Chinese language spelled out in Western characters, part of Mao Zedong's flirtation with the Occident. China had had four such periods of flirtation over the years, and so there are four distinct versions of transliteration, further complicating an already unimaginably complex linguistic agglomeration. (Chou K'ou Tien, for example, is now written Zhoukoudian.) Clayton tried unsuccessfully to get owner's manuals for the Chinese equipment purchased for the field camp. He found that there was no such thing as an English-language owner's manual in China. Virtually every vehicle in the country was a government vehicle, driven by a government driver. If a vehicle required major repairs, it was generally scrapped or scavenged for parts for another vehicle. A few years earlier, the Red Army-owned Da Du Hotel, where Clayton and Brian had been put up, had purchased a fleet of two dozen white Volvos as taxis. Only six of them were still roadworthy; the rest were in the Da Du parking lot in various states of disrepair, their internal organs donated to keep the other six running. Clayton kept himself busy attending meetings with Brian and meeting people at the IVPP and hoped for the best.

Brian's task was only slightly less inconclusive. Since January he had been trying to organize an event that would symbolize the spirit of cooperation between the two countries, something tangible to express the philosophy of the Dinosaur Project. As an anthropologist, he was aware that the Dinosaur Project was working in parts of the world that shared many geographical and cultural characteristics. Both Xinjiang and Alberta were populated by minority groups — Blackfoot in Alberta, Kazakhs and Mongols in China — living in remote regions controlled by a strong central government; both minority cultures were traditionally fine horsemen and lived nomadic lives in similar terrain. And both the Blackfoot and the Kazakhs and Mongols shared at least one thing with members of the Dinosaur Project: they all lived in tents. Brian had come up with the Tipi-Yurt Exchange. Sometime that summer, a group of Native people from Alberta would be flown to Xinjiang to present their Kazakh counterparts with a North American tipi. Later,

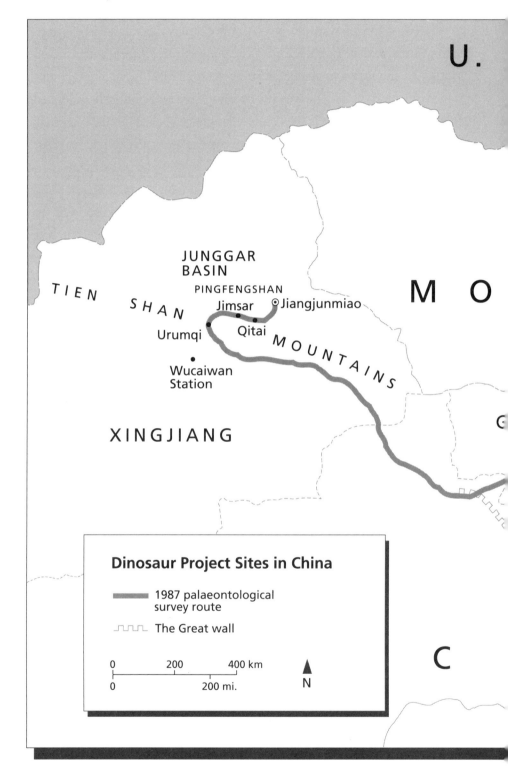

U.

JUNGGAR
BASIN

PINGFENGSHAN

M O

Jimsar ⊙ Jiangjunmiao

TIEN

SHAN

Urumqi   Qitai

M O U N T A I N S

Wucaiwan
Station

XINGJIANG

G

Dinosaur Project Sites in China

1987 palaeontological
survey route

The Great wall

0	200	400 km
0		200 mi.

N

C

R.

Ulaan
Baator •

O L I A

INNER MONGOLIA

habarakh Usu
Flaming Cliffs)

Erenhot ⊚

I

⊚ Bayan Mandahu

Urad •
Houqi
        Linhe

Hohhot

Dongsheng •
                    • Beijing

ORDOS
BASIN

N A

Yellow   River

a similar ceremony could be held in Inner Mongolia between Alberta Indians and Mongols. In exchange, a group of Kazakh and Mongolian representatives from China could fly to Alberta to present their North American brethren with two yurts.

In April, Brian had signed a Letter of Agreement with the Indian Association of Alberta (IAA) outlining the exchange. The IAA agreed to deliver four tipis to Ex Terra that summer. In June, Brian met with two Peigan elders, Joe Crowshoe and his son Reg, who agreed to go to China to perform a traditional tipi-raising ceremony. Joe also said he would paint two of the tipis with motifs designed by his grandmother to illustrate the Snake-People legend, a Blackfoot creation myth explaining the origin of life on earth. Creator Sun was lonely, according to the legend, so he made Moon and took her as his wife. Their sons were the stars. Then he made earth by spitting into a ball of cosmic dust, and he made the Snake People to live on it. When Sun discovered that Moon was meeting secretly with a Snake Man, he destroyed all but two Snake People and buried them under the prairie, where their bones are now being dug up by scientists, who mistakenly believe them to be the bones of dinosaurs.

Brian had written to the Chinese Embassy in Ottawa, asking for "views on this exchange, and particularly whether it might involve sensitive issues in China" but had received no written reply to this question, so now, in Beijing, he set about finding a venue for the ceremony and getting the necessary permission from an incredible array of seemingly unconnected government departments, none of which appeared willing or able to assume responsibility for the go-ahead. Xinjiang is a mostly restricted area — not open to foreigners without travel permits — and Brian's plans were not definite enough to be convincing. He met with Chang Meeman on August 5 and asked her help with transport arrangements for the tipis from Beijing to Urumqi, with customs, and with letters of invitation to Reg and Joe Crowshoe that would facilitate their getting visas and travel permits. Finally, representatives of the local government of Jimsar County in Xinjiang, an autonomous region, agreed to the idea of the ceremony. But, just as Brian and Clayton were leaving the hotel, a message came from Ex Terra saying that it might be difficult to go through with the exchange.

Nonetheless, Brian decided to bank on Jimsar's permission and to find a location for the ceremony when he got there. When he and Clayton boarded the plane

Canadians accustomed to working in Alberta's Dinosaur Provincial Park (top) felt
at home with their Chinese colleagues in the Junggar Basin in northwestern
China (lower left). In fact, the two areas were quite different: this quarry in the Jurassic
sandstone of the Junggar yielded the sauropod *Mamenchisaurus*, a family
of dinosaurs unknown in the Cretaceous formations of Alberta.

After landing in Xinjiang, Project members traveled by truck and jeep through Jimsar (opposite page,top) at the foot of the Tien Shan Mountains, stopping at local Chinese inns (opposite page, bottom) on their way north to Jiangjunmiao in the Junggar Basin (this page, top). With hammers and chisels, Dennis Bramen and Don Brinkman (lower left) chip away at the 100-million-year-old sandstone encasing a fossilized turtle.

Exploring the cultural as well as the paleontological links between China and Canada, at a ceremony in the Tien Shan Mountains, Dinosaur Project members exchanged tipis from the Native Peoples of Alberta for yurts from Xinjiang. As well as Khazak horsemen and their families, the celebrations were attended by representatives of local governments and Academia Sinica.

Setting up the Sprung Structure in Xinjiang's Junggar Basin in 1987, where high winds and 54-degree Celsius temperatures often called for innovative procedures.

to Urumqi, both were feeling somewhat uneasy about the future. In Urumqi they were met by Dong Zhiming and Zhao Xijin. Brian asked Dong Zhiming to help him sort things out with the proper authorities in Beijing.

"It is very dangerous," Dong Zhiming replied, using his favorite word. "You can't understand. But I'll try, I'll try."

After a short stay in Urumqi, they drove to Jiangjunmiao. The Chinese had been there for a week and had already set up their own tents in Chinese fashion: straight rows, close together. In all, there were thirty members of the Chinese team, including Dong Zhiming and Zhao Xijin as chief scientists; Hou Lianhai, a fossil lizard specialist and one of the IVPP's senior scientists; paleontologist Cui Gui Hai; Huang Daifu, the camp doctor, a thin, fragile, perpetually smiling man who had learned his profession in Korea during the war; several students and technicians; and, of course, Tang Zhilu, the camp's chief technician. The crates were still on the back of the truck, waiting for Clayton and his manuals so that the

The base camp at Jiangjunmiao was close to several important dinosaur localities, but exposed to fierce sandstorms.

Sprung Structure, generator, freezer, and air conditioners could be set up.

The Sprung Structure presented a problem right away. First, about a dozen of the bolts to hold the aluminum ribs together were missing. Second, there was no scaffolding. Third, none of the manuals were in Chinese, and none of the Chinese could read English. Several plans were launched and aborted. Clayton had done this before, but no one in camp could understand his instructions. Someone suggested bolting the ribs together upside down and then flipping over the whole frame with the truck. Finally they decided to use the truck as a scaffold. Two two-hundred-liter drums were placed atop one another on the cab roof, and a technician with a wrench stood on the top drum, bolting the ridge together as the truck moved slowly along the ten-meter length of the arch. No one was killed.

Once the skeleton was up, they rested before tackling the skin. The temperature was 54 degrees Celsius. The lightweight fabric had to be cleated into channeling in the ribs of the structure, "exactly like a sail over a mast," says Clayton.

The high wind added to their difficulties; Clayton recalls that it was sand-blasting the hair off his legs. Two people had to climb from the top of the truck onto the aluminum frame and hold on while the panels were pulled into place by ropes from below. Somehow this was done. When the skin was in place, the technicians on top had to ease themselves slowly down the side of the tent. By then the temperature of the fabric was 60 degrees Celsius. They burned their legs. Then the wind tried to pick up the tent and transport it to Inner Mongolia. When they tried to anchor the ribs in the sand, they found that the ninety-centimeter anchor-rods hit solid bedrock fifteen centimeters below the surface. But for the moment that seemed to be enough to hold the tent in place.

When they went inside, however, the heat was so great they immediately began to sweat. They quickly strung up the lights and air conditioners and connected them to the generator. They then realized that the generator's head gaskets had not been tightened. They tightened them and switched on the generator, only to find that it was powerful enough to run the lights but not the air conditioners. The tent, they then discovered, had come without the specially coated liner recommended for desert conditions and without the clips needed to connect the specially designed floor to the rods. As a result, the tent interior was both hot and dusty; sitting in it was like sitting in a huge vacuum-cleaner bag. Even with the windows open, they couldn't enter the tent for a week. A kind of lean-to built against the truck served as a cook shack, and they strung lights to it from the generator. When it was started up, the generator guzzled thirteen liters of gasoline an hour.

By the time the tent cooled, the rest of the Canadians had arrived: Dale Russell, Rick Day, and Francis Chan from the National Museum in Ottawa; Don Brinkman, Dennis Braman, Gilles Danis, and Linda Strong-Watson from the Tyrrell Museum. Phil Currie had stayed behind in Urumqi with Dong Zhiming to attend a conference on geological correlation. There was also a film crew — Alan Bibby, Jim Jeffrey and Andy Thomson of Terra North Productions, accompanied by two technicians from the Shanghai Educational and Scientific Film Studio who were making a two-hour documentary about the Dinosaur Project.

The desert was a sea of light-colored sand framed by bright red sandstone cliffs. There was practically no green. The camp had been established very close to the fossil forest that Phil, Dale, and Brian had visited the previous year, and not far from the adobe ruins that were first thought to be the remains of a shrine to Jiang Jun, a twelfth-century general who had been killed in battle near the site and whose name had been given to it. In fact, explained Zhao Xijin, the ruins were those of a hotel in which he had stayed during his first trip to the area in the mid-1960s: he said he had slept with a pistol under his pillow. The owners had been shot to death by a gang of bandits in 1965, and now the buildings had been abandoned to the desert, which was quickly returning them to sand.

The Canadians set up their domed nylon tents North American style — everyone trying to find a secluded spot away from the main camp. A strong wind made the task of pitching the light tents difficult, and by bedtime a severe sandstorm was blowing in from the desert. The wind, unbelievably fierce, whipped along at ground level and filled the air with a fine, yellow dust that sifted into the tiniest cracks and crevices. Cameras and shortwave radios were hastily sealed in Ziploc bags, but packs and tents were soon filled with sand. Some of the tents were not anchored as well as they might have been; Linda Strong-Watson spent the night lying across the opening of hers to prevent its blowing away. Francis Chan lay spread-eagled in his sleeping bag, his tent hovering thirty centimeters off the ground and tethered by a single cord, like a helium-filled balloon. Stories about murderous bandits and now the wind made it a stormy welcome to the Gobi.

The next morning the wind was still strong and it had begun to rain, so that the air seemed filled with bright yellow mud. While Gilles Danis remained in camp to work on the compressor, which was still not functioning properly, several of the others scouted around for stones big enough to hold down the tents. They came back with fossil logs from the petrified forest. Then Zhao Xijin took everyone on a tour of the localities in the area, including the Wucaiwan Formation, a Middle Jurassic exposure of red mudstones intermixed with yellow-green siltstones about thirty kilometers to the northwest of camp. Wucaiwan means "five colors" in Chinese: the 122-m cliff faces are mainly red, but have horizontal bands of white, black, blue, and green. A few years earlier, Dale noted in his field book, a *Kelmayisaurus gigantus*, a huge theropod measuring twenty-one meters from neck to tailtip (there was no skull) had been found there.

The group spread out to prospect for more bones, and very soon Dennis Braman discovered a small humerus, or upper forelimb bone, which Zhao Xijin identified as that of a stegosaur. Although relatively rare in North America, stegosaurs are well known in the Middle Jurassic in China. The most common, and most primitive, is *Huayangosaurus taibaii*, a smallish, low-headed creature measuring about four and a half meters in length, with the stegosaurs' double row of sharp bony plates running along its spine and down its tail. Each hip and the end of its tail were further armed with sharp spikes.

Stegosaurs were slow-moving herbivores with brains about the size of grapefruits, but the group survived for many millions of years under not very promising conditions; Jurassic stegosaurs are found just about everywhere, a few Early Cretaceous stegosaurs have turned up in China and East Africa, and there are some Late Cretaceous stegosaurs in India.

One of the first locations visited in the 1987 field season was here in the Wucaiwan Formation, a middle-Jurassic exposure of red sandstone mixed with horizontal stripes of white, blue, black, and green. The formation is known for its abundance of fossil stegosaurs.

Dong Zhiming considers Asia to be the ancestral home of all stegosaurs. Originating in China 150 million years ago, he believes, they spread out through northern Asia into Europe, and across Greenland into North America. Zhao Xijin's find did not increase the world's knowledge of stegosaurs by much, but it did help to confirm the age of the formation and correlate it with other formations in the area.

Tang Zhilu, meanwhile, was prospecting in the Early Cretaceous beds of the Tugulu Group, about thirteen kilometers west of the base camp. He had found a bonebed — a 275-m stretch of gravel at the base of the exposure containing hundreds of disarticulated small bones, probably in a spot where a stream emptied into a lagoon or lake. There were lots of turtle bones and a possible lizard, also a sauropod cervical vertebra more than ninety centimeters long. All in all it was an eventful first day. That night even the weather seemed to celebrate: the wind died down, the rain stopped, and the sky cleared.

Two days later, however, the wind started up again. In his field book, Dale called it "a memorable day": the cook slaughtered one of the sheep for dinner; Dale saw his first desert snake — a sand boa, light brown with dark, horizontal stripes, about a meter long — that was "running" by throwing its neck and head forward. "It was raising its head in my direction," writes Dale, "when the driver told me to get in the jeep and leave it alone." He scrambled into the jeep. "Oh yes," he added at the end of that day's entry, "and the cook-shack roof caught fire."

It was also the day that Zhao Xijin found a sauropod rib sticking out of the side of a sandstone cliff face. It did not seem a very significant discovery at the time. Dennis and Don went to investigate. It was a cervical rib, in life attached to the neck vertebrae of sauropods to support the animal's windpipe and arteries. It was sticking out about halfway up a high butte, and they estimated that there were nearly a hundred tonnes of very hard overburden above it. They said there was no way to remove the overburden without the jackhammer, and they couldn't use it because there were no fittings for the compressor. Besides, it looked as though it was an isolated rib; they could remove the overburden and find nothing more than that one bone. They decided to think about it for a few days.

During those few days, Rick Day spent his breaks sitting in the shade of the butte looking up at the rib, watching it dance in the heat waves shimmering from the rock. After a day or two he noticed a small nodule sticking out of the cliff beside the rib. He climbed up to take a closer look: it was a cervical vertebra, the part of the neck to which the rib would have been attached. Maybe the rib was not so isolated after all. The quarry suddenly became worth working. The Chinese technicians proposed a solution to the overburden problem. They called it *fan pao*, an onomatopoetic word for an ancient Chinese invention. It means dynamite.

The Lost Continent

FOR DALE, FOLLOWING THE NECK OF THIS IMMENSE SAUROPOD INTO THE CLIFF TO see if it ended with a skull became extremely important. If there was a skull, and if the skull contained teeth, and if those teeth were a certain shape, then his whole picture of what earth looked like 200 million years ago would be radically changed.

On a wall outside his office in Ottawa hangs a map showing the huge supercontinent of Gondwanaland, which seems to be made up of a conglomeration of smaller land masses, like islands, so that the whole thing looks like a vast field of ice floes crammed tightly together. The shapes of some of the floes seem vaguely familiar, if you turn your head the right way. In the center there's a piece that looks like Antarctica turned on its side; above it, Africa tilts crazily with its tail under Antarctica's head and its own head resting on South America's shoulder. In the west, the bottom of Australia nestles against Antarctica. In the north, a pointed piece of peninsula that looks like India juts into a

The first major find of 1987: a neck rib from the huge sauropod *Mamenchisaurus* projecting from a cliff face with one hundred tonnes of hard sandstone above it. Dinosaur Project members would spend the next four summers exhuming the animal from its 150-million-year-old gravesite.

gap created by the diverging coastlines of Africa and Madagascar.

Although Gondwanaland existed more than 200 million years ago, it has been possible to produce a map of it only in the past twenty years, when its theoretical existence began to gain general acceptance among geographers. Its name was coined by the nineteenth-century Austrian geologist Eduard Suess, who noticed striking similarities in the rocks and fossils from certain localities in southern Africa, the Indian subcontinent, and Madagascar. From the age of the rocks, Suess postulated that during late Permian and early Triassic times, those three land masses had formed a single body that he called Gondwanaland, after Gond, in India, where he had first noticed the similarities. Suess was dismissed as a crank; in the nineteenth century, rocks did not move. And continents were large rocks.

In 1912, however, the German geographer Alfred Wegener took Suess's theory seriously. By comparing the western coastline of South America with the eastern coastline of Africa — not just their shapes, but also their rock types, fault lines, and various other geological peculiarities — he concluded that the two continents had in fact been one at some distant time. He thought that the only way the land mass could have separated was if it were made up of vast chunks of rock floating on the earth's molten core; at some point in geological history, he explained, a crack had developed along what is now the coastline between the land masses, and the two halves had simply drifted apart — hence Wegener's term for the phenomenon: continental drift. Wegener was no more popular with other geologists than Suess had been. In 1912, continents did not float.

Continental drift was not fully accepted by geologists until paleontologists began bringing in the fossil evidence. This first came in the form of a large, early Triassic reptile known as *Lystrosaurus*. A low, barrel-chested, snub-nosed creature, a primitive dicynodont — which means it was a herbivore, toothless except for two ("*di*") canine ("*cynos*") teeth ("*dont*") protruding from its upper jaw like vampire fangs. It lived on land and stayed close to fresh water, and its bones are found just about everywhere in the southern hemisphere, including Antarctica, India, and southern Africa. (It was the discovery of this creature in Antarctica in 1968 that helped clinch the Gondwanaland controversy.) *Lystrosaurus* is so common it is now the index fossil for the Early Triassic; its presence confirms the date of the exposures in which they are found.

The fact that *Lystrosaurus* was a dry land and freshwater animal meant that it could not have spread out over such vast areas unless those areas had been connected by land. These might have been land bridges, like Beringia or the Isthmus of Panama, but it was difficult to imagine such an intricate pattern of linkages connecting all the land in the southern hemisphere. Benthotic, or sea-floor, evidence didn't support the idea; what the sea floor did show, however, was that at the one-thousand-fathom level, all the land masses in the southern hemisphere fit together like pieces in an enormous jigsaw puzzle. *Lystrosaurus* provided strong evidence that Gondwanaland existed; the sea floor showed what it looked like.

It is now known that in the Late Permian and Early Triassic, all land on earth was one huge land mass called Pangaea. Half of Pangaea existed above the equator and is called Laurasia; the other half was below the equator and is called Gondwanaland. In the far east, between what is now Australia and Indochina, a vast inland sea, called Tethys, separated Laurasia from Gondwanaland, but the two

***Mamenchisaurus* had nineteen neck vertebrae, giving it the longest neck of any animal that ever lived. The specimen found by Dinosaur Project members in Xinjiang was critical to Dale's theory that Chinese and North American sauropods were related but not identical.**

halves were joined in the west at what is now northern Africa and southern Europe.

The evidence for all this — benthotic, geologic, and fossil — is fairly concrete. On the map in Dale's office, most of the major land masses are drawn in with a firm hand. The lines leading to what is now northern India and southeast Asia, however, are dotted and vague, like the lines west of Baffin Island on sixteenth-century explorers' charts. *Terra incognita.* There be dragons here. How did northern India and southern China fit into this ancient pattern? *Lystrosaurus* specimens have been found only in Gondwanaland — with one exception. In Xinjiang, a few kilometers south of Urumqi, in the 1980s, Dong Zhiming and other IVPP paleontologists found a magnificent, virtually complete *Lystrosaurus* skeleton in red sandstone sediments dating (of course) from the Early Triassic. Was western China, then, part of Gondwanaland? Or was *Lystrosaurus* so widespread that it wandered into eastern Laurasia through some route involving northern Africa, as primitive man did nearly 200 million years later? Or did *Lystrosaurus* originate over a

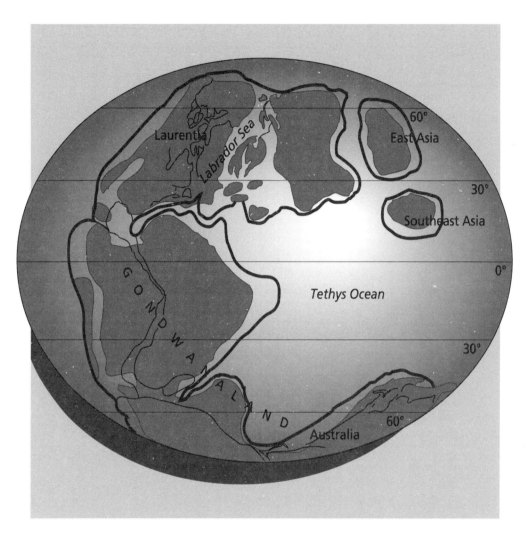

The earth's land masses as they appeared 200 million years ago. All the present continents were joined to form a single supercontinent called Gondwanaland. Dale Russell believes that present-day China was separated from Gondwanaland during a crucial time in dinosaur evolution.

wide area before China separated from Gondwanaland, leaving a remnant population on both land masses? One goal of the Dinosaur Project was to fill in a bit of the *terra incognita* on the north side of the Tethys Sea. And one Jurassic sauropod skull could help them realize it.

Whether western China was connected to Gondwanaland or Laurasia during the Early Triassic, at least it was known to have been connected to *something*. It is not clear that that continued to be the case. Skipping ahead to the Late Jurassic, faunal differences between North America and Asia make it look as though China by then was isolated from other land masses. Certain dinosaur lineages disappear; others spring up that are not found anywhere else. Did mainland China become separated from both Laurasia and Gondwanaland? Or are the faunal differences merely the result of completely different environments with natural barriers — mountains, inland seas, deserts — preventing the migration of animals from China to other regions? If China was isolated, when did it separate? And when did it join up again? And when the natural barriers were removed, or when China once again became connected to other continents, was it Asian dinosaurs that spread into North America, or North American dinosaurs that spread into China? Or both?

To answer some of these questions, Dale needed a sauropod skull from the Late Jurassic in China in order to compare its teeth to those of sauropods found in North America. The dinosaur that best filled that bill was *Mamenchisaurus*. From the partial skeletons already found in other parts of China, it appeared that *Mamenchisaurus* was remarkably like the North American sauropod *Diplodocus*. In fact, many paleontologists still classify *Mamenchisaurus* as a member of the family Diplodocidae. Both were very large plant-eating quadrupeds with long tails and even longer necks — the *Mamenchisaurus* neck was the longest of any dinosaur: it had nineteen vertebrae and was up to fourteen meters long, half the total length of the animal. Making *Mamenchisaurus* and *Diplodocus* members of the same family, however, means that there must have been some congress between them; if there were diplodocids in Asia in the Late Jurassic, then the two continents must have been connected at that time. If *Mamenchisaurus* was not a diplodocid, then there were no diplodocids in Asia until *Nemegtosaurus* showed up in the Late Cretaceous. And that would mean that the two continents must have been separated before or during the Late Jurassic.

The best way to compare two similar species is by the skull, since it is in the head that evolutionary changes are easiest to detect. Teeth are particularly useful. Dinosaurs from different environments may be identical in almost every respect but have completely different teeth, either because they have a different ancestry or because their anatomy has adapted to process different kinds of food. North American sauropods — diplodocids, camarasaurids, brachiosaurids, and titano-

With the gas-powered compressor out of commission, the only way to get the overburden off the *Mamenchisaurus* quarry was with dynamite. The Chinese were experts at this method, but dynamite had not been used in Canada since the days of Sternberg.

saurids — had narrow, pointed, pencil-shaped teeth at the front of their jaws; early Asian sauropods — such as *Euhelopus* and *Omeisaurus* — although impossible to distinguish from New World sauropods from a distance, had broad, flat, spatulate teeth. All paleontologists have to do, then, is look at the teeth in a *Mamenchisaurus* jaw and see if they are round and sharp or flat and chisel-shaped, to determine whether *Mamenchisaurus* was related to Chinese sauropods or North American sauropods.

The problem with that is known (by Dale) as Russell's Law: "The skull of a sauropod is never found." Compared to the enormous body, a sauropod skull is a tiny, fragile thing that does not appear to have been very securely attached to its neck. Although many nearly complete sauropod skeletons have been found, a surprising number of them have been headless: the type *Brontosaurus* specimen (now known by most scientists as *Apatosaurus*) mounted in the American Museum, for example, was fitted with a *Camarasaurus* skull for nearly half a century before a properly identified *Brontosaurus* skull was found. This dearth has led some paleontologists to speculate that sauropod heads were the tastiest parts of their bodies, and carnivores crunched them off first before tackling the tougher meat farther down. Others say that sauropods lived, and therefore usually died, near water, and that when they fell in water, the swift-moving currents eventually dislodged the skulls but left the heavier bones of their bodies intact.

Russell's Law does not apply universally — sauropod skulls have been found, although not always in the same place as the rest of the skeleton — but it holds when it comes to *Mamenchisaurus*; one possible skull of that animal had been found near Zigong, but it had contained no teeth, so no dental comparisons had been possible. Finding a toothed skull from a verifiable *Mamenchisaurus* would go a long way toward helping Dale solve the riddle of the lost continent.

The Big Quarry

THE CANADIANS WERE LEERY ABOUT USING DYNAMITE IN A DINOSAUR QUARRY. IT seemed to them a fairly primitive technique. Although the charges would be set well above specimen level, dynamite works by shattering rock along fault lines, and dinosaur bones are often found along fault lines. Besides, one of the objects of the Dinosaur Project was to train Chinese paleontologists and technicians in Western quarrying techniques. It did not make much sense that the first potentially important quarry in Xinjiang should be excavated with anything as potentially risky as dynamite.

On the other hand, the compressor was not working, and the Scientific Agreement specifically stated that while the Dinosaur Project was in China, the Chinese technicians called the shots. And Tang Zhilu, the head technician, was calling for *fan pao*.

The first blast produced what Dale called "a rain of turtles": the rock layer above the sauropod neck was full of fossil turtle bones. Blasting was halted while Don Brinkman — the Tyrrell's turtle specialist — carefully collected the bits and tried to identify them. They seemed to be mostly a species of *Xinjiangchelys*, known to be common in the vicinity. They remained at the quarry picking up turtle fragments until eight o'clock in the evening, then went back to camp, chased by strong winds and whipping sand.

The next morning they returned to the quarry and found a second rib, next to the first and also disappearing into the cliff. There was no blasting that day. At breakfast the next morning, August 30, Zhao Xijin announced that he was taking the Canadians to a place west of camp called Lao Yin Gou, where he would show them some interesting exposures he had worked in 1983. They set off at ten o'clock in two jeeps, Zhao Xijin giving directions in the lead jeep. Since his last trip in 1983, however, oil exploration roads in the Junggar had proliferated astronomically, and it was soon apparent that they were lost.

At one o'clock they stopped at an abandoned oil rig over a capped well and had lunch. Don and Dale climbed halfway up the rig but could not see any exposures. After lunch they decided to head back to camp, but instead they became even more lost. Vague two-wheeled tracks in the sand crisscrossed the desert, each one looking more traveled than the last, each one leading nowhere. They struck off across the desert, cresting rises and following troughs. The jeeps became stuck as if in snow, the wheels spinning in the soft sand as they climbed up the ridges. Everyone got out and pushed. Eventually, knowing they must be west of camp, they simply put the setting sun at their backs and headed due east along a seismic line, trying to keep on the graveled parts of the desert. Looking north, they could see the line of mountains that formed the Sino-Mongolian border. Zhao Xijin looked worried. Wang Ping, driving the lead jeep, kept his radio open but was picking up nothing but static. They passed endless white ledges of the Tugulu Group, but did not dare stop. They were getting low on gas. The sun had set and they were still steering east by Dale's compass. Finally, at ten o'clock, the surroundings began to look familiar. They saw the lights of an oil camp that they knew was close to their own, and then they rounded a curve, shot over a hill, and saw their camp below them. They were all exhausted — they had been driving steadily for nearly twelve hours without the slightest idea where they had been.

When they got out of the jeep, they found that Dong Zhiming and Phil had been in camp since six o'clock. They also learned that further blasting in the sauropod quarry had gone on all day.

Phil was curious about the sauropod, but he was more interested in finding a large carnivore, such as the theropod found by the Chinese in 1984 in the Junggar

Basin and temporarily referred to as "Jiangjunmiaosaurus." His principal area of interest was dinosaur dispersal, tracking the possible movements of dinosaurs between Asia and North America, and he felt that the best way to tackle that vast subject was by studying the theropods. He knew there were remarkable similarities between the dinosaur families of Asia and those of North America, and he was willing to leave the sauropods to Dale. Theropods, he thought, might provide more clues about family relationships between the continents.

"I haven't looked into this yet to see if it works for modern animals," he says, "but I suspect it does. Herbivores — like deer, for instance — very often get tied into certain plant resources, they become more environmentally specific, so they differ from environment to environment. You get caribou in one environment, reindeer in another, white-tailed deer in another, and so on. Meat eaters, on the other hand, take down meat, period; it doesn't matter whether it's an antelope on the plains or a deer in the forest. A wolf, for example, will take down either animal, and so it can live in either environment. A wolf from Siberia is virtually identical to a wolf from northern Canada." Carnivores, in other words, tend to have bigger ranges and be less environmentally specific. They also tend to be more active, more mobile, bigger, and faster. It follows that a good way to plot herbivore migration patterns is to track carnivore dispersal.

"There is no question that the Asian carnivores got into the north," says Phil, "into Alaska and the Yukon, just as a lot of our herbivores did. But what we're seeing is that the Asian carnivores are an awful lot closer to the Alberta carnivores than the Asian herbivores are to the Alberta herbivores. At first glance, it's very hard to tell *Tarbosaurus* from *Tyrannosaurus*. And it's very hard to tell *Velociraptor* from *Saurornitholestes* — in fact, it's impossible because they may be exactly the same animal."

By studying the carnivores closely, in order to determine just how similar they were, Phil hoped to be able to state positively that dinosaurs from Asia spread into North America, rather than vice versa. Without secure dating of the geological strata, it is still impossible to say for sure, but from the faunal evidence, "it *appears*," says Phil, "that during the Cretaceous Period there was a major invasion of Asian dinosaurs into North America." *Velociraptor* may indeed be *Saurornitholestes*, but a lot more evidence is needed before such statements can be made out loud. "We'll probably never know for sure that the two animals were the same species. Even identical skeletons would only tell us that they were the same genus — one could have been bright green and the other one bright purple. But suppose there's a rare trace element found only in the earth in Mongolia: and if you picked it up in a bone found in Alberta you'd have some proof that they came across. But that kind of thing is way beyond our technology now. All we can say now is that *Velociraptor* is 99.9 percent within the range of variation of *Saurornitholestes*, that probably they're the same animal. Still, I think that if we can come up with those levels of probability we're going to do it with the carnivores, not the herbivores."

A distinction should be made here between two meanings of the word migration. We are all familiar with the ordinary kind of migration: the migratory patterns birds follow twice a year, which brings them north in the summer months and south in the winter. Some mammals also migrate: herds of caribou, for example, make annual east-west migrations of many thousands of kilometers across the Canadian tundra. Plant ecologists have mapped the probable migration routes of the vast buffalo herds that once filled the prairies by charting the ripening patterns of the various types of grasses found in different parts of the region.

When Darwin spoke of species migration, however, he meant something that is more accurately called species *dispersal*: a group of animals of the same species separates from the main body of its kind and migrates to a different environment, where it remains reproductively cut off from the rest of its species. Gradually, over many hundreds of generations, this group evolves into a new species. It usually retains many of the characteristics of the parent group, but modifies others in response to its new environment: different coloration, for instance. This second kind of migration, followed by descent with modification, is, almost literally, "the origin of species."

The scientists of the Dinosaur Project believe that dinosaurs participated in both kinds of migration. Both Dale and Phil were in China looking for ancient links between Asia and North America, and herd migration as well as species migration would have provided those links — indeed, one would have resulted in the other. Neither doubted that the links were there, but each was trying to identify them from a different perspective. Dale was looking for sauropod evidence of a separation of Asia and North America in the Early Cretaceous; Phil was seeking theropod evidence for a re-establishment of the links during the Late Cretaceous.

Fan pao

THE MORNING AFTER PHIL AND DONG ZHIMING ARRIVED IN CAMP, WORK RESUMED on the sauropod quarry. Gilles Danis, meanwhile, prospecting a short distance away, found a second sauropod; four tail bones from an animal much smaller than the *Mamenchisaurus* in the big quarry, possibly a juvenile. More of the tail could be seen disappearing into the cliff. Phil noted the site in his journal as "especially interesting" and assigned Gilles and Linda to continue to work on it.

In the afternoon, the slow work of drilling holes for dynamite above the small sauropod began. The crew had to drill twelve holes, and before they were finished the drill bit broke. It would have taken too long to go back to camp for a new one, so they spent the rest of the afternoon splitting rock with their chisels. Brian had gone to Urumqi and was due back the next day. "I sure hope Brian brings the fittings for the compressor," Gilles wrote in his logbook that night, "or I'll spend my summer sitting on a rock waiting for a blast."

Before leaving Urumqi, Phil and Dong Zhiming had met with Brian to discuss plans for the Tipi-Yurt Exchange. Brian had finally arranged for the ceremony to take place in a pasture high in the Tien Shan Mountains, south of Jimsar, on September 22 and 23. The tipis would be set up on the twenty-second, and the ceremony would take place at sunrise on the twenty-third, after which fifty Kazakh horsemen would demonstrate traditional games and sports. A dinner would ensue. After another night spent in the tipis, the Dinosaur People would go back to Jiangjunmiao. Ex Terra agreed to pay 5,000 yuan (about $1,250 CDN) for the meals and accommodation (including 1,000 yuan for the horsemen), and another 1,000 yuan for poles for the two tipis which had to be cut and transported from a great distance.

As they were leaving Urumqi to return to camp, Brian asked Dong Zhiming to buy a blackboard so that at future meetings he could have something to write on. Dong Zhiming refused, saying the IVPP had already provided large sheets of paper for that purpose. This exchange precipitated a heated argument between the two men, during which a number of frustrations were aired. Dong Zhiming felt that schedule changes and the Tipi-Yurt Exchange were eating into valuable field time; the film crew was interrupting field work; extra expenses — for blackboards and tipi poles — were eating into the money needed for scientific work. If Brian wanted a blackboard, he could go out and buy one himself, with his own money. However, as they were leaving the city, Dong Zhiming told the driver to stop at a department store. He came out carrying a blackboard. He apologized to Phil for his outburst, but the incident clouded the trip to Jiangjunmiao.

The first day of September was cool, breezy, and overcast, perfect for desert work. In the morning, Phil and Dong Zhiming went with Zhao Xijin to the Wucaiwan Formation, where Zhao Xijin had found a sauropod femur the day before. From there they visited a site in the Tugulu Group, where Clayton, Dennis Braman, and Linda were collecting three crocodiles. They had also found four sauropod vertebrae — there seemed to be sauropods everywhere.

Dale joined Tang Zhilu and Gilles at this second sauropod quarry. They had replaced the drill bit, but the new one broke after two minutes with only three holes prepared for dynamite. They blasted anyway, and dislodged four carnivore teeth. Since carnivorous dinosaurs shed their teeth fairly easily — like sharks — finding their teeth did not necessarily mean there was a theropod skeleton close by and, since the dynamite had been placed well above the sauropod, there was little chance that the teeth were associated with it.

When Phil examined the teeth the next day, he saw immediately that they were similar to *Allosaurus* teeth: curved and barbed and containing "blood grooves" down the sides. *Allosaurus* was a relatively primitive carnivore from the Late Jurassic in North America, one of the most common predators of its era. Measuring about eleven meters in length from the tip of its stiff tail to the snout on its huge head, it may have hunted in packs, pulling down sauropods much as wolves pull down moose. The only allosaurids known from China were *Chilantaisaurus* and *Szechuanosaurus*, neither of which had been found in Xinjiang. Phil dropped the teeth into a Ziploc bag for safekeeping. More pieces in a growing puzzle to be worked out later.

Meanwhile, Brian's wife, Marna, arrived in camp along with Teng Tingkang, vice-president of the Urumqi branch of Academia Sinica. And they came bearing gifts: compressor fittings and two bottles of Johnny Walker scotch. The Chinese opened a few bottles of *bai-jo* and there was, noted Dale, "much celebrating after a supper of little interest: the cook doesn't like whisky." Outside the big tent — which had become a kind of community center, where people got together to talk and play chess — the wind died down, the sky cleared, and the temperature dropped to 12 degrees Celsius. Everyone began to feel the chill. The Chinese spent much of the night sitting in the jeeps with the motors running, smoking cigarettes and listening to tapes of Western music. With the cold and the scotch and the music, no one slept much that night.

The next day the sky remained clear and the temperature rose to 26 degrees. Gilles worked on the compressor and had it going by supper time, which meant that next day they'd be able to use the jackhammers instead of dynamite. By now everyone's attention was on the big sauropod. Judging from the angle at which it was lying, Dale guessed that the animal had died on the shore of a river with the head sloping down into the water, but he thought there was an outside chance that the neck was complete and the skull preserved. Clearing rubble after dynamite blasts had exposed two neck ribs and nine neck vertebrae. Each rib was more than 180 cm long. Removing the overburden became a priority. However, there was still something wrong with the compressor: the pressure regulator was strong enough to work the "zip guns" — hand-held jackhammers small enough for taking rock off the bones themselves — but not to run the big jackhammers, or "whackers," that were needed to remove almost the whole cliff from above the specimen. That meant more *fan pao*.

More theropod teeth were found in the second sauropod quarry: a total of nine so far, all apparently allosaurid. Would a single theropod shed so many teeth at one kill site, Phil wondered, or was he holding evidence that the sauropod carcass had been feasted on by an allosaurid pack?

Then Dennis found a small theropod near the spot where he had been excavating a crocodile. Phil went to look and dug out two vertebrae, a scapulacoracoid or shoulder blade, a toe bone, and the end of what looked like a fibula. All the bones were badly weathered, but the shoulder blade disappeared into rock to show where the rest of the skeleton was. Phil decided to excavate the rest of the theropod and named the site Quarry 6.

Work continued in the big quarry, presided over for the most part by Dale. The sauropod had been found at about mid-neck, with the vertebrae disappearing into the cliff in the direction of the skull. The rest of the body had been eroded away. The rock was very hard. The zip guns worked well, but they were run by the

Using jackhammers, shovels, chisels, and paintbrushes, the field crew works its way down to the *Mamenchisaurus*. The large sauropod had been found at mid-neck, with the vertebrae disappearing into the cliff in the direction of the skull. The big question: would there be a skull?

compressor, which was run by the generator, which soaked up gasoline at a nail-biting rate. Finally, the gas ran out and they had to revert to dynamite. Each new blast shattered rock as well as nerves, but eventually enough overburden was removed to allow the workers to get down to bone level. Linda began to quarry a second tritylodont she had found — not a dinosaur but one of the small, mammal-like or therapsid reptiles known previously from the Upper Triassic beds in Lufeng Province, and in the Jurassic beds of Sichuan but common elsewhere among Gondwanaland fauna. Don was finding so many turtles that Dong Zhiming jokingly suggested renaming the venture the China-Canada Turtle Project. The weather was turning decidedly fallish, but despite the wind, the spates of rain, and continued friction between Brian and Dong Zhiming — who was refusing to take part in the Tipi-Yurt Exchange — spirits in camp rose.

At Quarry 6, Marna, Dong Zhiming, and Dale took out a scapula and in the process found another, smaller allosaurid tooth and an enormous tibia. Phil, Clayton, Rick Day, Alan Bibby, and Jim Jeffrey joined them, and before the day ended three ribs, six phalanges, a humerus, four metatarsals, and a claw nearly eight centimeters long had been added to the list of specimens. Phil also found a calcaneum and an astragalus — two ankle bones that, when cleaned off in camp that night, fit together perfectly. The shortage of gasoline produced talk about dynamiting the theropod quarry, but Phil objected strenuously: "Out of the question."

The next day — September 13 — Zhao Xijin once again piled the Canadians into the jeeps, this time for an extended four-day trip to dinosaur localities near an oil camp at Wucaiwan Station, about 160 km to the west and 96 km north of

Jimsar. Three Cherokees and the Beijing jeep were loaded. At the last minute, Phil decided not to go. He had been there the year before, and he was anxious to keep an eye on the theropod quarry. Tang Zhilu had decided to use dynamite, despite Phil's objections, and Phil wanted at least to be there to pick up the pieces.

The caravan made four stops along the way to the oil camp: at a Permian fish site, a Triassic-Jurassic boundary site, a fossil mammal site in the Wucaiwan Formation, and in Dinosaur Valley, the Middle Jurassic shopping center where Dong Zhiming had found what he tentatively identified as a *Bellusaurus*, a very small (five meters long) sauropod that may or may not be the juvenile of a larger species. The oil camp, when they reached it ten hours later, had tripled in size since Dale's visit the year before. There were public showers, good food, and, as the *bai-jo* flowed, a boisterous round of songs from Beijing Opera sung by members of the oil crew. Their accommodations at the station were in "a little adobe hut with rooms in it," Linda recalls, "and beds and bare floors. I was sort of turned over to the women who were there cooking and looking after the rooms. They came over to me and put their arms around me, they took me into a room and sat me on the bed; they touched my hair and hands and looked at my skin. I could feel them feeling sorry for me. They thought it was awful for me to be out in the desert with all these men. My skin was dry and cracked, my hair was absolutely dried out. They thought I was in deep trouble."

The next day at a Tugulu site — an ancient freshwater lake bed — Dong Zhiming found a skull of the pterosaur *Dsungaripterus* and, about seven meters away, an excellent turtle. Linda found a second pterosaur skull that was even better than the one Dong Zhiming had found. "We were prospecting intensively," she says. "We knew the site was rich in pterosaur material, and we were finding bits and pieces of limb bones. Then I saw some teeth and I followed them to the skull." It wasn't a complete skull — about one-third of it had been eroded away — but pterosaur material is generally scarce, and *Dsungaripterus* skulls are downright rare. The fact that it had teeth meant that it was probably a juvenile, as the teeth in adults are covered by bone, which makes them strong enough to crunch molluscs.

They also visited Wucaiwan Gorge, a spectacular badlands area containing the most colorful banded sediments Dale had ever seen. At Pingfengshan, a locality that gave them access to two exposures — one from the Upper Jurassic and anoth-

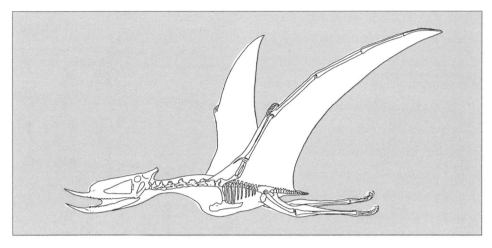

**A distant relative of the North American *Pteranodon*, this
Dsungaripterus was a flying dinosaur found in the Junggar Basin. Skulls of
this animal are extremely rare; those with teeth were from juveniles, as
the adults developed bony plates for crushing clam and turtle shells.**

er from the Lower Cretaceous — they visited a site where an earlier Chinese team
had found part of a sauropod, as well as some large turtles and crocodiles. At last
they headed back to the Jiangjunmiao camp, another ten-hour cross-country drive.

Phil, meanwhile, was the only Canadian left in camp. He hung around the
theropod quarry, but Tang Zhilu's dynamiting kept him pretty much away from
the bone. He would watch the Chinese technicians set the charges, then walk
around the exposure to the sauropod quarry in order not to watch the blasts. On
September 14 he managed to open up the quarry a bit farther to get at the
metatarsals. What he had thought was a fibula was in fact part of a femur, but he
did not have time to remove it. It was a frustrating three days. By the time the others returned from Wucaiwan on the fifteenth, he had exposed two more
metatarsals, two phalanges, a distal tarsal, and the end of a fibula. He now had a
nearly complete foot and was very anxious to assemble and study it.

At the sauropod quarry, a fourth neck rib had been exposed — it was more
than three meters long. This was obviously going to be one colossal animal if they
ever got it out of the ground.

Work continued in both quarries during the week before the Tipi-Yurt ceremony. On September 18, Brian went to Urumqi to meet Reg and Joe Crowshoe,
the Peigan elders who were to lead the ceremony. With them came Emlyn Koster

from the Tyrrell Museum, Chuck Gruchy from the National Museum, and Kevin Taft, whom Brian had brought aboard Ex Terra as the administrative CEO. All three had come to join Brian, Phil, Dale, and Dong Zhiming in a reconnaissance trip across northern China to scout locations in Inner Mongolia for the next field season. Emlyn Koster, a sedimentologist, was very interested in the Xinjiang sediments, which had never been examined by a Western geologist. "I felt like Joseph Burr Tyrrell must have felt the first time he laid eyes on Alberta," he says. "This was frontier geology with a vengeance."

Dynamiting continued in the theropod quarry — two or three blasts

Phil Currie demonstrates the difference in size between his own tibia and that of the theropod, later named *Sinraptor*, unearthed at Jiangjunmiao. Although sauropods dominated the site, theropod material was also plentiful.

a day, with an average of eight sticks of dynamite per blast — but Emlyn had brought a pressure gauge for the compressor, so it could finally be fired up enough to run the whackers; these were used in the sauropod quarry, where a push was on to get as much bone out as possible. Vertebrae were still coming out of the rock and hope was increasing that a skull would be found at the end of them. Rick Day "had a gut feeling that the skull would be there."

Trouble between Brian and Dong Zhiming also seemed to be coming to a head. Dong Zhiming was still objecting to the Tipi-Yurt Exchange as a waste of time and money — both of which, he said, were running out and could be put to better use in the field. The second transfer of cash from Ex Terra into the IVPP's account had not been made (there had been a mix-up with the banks), and Dong Zhiming was short of funds with which to continue the field program. Where would the money for the ceremony come from? Dale and Chuck Gruchy sided with Dong Zhiming, with everyone else doing his or her best to stay out of the dis-

**These foot bones from *Sinraptor* gave paleontologists their first look
at the digitigrade structure of this bipedal dinosaur. *Sinraptor's* three-toed
hind foot had a straight hinge line between the bones of the foot and
the heel (left), which allowed it to move quickly over rough ground.**

cussion altogether. Brian felt isolated, even betrayed, and confided to Phil that he
was considering backing out of the trip to Inner Mongolia, which was scheduled
to begin on September 27, a few days after the ceremony.

PERHAPS IT WAS THE FIERCE WINDSTORM THAT RIPPED THROUGH THE CAMP ON THE
nineteenth: the winds and rain were so strong that visibility was nil. Marna's glasses were blown off her face and nearly buried forever, and Andy Thomson's tent
was yanked off its moorings and later found three kilometers away, caught on a
bush halfway down an exposure. Perhaps it was the strange calm that followed the
storm on the twentieth, with the temperature shooting up to more than 37 degrees,
the sun a yellow ball of mud in a troubled sky. Or maybe it was the second windstorm that besieged the camp again that night. No one slept. In the morning everything was packed with dust, and the temperature had plunged to under 10 degrees.
Perhaps it was the thought of three days high in the Tien Shan Mountains, with

their gentle, moist breezes, the sight of flowing rivers and green grass and real trees. Or perhaps it was a gentle hint from the Jimsar officials that if the ceremony were canceled it might be difficult to arrange for the shipment of fossils out of their province. Whatever it was, when the time came to depart on the morning of the twenty-second for the Tipi-Yurt Exchange, everyone, including Dong Zhiming, Dale, and Chuck Gruchy, boarded the jeeps. Zhao Xijin, Tang Zhilu, and two Chinese technicians stayed behind to look after camp, but when the cavalcade of nine vehicles headed south into the mountains, there was a distinct feeling of festivity in the air. For most of the crew, it was the first time they had had a day off in more than six weeks.

The weekend got off to a good start, even though those gentle mountain breezes had turned into icy autumn gusts. The temperature was 7 degrees and it had rained hard for two days. Dozens of people had arrived at the site already: Kazakh families from across Xinjiang, government officials from Urumqi and Jimsar, Academia Sinica representatives, a platoon of Red Army police. Army tents and civilian trailers were scattered around a central clearing where the games were to take place. Signs had been put up everywhere, in Chinese and English: "PEACE, FRIENDSHIP, COOPERATION" and "FRIENDSHIP BETWEEN THE PEOPLE OF CHINA AND CANADA."

Two tipis and two official yurts had been set up in the pasture, and everyone gathered in them for an enormous ceremonial dinner of boiled sheep. The Kazakhs are Muslims, so there was no *bai-jo*, for which everyone was thankful. Joe Crowshoe, who was in his eighties, was the Canadian elder, and so was given the honorific first slab of mutton fat. Kazakhs raise fat-tailed sheep, and the custom is for guests to receive a slab cut from along the animal's back and down its tail — a thirty-centimeter-long, two-and-a-half-centimeter-thick slice of pure white fat that slides down the throat without being chewed. The ritual takes some practice. Dale, ordinarily the elder statesman, was relieved that Joe was there. There was a trace of alarm on Joe's face as the slab of fat was placed in his hand and along the underside of his arm, but he wriggled the end of it into his throat and swallowed with great dignity. Then it was the others' turn.

The meal lasted until after midnight, and then the floors of the tipis and yurts were spread with thick felt Kazakh blankets, and everyone crawled into their sleep-

Field camp conditions were often challenging; here the Chinese chefs cope with high winds as they cook noodles on a makeshift coal-burning oil drum. Water had to be hauled from distant oil-drilling stations and was always boiled before drinking.

ing bags and slept. Coal-burning braziers kept the tents warm. Phil lay on his back in the darkened yurt for a while, listening to the wind and thinking that "it was pretty incredible to be lying on the floor of a yurt, next to a Peigan medicine man from Brocket, Alberta, gazing through the smoke-hole in the roof at the stars over northwestern China."

Breakfast in the morning consisted of deep-fried hollow bread filled with delicious strawberry jam, washed down with milk tea. Milk tea is a traditional desert specialty: green tea leaves are steeped in hot milk instead of water, and quantities of salt and butter are added to it. It is served in bowls, quite often with chunks of goat cheese and raw millet grains thrown in for good measure. It is not delicious, but it keeps the body's salt content up, and the mutton fat prevents the lips from chapping in the arid desert winds.

After breakfast it began to get dark. The solar system had decided to participate in the festivities by staging a full-scale eclipse and, as it turned out, the Tien Shan Mountains between Jimsar and Urumqi were just about the best place in the world from which to view it. Phil and Don Brinkman left the breakfast tent and crossed a raging mountain stream — Phil hopping from rock to rock, Don walking fifty or sixty meters upstream to a bridge — and climbed the steep side of the valley on the other side. About a third of the way up they emerged into bright sunlight, but the eclipse was approaching quickly. Dale and Linda followed a few seconds later with two IVPP graduate students, Zheng Zhong and Peng Jianghua. Emlyn Koster found a knoll. Several Chinese people who had come just to see the eclipse passed around rolls of exposed film, which they used to shield their eyes as they watched the moon's progress across the sun. The eclipse was nearly total. The Canadians and Chinese scientists stood in their separate darknesses and watched in silence as the heavens performed their ancient ritual. Slowly, a thin crescent of sun appeared behind the moon, and, as if on cue, there came a great thundering of hooves from the floor of the valley below. The Kazakh horsemen had arrived.

The Tipi Ceremony began shortly thereafter, with Joe Crowshoe dedicating the Snake People tipi and passing a peace pipe to the Kazakh elders, many of whom politely declined to smoke it. After that came a semi-official exchange of gifts, food, and song; two Kazakh elders performed a Bear Dance; Kazakh schoolchildren recited poems of friendship between China and Canada; Emlyn Koster sang Joni Mitchell's "Both Sides Now"; he and Linda, Don Brinkman, and Gilles Danis joined in a traditional Kazakh folk dance. The Kazakhs displayed their superb horsemanship as women on horseback chased men on horseback up and down the valley. There followed a demonstration of the ancient Mongolian sport of goat-pulling, a kind of tug-of-war between the men using a dead goat for a rope.

When the tug-of-war ended just before six o'clock, the camp began to break up. The Kazakhs dispersed to their winter encampments, the Canadian and Chinese scientists in their caravan of jeeps filed north to Jimsar, where they spent the night in the Beiting Hotel. By five-thirty the next evening they were back in camp in Jiangjunmiao. Despite the controversy, most of the Canadians were glad that Brian had, as Linda puts it, "ramrodded the Tipi-Yurt Exchange through." And she adds that participating in the ceremony and witnessing the traditional Kazakh games "was one of the most special times in my life. We were in a place lost in time."

Work on the theropod quarry progressed for the next few days. More overburden was removed, and some broken vertebrae and ribs were exposed. A fifth metatarsal showed up. Scattered gastralia — long, rib-like scutes that protected the stomach — began to appear. The gastralia meant the animal was a theropod, but until they found a skull the genus could not be identified. When the jeeps left on their cross-country scouting trip on the morning of September 27, the decision had already been made for the others to continue work on the sauropod and theropod quarries until October 10, at which time all sites would be sealed up until the following year. Neither Dale nor Phil wanted the skeletons taken out in their absence.

The Silk Road

WHILE THE REST OF THE DINOSAUR PEOPLE CLEANED UP THE QUARRIES AND PRE-
pared to break camp, five of the organizers — Phil, Dale, Dong Zhiming, Chuck
Gruchy, and Emlyn Koster — and two drivers left Jiangjunmiao to spend the next
three weeks driving from Xinjiang to Beijing. After passing through Urumqi, the
jeeps headed southeast and descended through the White Poplar Gully toward
Turpan, an oasis of grape arbors surrounded by the lowest desert basin in the world.

Turpan is called the "Bright Pearl of the Silk Road." The entire city is irrigated by underground streams, or *karez*, that originate in the mountains to the north.
Green "mare's-nipple" grapes have been growing there for two thousand years;
during the Tang Dynasty, the city paid its annual tribute to the emperor with them,
shipping them across the desert to Chang'an in lead-lined boxes packed with snow
from the Tien Shan Mountains. Dale bought bunches of the grapes in the market
in the morning and declared them "delicious."

They left early for Hami, following the paved road to Gaochang, running
south of the Flaming Mountains through brilliant red sandstone badlands of
Eocene age that, Phil noted, "have produced only poor fossils." But they were on
the Silk Road. Sven Hedin, the Swedish paleontologist who spent the latter part
of the 1920s and early 1930s exploring northern China, called the Silk Road "the
longest, and from a cultural-historical standpoint the most significant connecting
link between peoples and continents that has ever existed on earth." The Imperial
Highway, as the trade route was called by the Chinese (the term "Silk Road" was
invented in this century), stretches from the Middle East to Beijing, passing
through the hot heart of central Asia. It was so vital a lifeline for ancient China
that the Han Emperor Shi Huangdi began building the Great Wall during the Qin
Dynasty (221-207 B.C.) to protect it from Mongolian invaders. Its total length is
nearly 8,850 km — one-quarter of the earth's circumference. On this trip, the
Dinosaur Project team would cover 6,172 km of it.

The road climbed swiftly out of the Turpan Basin through a green gorge
framed by high, treeless hills of more red sandstone. The truck overheated during the climb, and they all stopped to allow it to cool, spending the time in conversation with a Kazakh camel herder who could speak neither English nor

Chinese. Pressing on, they drove through villages in which old men played billiards on dusty, outdoor tables. They arrived in Hami at ten-thirty at night, tired and covered in yellow Gobi dust.

Hami — Kumul in Uygur — is Xinjiang's eastern gateway, the last desert oasis and the melon capital of China. Thirty types are grown in the lush fields surrounding the city. Marco Polo noted in the thirteenth century that the inhabitants of Hami "subsist on the fruits of the earth, which they possess in abundance, and are enabled to supply the wants of travelers." Phil's hotel room had "a bathtub with no plug" and "cold water you can't turn off and hot water you can't turn on."

The next day they left the paved highway and the shadow of the Tien Shan Mountains and entered the granite pass into Gansu Province, following a narrow desert track no better than the one to Jiangjunmiao. In Gansu, the dirt road improved, but their speed did not; Chinese drivers like to speed up to ninety-six kilometers an hour, then shift into neutral and coast until the jeep all but stalls, then speed up again, then coast. The Canadians found the habit annoying, but the drivers believed it saved gas — as indeed it does. They also claimed that not using the windshield wipers during a rainstorm saved the battery, that the air conditioning worked better when all the windows were open, and that, after dark, headlights were only to be used when approaching other vehicles, in order to warn them of their presence. "Each time this happened," Phil noted, "the cars would practically have to stop because the drivers were blinded in the dark." Still, after four days on the road, the caravan had covered 1,930 km.

They continued in this fashion for three more days, staying in clean hotels with indoor plumbing for the first time in two months; the hotel in Yumen even had hot water. They crossed the western end of the Great Wall on October 2 and shot straight north into Inner Mongolia. The desert was flat and, well, deserted: an occasional well, a nomad's house, but no villages, no signs of agriculture, no evidence of human habitation for kilometer after kilometer. At Ejin Qi, almost at the Mongolian border, they were joined by Li Rong, who had come from Hohhot by bus to join them. He would be their guide for the rest of the trip.

From Ejin Qi they dipped south and east toward the Yellow River and climbed into the Ordos Basin. The Ordos is a kind of sub-desert within the Gobi, the only part of the Gobi's 800,000 square kilometers that lies south of the Yellow River.

Depending on which map of China you look at, the Ordos is called either a plateau or a basin. In a sense, it is neither; in another sense, it is both. A plateau ought to be higher than the land that surrounds it: the Ordos is completely surrounded by higher mountains, and the ring of peaks makes the Ordos seem like a basin. At one time the land was at a much higher elevation, but at some point in its pre-history it sank to its present level. Although it is lower than the surrounding ranges, it is still 1,120 m above sea level, making it a plateau. A basin ought to drain into itself; if it has rivers, they should flow inward to a central lake that seasonally fills with water then evaporates to salt, as happens in the Junggar Basin. There are seven rivers in the Ordos; each of them drains outward, six into the Yellow River, the seventh southward into the Wei He. The Yellow River courses down from the highlands of Qinhai Province, which are the northern extensions of the Himalayas of Tibet. Near Langzhou, it makes an abrupt northward detour, the beginning of a 2,400-km curve in its otherwise headlong rush to the Yellow Sea. It runs north into Inner Mongolia until it hits the Yin Shan mountains, then veers east again for several hundred kilometers before dropping south to join up with the Wei He and continue its slightly northeasterly trek to the sea. When it leaves Langzhou, the Yellow River still retains plenty of its cascading energy; by the time it finishes its loop through the Gobi, its waters are flat and sluggish and yellow-brown, having picked up the highest silt content of any river in the world. The neat rectangle formed by the river's northern detour is the Ordos, basin or plateau, take your pick.

The team spent the next four days touring the Ordos, prospecting sites earlier identified by Li Rong — in fact, all the sites they examined along the way were pre-selected by the IVPP, sites the Chinese had long wanted to explore more fully but for which they had never had enough money. They examined an outcrop of low, reddish cliffs from the Suhongtu Formation, where Dong Zhiming had spent a brief time the previous year and had found some protoceratopsian and theropod specimens. Dale saw only a few unidentifiable bone fragments and many, many camels. Donkeys and goats also enlivened the landscape. Several times the vehicles became stuck in the sand and were once pulled out by a bulldozer from a nearby road construction crew. Roads in the Ordos are little more than lines gouged in the sand and filled with clay from the nearest badland.

A highlight of the Ordos segment of the trip was the dinosaur trackway near

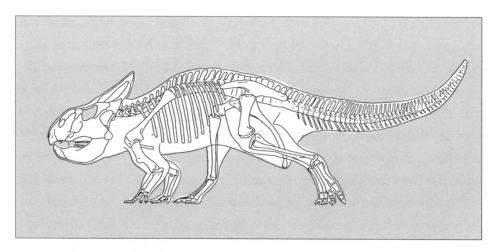

Although they lived at the same time as their cousins the North American _Leptoceratops_, _Protoceratops_ (the name means "first horned face") retained such primitive characteristics as forehead bumps instead of horns. The first specimens were found by Roy Chapman Andrews in Outer Mongolia.

Chabusumu, the one Li Rong had discovered in 1978. They parked their vehicles near a rammed-earth wall surrounding a shallow well, then walked up a gradual incline to a wave-patterned exposure at the crest of a low hill, where Li Rong showed them more than four hundred fossil footprints. Later, they lunched in the village — the first Westerners ever to have done so. They found a noodle-house and were given milk tea to which they added sugar, millet, mare's milk cheese, slices of boiled mutton, and crackers. After that, they ate onions wrapped in lichen and bamboo shoots wrapped in chicken, as well as shrimp, mutton, steamed bread, and vegetables. They concluded that Mongolian food surpassed Kazakh food in taste and edibility and that Mongolian _bai-jo_ was virtually indistinguishable from the Chinese variety, both in its taste and its effect on the head.

On October 7 they drove north from the brand new city of Linhe (built in 1970 at the hub of a network of train tracks), accompanied by a third jeep carrying party officials from the Foreign Affairs Department, the Department of Culture, and the Historical Relics Department. Near Urad Houqi, where they would spend the next three days, they prospected in an ancient, dry river valley containing redbeds of Late Cretaceous age. Earlier that summer Li Rong, who apparently could find fossils in his sleep, had turned up a dozen _Protoceratops_ skulls and the bones of what Phil thought was a small theropod, perhaps a _Velociraptor_, in an area called

Bayan Mandahu, a Mongolian name meaning "richly developed plants," although they saw no plants more richly developed than a thorn bush. In two hours of walking the cliffs, Phil found another *Protoceratops* skull, a partial *Protoceratops* skeleton with vertebrae, ribs, and parts of one foot sticking out of the cliff, and evidence of another small theropod. Emlyn Koster determined that the beds were mostly wind-deposited, formed from large, moving sand dunes that had once had rivers carrying sheet wash gravel running between them — which made sense, because such a wealth of dinosaur material is usually associated with fluvial environments.

The next day they returned to the site, and everyone spread out to prospect as wide an area as possible. At five o'clock, Phil tallied their finds for the two days: twenty-one *Protoceratops* specimens, either skulls or whole skeletons; three turtles; two small theropods; two lizard jaws (each from a different species); one lizard vertebral column; one mammal jaw, very tiny, about the size of a bat's; and one possible iguanodont tooth. There was no doubt in anyone's mind that Bayan Mandahu would be high on the list of sites for the 1988 field season.

Leaving Bayan Mandahu, they returned through Linhe and struck eastward again, arriving in Hohhot (pronounced Ho-ho-hot) on the night of October 12. They had traveled 4,473 km since leaving Jiangjunmiao two weeks earlier. Hohhot, the capital of Inner Mongolia, is a city of 2 million people. When Marco Polo visited it in the thirteenth century, it was called Tenduk, and was said to be ruled by a descendant of Prester John, an enigmatic figure in Chinese history. The reign of Genghis Khan in Mongolia coincided with the Crusades, and Prester John, according to legend, was a Christian Knight Errant who wandered from the Holy Land into Asia after tiring of slaying Saracens. Tenduk was a Christian stronghold in northeastern China, although Christianity had existed in China since the seventh century, having been introduced by Syrian monks. In 1269, during the Mongol Dynasty, Kublai Khan convened a great conference of religious leaders in China in order to determine the official religion of the country. He sent an envoy to the Pope inviting a deputation of one hundred learned men who would expound on the Christian faith. The envoy was Marco Polo's father. The Pope sent no reply at all to the Chinese Emperor, and Kublai Khan declared his country Buddhist, which, despite the People's Republic and the ravages of the Red Guard, it remains to this day.

Hohhot, the capital of Inner Mongolia, is a city of 2 million people. The Canadian members of the Dinosaur Project first passed through it on their six-thousand-kilometer trek across the Gobi Desert in October 1987, as they scouted sites for future excavations.

In Hohhot, Phil, Dale, and Emlyn were joined by their wives, who had flown from Canada to participate in the last leg of the journey — north to Erenhot and then back to Beijing. While the others went sightseeing in the Inner Mongolian capital, Dale spent most of his time in the paleo section of the Inner Mongolian Museum, Li Rong's domain. He noted an "excellent" skull identified as *Psittacosaurus*, a small, primitive, Early Cretaceous dinosaur, a relative of the later ceratopsians, and a creature with which the Dinosaur Project would become very familiar during the next three years. Dale also saw a *Bactrosaurus* and *Alectrosaurus* from Erenhot. That evening, Li Rong invited them all to join him and his Mongolian wife, Sarinxixiga — who claims direct descendancy from Genghis Khan — at their apartment for dinner.

From Hohhot they headed north to Erenhot — Roy Chapman Andrews's Iren Dabasu. Fog and drizzle followed them into the Yin Shan Mountains, which divide Inner Mongolia from China. As they rose to the Mongolian plateau, they found

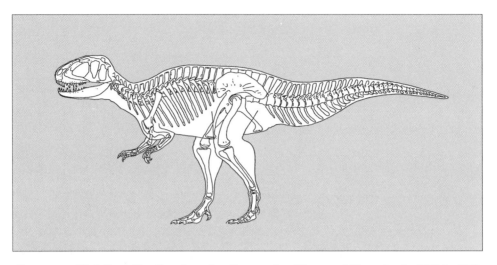

Known unofficially as the Jiangjunmiao theropod until named *Sinraptor* in 1993 by Phil and Zhao Xijin, this large carnivorous dinosaur from Jurassic China was one of the most perfectly preserved of the Project's finds. It is related to the North American allosaurids.

themselves on grassland, driving on country tracks past abandoned lamaseries and isolated yurts. The red-brick, walled villages appeared unwelcoming. The cold rain seemed to draw a curtain over the entire countryside. They tried to visit a sauropod locality near Qagan Nor, a mining town that rose, according to Dale, "like a mushroom out of a sea of mud," but they got lost in its maze of ditches and roads that seemed to be under perpetual construction. From their hotel that night in Jining, they could see the cliffs of the Early Cretaceous formation in which a sauropod had been found by a road-construction crew a year earlier, and learned from the local banner leader (a banner in China is a sort of county) that the quarry had since been paved over.

As they continued north toward Erenhot, the rain continued and the temperature dropped. They reached the city at three o'clock in the afternoon and proceeded directly to the badlands between Erenhot and the Outer Mongolian border, where Andrews had set up his camp more than sixty years before. Iren Dabasu, the "shining telegraph office" near the Americans' camp, was gone, the salt lake in the center of the wind-scoured basin was blighted by a disused soda factory built on a land-filled peninsula. The cold rain kept everyone except Phil in the jeeps — for some reason, he had brought along a down-filled parka. He also had Roy Chapman Andrews's map. In the half hour he spent prospecting, he found "a great deal of

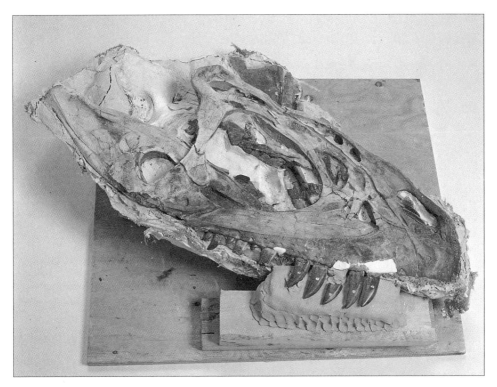

The Dinosaur Project's Gilles Danis found an almost complete *Sinraptor* skeleton, including this skull, its teeth coated in gypsum, in Jiangjunmiao in 1987.

bone, mostly ornithomimid, soft-shelled turtle and one *Myledaphus* tooth," enough to tell him not only that this was a very fruitful site, but also that it was one of the first dinosaur sites in northern Asia, the one discovered by the Central Asiatic Expedition in the 1920s. And most exciting was the fact that the dinosaurs there were almost identical to those found in Alberta. Emlyn remembers Phil coming back to the jeep with a handful of small fossil bones and saying, "I could have picked up this same handful in Dinosaur Provincial Park." Erenhot would definitely be another important locality for the 1988 season. In the morning, after gassing up the jeeps from drums on the back of the truck, they headed south again, en route to Beijing.

In the capital, they met up with Linda and the others from Xinjiang who had stayed on to do some sightseeing and shopping after visiting Turpan and Xian. The first thing they learned was that two hours after they had left Jiangjunmiao, Gilles Danis had found the theropod skull — a beautiful, nearly

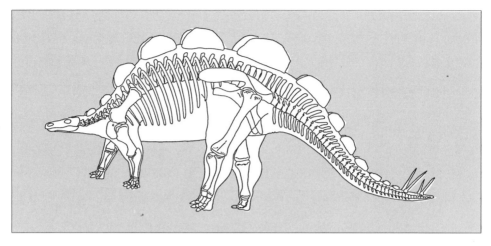

A new species of *Wuerhosaurus*, a stegosaur, was discovered by the Dinosaur Project in the Junggar Basin. Stegosaurs were slow-moving, heavily armored animals with tiny brains; they may have originated in Asia during the Middle Jurassic, but this one lived during the Early Cretaceous.

complete, monstrous allosaurid head — and Linda and Zhao Xijin had excavated it. During fossilization, the teeth had been covered by gypsum that made them seem translucent, like crystal daggers. They sparkled in the sunlight like prisms. No one had ever seen anything like it before.

At a press conference at the Sheraton Great Wall Hotel, Brian, Phil, Dale, Emlyn Koster, Chuck Gruchy, and Dong Zhiming announced their finds to twenty-five journalists representing most of the world's major news services, from the Los Angeles *Times* and Miami *Herald* to the Hoddaido *News* and Agence France Presse. The Canadians then attended a banquet at the Main Sichuan Restaurant. During the usual interminable rounds of *bai-jo* toasts, former IVPP chairman Zhou Mingzhen informed them that it was in this same restaurant that the ill-fated Sino-Soviet Expedition had been launched in 1959.

Media reaction to the Dinosaur Project's first full field season was swift and excited. In the two months the team had spent in the Junggar Basin, reported the *Japan Times*, two dozen skeletons had been excavated, including "what could be the largest sauropod ever found in Asia" — the *Mamenchisaurus* neck — as well as the "foot and ankle bones of what could be an entirely new species of carnivorous dinosaur," or what came to be known unofficially as the Jiangjunmiao theropod. Dale noted that the rock in which the sauropod had been found was extraordinarily hard and the bones particularly fragile; "It was like digging a poached egg out of concrete," he said. Phil told the Toronto *Star* that dinosaurs went right to the heart of our quest for knowledge of ourselves and our future. "They died off after being on top for so long," he said, "and that bothers people. It says something about our own chances of survival."

In some ways, the various newspaper articles reflected the differing interests of the scientists themselves. According to the Los Angeles *Times*, for example, Phil held up a plastic bag of assorted fossil teeth, claws, and vertebrae from the Gobi Desert and said, "These bones are all recognizable as Alberta dinosaurs." But in the Toronto *Globe and Mail*, Dale noted the "gross physiological differences" between Asian and Canadian dinosaurs, probably resulting from the vastly different climatic conditions in which they lived; "I was stunned," he said, "by how different the environment was in central Asia."

According to the *Globe and Mail* and *Maclean's* magazine, which also referred to "vast differences in Central Asian and North American dinosaur habitats," the 1987 expedition "scotched theories that herds of migrating Asian and North American dinosaurs mingled annually in Arctic feeding grounds." Both publications pointed out that "while Alberta dinosaurs were browsing on the lush edges of a large inland sea, in China they had adapted tens of millions of years earlier to semi-deserts and brackish inland lakes." *Maclean's* added that "Alberta dinosaurs lived in a swampy, coastal plain, while similar Chinese specimens evolved in inland basins comparable to Utah's Great Salt Lake area." All the news reports were correct about one thing: as the Boston *Globe* put it, the specimens found in China in 1987 were "so numerous and novel they are likely to force drastic revisions in our picture of the dinosaurs' evolution and diversity."

On October 27, the Tyrrell group flew home via Hong Kong, all except Don Brinkman, who decided to stay on to look at turtle specimens in the IVPP storerooms. The National Museum group — Chuck, Clayton, Francis Chan — also remained a few days longer. On October 29, the last of the Dinosaur People left Beijing. The next phase of the Dinosaur Project would take place in Canada.

CHAPTER 4

Devil's Coulee
Kevin Aulenback's eggs and dinosaur behavior

ABOUT 160 KM DUE SOUTH OF DINOSAUR PROVINCIAL PARK, CLOSE TO THE Alberta-Montana border, the Milk River snakes its way through Palliser's Triangle, a part of the prairie so dry and inhospitable that John Palliser himself, who first surveyed the area in the 1850s, declared it unfit for habitation by European settlers. That alone should identify it as a good place for dinosaurs. The river cuts a shallow gorge into the soft sandstone substrate, filling its water with the chalky silt that gives it its name. It is almost as silt-laden as the Yellow River in China, and for much the same reason. In its valley is a small badland that was sacred to the Plains Indians, who used its walls for the petroglyphs now preserved in Writing-on-Stone Provincial Park, the oldest of which show stick men with pointed shoulders standing beside horses that barely reach their shoulders. They show tipis, and men with shields and spears hunting buffalo, wapiti, and mountain sheep. The more recent ones show men with rifles. Huge fossilized bones found in the badlands were also sacred to the Plains Cree. They were said to have belonged to the giant buffalo that once roamed the prairies.

In the summer of 1987, a few weeks before they went to China, several people from the Tyrrell Museum were prospecting at the western end of the Milk River system, in a stretch of valley below Milk River Ridge. The group was led by Phil Currie. That May, a nineteen-year-old student named Wendy Sloboda and her boyfriend had been walking in the badlands near her father's ranch when they came across a patch of ground littered with little bits of what looked like blackened eggshell. Wendy had already had some experience in fossil hunting; dinosaur

**In 1923 in Mongolia, Roy Chapman Andrews (right) and George Olsen
(left, on ground) found what Andrews called "the first dinosaur eggs
ever seen by a human being." He declared them to be *Protoceratops* eggs.
Since then nearly twenty types of dinosaur eggs have been found.**

bones are not uncommon in the Milk River Valley, and she had earlier found stone nodules which, when split open, contained the tiny impressions of fossil fish. As soon as she picked up the eggshell fragments, she knew they were fossil. Black and slightly curved, they had tiny pinpricks that made a tight, regular pattern across them. They looked like pottery shards from a child's tea set.

She took a handful of them to Len Hills, a geologist friend at the University of Calgary, and he called the Tyrrell Museum and asked for Phil. Hills told Phil that he had what looked like dinosaur eggshell, and the two men met the next evening, a Friday, in the foyer of the Jack Singer Concert Hall in Calgary. When Hills held out his hand, Phil took one look at the mound of shell fragments in it and said, "Yup, that's eggshell," and on Monday, Phil and three technicians — Kevin Aulenback, Gerhard Maier, and Kent Wallis — drove south to meet Wendy on Milk River Ridge.

In the park, as elsewhere in North America, eggshell fragments are known but not common. There is no doubt that eggs were laid there, but not many of them fossilized. Rotting vegetation produced acidic groundwater, and volcanic activity in the nearby Rockies created acid rain conditions — precipitation high in sulfuric acid — that dissolved the shells of hatched eggs before they could turn into stone. In some cases, calcium carbonate from mollusc shells neutralized the acid precipitation, and in those areas eggshell is found from eggs either laid near-by or washed down from higher land. Away from the lime-laden water, however, shell fragments are rare.

Intact dinosaur eggs are rare everywhere. Although nearly 350 genera of dinosaurs are known worldwide, most of them presumably egg-layers (although there are some living reptiles who bear their young alive), only a few dozen dif-ferent types of eggs have been found. The first was discovered in France in 1869 by Philippe Matheron, an amateur fossil collector who lived near Aix-en-Provence. Matheron conjectured that the egg had been laid either by a large, ostrich-like bird, or by the sauropod *Hypselosaurus*, whose skeletal remains had been unearthed in the same area. But Matheron's discovery, announced in a brief article in an obscure journal, went unnoticed until 1950, when the director of the Musée d'Histoire Naturelle in Aix-en-Provence, Raymond Dughi, came upon the article by chance.

Until then, it had been assumed that the discoverer of the first dinosaur egg was Roy Chapman Andrews, who was not a man to publish brief articles in obscure journals. When Andrews and the members of his Central Asiatic Expedition pitched their tents beneath the Flaming Cliffs in Outer Mongolia on July 8, 1923, there had been no rain in the area for a year. "The scanty vegetation lay brown and shriveled by the pitiless sun," Andrews wrote in *On the Trail of Ancient Man*; "white rims of alkali marked the beds of former ponds; the desert swam in a maddening, dancing mirage that mirrored reedy lakes and cool, forest-ed islets where we knew there was only sand." In these red Late Cretaceous cliffs ten months earlier, Andrews's team had discovered "the ancestral dinosaur" — the first known skeleton of a *Protoceratops*, which they believed was the granddaddy of all the ceratopsians, a family of dinosaurs that had previously been known only in North America — and now they had returned to see what other treasures lay hidden in the basin.

That evening, when they gathered in the mess tent for dinner, every single

Wendy Sloboda and Phil examining an ankylosaur skull from Dinosaur Provincial Park. It was Wendy's discovery of dinosaur eggshell fragments in the Milk River area that first led Phil and other Tyrrell Museum crew members to Devil's Coulee in 1987.

member of the expedition reported finding a ceratopsian skull. Andrews himself discovered the skull and dentaries of a *Protoceratops* lying fully exposed on the surface; others reported finding complete skulls on the tops of hoodoos like so many Ming vases on pedestals. Clearly the team had stumbled upon a ceratopsian graveyard. Fragments of eggshell mixed in with the skull remains suggested to them that the Flaming Cliffs might also have been a nesting site for birds. Although the bird-like *Archaeopteryx* was known from the Jurassic, at that time no birds had been found in Cretaceous beds in Asia.

"Our real thrill," records Andrews, "came on the second day, when George Olsen reported at tiffin that he was sure he had found fossil eggs. We joked with him a good deal, but nevertheless all of us were curious enough to walk down with him after luncheon. Then our indifference suddenly evaporated; for we realized that we were looking at the first dinosaur eggs ever seen by a human being."

That Olsen had found true dinosaur eggs was confirmed partly by their shape and texture. Birds' eggs are large at one end and small at the other so that when they roll, Andrews speculated, they would roll in a circle and be less likely to fall out of a nest. Reptilian eggs are deposited in shallow depressions scooped out of sand, and so there is no evolutionary advantage to being "egg-shaped"; they are quite evenly elongated, more like rolled-out bread dough than like chicken eggs. The eggs found by the Andrews expedition were twenty centimeters long and eighteen centimeters in circumference, with shells two millimeters thick. The shells were more porous than birds' eggs; although buried under sand, they still had to let oxygen in and carbon dioxide out. Their surfaces are pock-marked — Andrews described them as "pebbled" — and sometimes striated.

That dinosaurs laid eggs had not been in much doubt; since most modern reptiles are egg-layers, it was assumed that most of their ancestors had been as well. There was some speculation that dinosaurs, like some modern reptiles — chameleons and snakes, for example — bore living young, but as John Noble Wilford observed in his book *The Riddle of the Dinosaur*, it would have been surprising if Andrews had discovered proof that dinosaurs did *not* lay eggs.

Another discovery was awaiting Andrews and his colleagues at the Flaming Cliffs. While other members of the expedition were digging into the cliff face to uncover the eggs from below, Olsen climbed up to the top of the ledge and began digging down from above. He soon came to the skeleton of a small dinosaur lying ten centimeters above the egg cluster. "It was a toothless species," Andrews noted, "and we believe that it may have been overtaken by a sand-storm in the very act of robbing the dinosaur nest." Osborn later named the creature *Oviraptor philoceratops*, meaning "egg-seizer with a fondness for ceratopsian eggs," for the twenty-five eggs the expedition collected were identified as those of *Protoceratops*. As we shall see, discoveries by the Dinosaur Project have cast doubt on both of Andrews's conclusions: that the eggs were *Protoceratops*, and that *Oviraptor* was scavenging them.

News that the American Museum expedition had discovered dinosaur eggs spread quickly, and when Andrews returned to the United States newspapers and magazines deluged him with requests for photographs and descriptions of them. Almost on the strength of the eggs alone he was able to raise the capital needed for his next trip into northern China — one egg was even sold at public auction for $5,000.

Andrews speculated on the circumstances under which the eggs were laid, and his speculation was, for the most part, highly colored by what was already known about *Protoceratops*. "Ten million years ago," he wrote in the January 1924 issue of *Asia* magazine (paleontologists in the 1920s still underestimated the age of the Cretaceous), "a goblin-like creature stood on the edge of a shallow basin in what now is called Mongolia. Its great round eyes stared unblinkingly from a thin, hatchet face, ending in a hooked beak. Its head sloped up and back into a circular boney frill, which formed a solid armature over the slender neck and almost covered the shoulders. Low in front and high behind, with its ten-foot body ending in a thick tail, it seemed like a horrid, nightmare fantasy. It gazed across a fertile upland with lush grass, where forest patches broke the sky-line and dotted the open savannas with islets of vivid green. Slowly it waddled down the slope and settled itself into the sand. And there in the hollow it left ten elliptical white eggs, fated, though warmed by the sun's rays, never to be hatched."

Had Andrews wondered how dinosaurs behaved when they were alive instead of what happened to them when they died, he might have asked himself — as American paleontologist Jack Horner did fifty years later — why juvenile dinosaurs and dinosaur eggs were so abundant in that one Mongolian basin and so maddeningly scarce everywhere else in the world. Horner reasoned that more dinosaurs must have died as babies than as adults — "That's what happens with most animals," he writes in *Digging Dinosaurs* — and he therefore wondered why adult skeletons are so much more common than those of juveniles. One explanation that came to mind was an earlier theory that the smaller bones of baby dinosaurs were too fragile to survive intact. "But, if that were the case," he reasoned, "why have paleontologists frequently found fossilized bones of lizards and other small reptiles?" Fossil debris in the microsites should contain juvenile dinosaur remains as well as lizard, fish, and turtle fragments, but it does not.

Eventually, Horner hit upon an explanation that made sense and led him to a preliminary evaluation of how dinosaurs lived. Adult Cretaceous dinosaurs spent most of their time in low, wet, coastal areas, either feeding off the abundant vegetation that grew there, or else preying on those that did. When they died, their carcasses were buried by river-borne sand and mud and were preserved long enough to fossilize. But areas that are repeatedly flooded are terrible places to lay eggs; eggs need air and would quickly drown if buried in saturated sand. Horner thought that adult dinosaurs would probably travel inland to higher, drier terrain in order to lay their eggs where they would be more likely to survive until hatched. And higher, drier plains do not lend themselves as readily as low, wet areas to preserving fossil remains. Even adult skeletons are rarely found in areas that were plains during the Cretaceous.

If the inland area were a desert, however, dotted with inland lakes and ephemeral streams, bones of animals that died there could be covered by a sandy stream-side matrix or dunes and stay buried long enough to fossilize. That is the case with the red sandstone in central Asia, which was semi-arid during the Cretaceous but seems to have been sprinkled with seasonal lakes or swampy areas. According to Zofia Kielan-Jaworowska, leader of the Polish-Mongolian expeditions in the mid-1970s, it has remained uncovered by sea for the past 135 million years. The Flaming Cliffs of Outer Mongolia and the Bayan Mandahu area in Inner Mongolia were as arid during the Cretaceous as they are today, but they are riddled with coarser-grained channels that indicate fast-moving, seasonal stream beds.

In North America, Jack Horner's reasoning led him to look for dinosaur eggs in areas that were high and dry and sandy during the Late Cretaceous but had indications of wetland microenvironments. He found such an area in northern Montana, several kilometers southwest of Choteau, within shouting distance of the Milk River across the border in Alberta. From 84 million to about 72 million years ago, this area was an upper coastal plain between the rising Rocky Mountains to the west and the retreating Western Interior Seaway 320 km to the east. Geologically it is known as the Two Medicine Formation, 488 m of sediment from the volcanic highlands and rugged hills that was pushed eastward by the rising mountains and carried down by torrential streams. The formation is made up of alternating bands of reddish sandstone and hard whitish rock. "During the rainy season," writes Dale Russell, "the verdant plain was dotted with ephemeral soda lakes, but during the dry season only vegetation growing near the streams remained green." This alternating wet and dry pattern formed a hard, white, substrate geologists call caliche and farmers curse as hardpan.

The first egg find there was made in July 1979 by a Princeton paleontology student, Fran Tannenbaum, one of thirteen volunteers doing summer fieldwork under Horner's direction. Tannenbaum found a perfectly preserved, 75-million-year-old egg belonging to a previously unknown species of small, fleet-footed herbivore that was later named *Orodromeus makelai*, or "Makela's mountain runner," by Horner, in honor of his late colleague, Bob Makela. For the rest of that summer, Horner and his students sifted the top layer of that first hill and a neighboring promontory — now famous among paleontologists as Egg Mountain and Egg Island, respectively. Grid by grid, tonne by tonne, they uncovered fifty-two eggs and a huge pile of small dinosaur and lizard bones; over the next few years, Horner and Makela found sixty-one eggs belonging to three different types of dinosaurs — a hadrosaur, *Troodon*, and *Orodromeus* — as well as fossils of shrew-like mammals, a varanid or monitor lizard, and an adult *Troodon*. They named the hadrosaur *Maiasaura*, or "good mother lizard," because, according to Horner, its nest spoke so eloquently of its maternal instincts. Egg Mountain, he writes, has "so far proved to be the most fertile territory in the world for uncovering evidence of nesting dinosaurs and details of their growth and life history."

Maiasaura, which flourished 80 million years ago, was a smallish, flat-headed hadrosaur that weighed about two tonnes at full growth and measured nearly seven and a half meters in length. It was bipedal, but went down on all fours to graze and rest. Its forehands had four fingers, and its "beak" was perhaps the most duck-like of all hadrosaurs, flat and rounded, concealing jaws that contained two hundred self-sharpening cheek teeth and an additional six hundred spares waiting to descend. Its forehead was marked by bony ridges that, according to Dale, "served probably as a support for fleshy structures used in trumpeting." Like most hadrosaurs, *Maiasaura* had large eyes — about twice the size of an ostrich's — and brains about twice the size of modern reptiles when adjusted for its larger body size.

Maiasaura bones and teeth reveal a lot about its natural history and growth rates; there are no clearly defined growth rings in the bones, for example, which suggests that the animal grew quickly and steadily rather than in sudden spurts. Its teeth had large grinding surfaces, indicating that their owner required proportionately as much vegetation each day as modern herbivores do, and this also suggests a high metabolic rate. "Maiasaurs," writes Dale, "and by implication hadrosaurs in general, were at least incipiently warm-blooded."

**Phil Currie hoped that the Milk River badlands south of Dinosaur Provincial
Park would yield Canada's first complete dinosaur eggs, and in the
summer of 1987, his search paid off. Fossil eggs were found in several sites,
close enough together to be considered evidence of a dinosaur nesting colony.**

Orodromeus is a member of the hypsilophodontid family, small, long-legged
sprinters known informally as "dinosaur gazelles," except that they were bipedal.
Their strong hind legs and large balancing tail enabled them to run up to thirty-
two kilometers an hour. It was a quick and agile herbivore and quite possibly
warm-blooded. Its hands and feet were clawed and its triangular tooth structure
suggests that it fed on fleshy fruits, pulpy foliage and, at least as a hatchling,
insects, such as beetles, numerous species of which existed at the time.

There are two *Maiasaura* sites. The bonebed, which is all that remains of a
great herd killed by a thick and obviously sudden fall of volcanic ash, spreads out
over one and a half square kilometers and contains animals at various stages of
development from yearlings to mature adults. A second site contains skeletons of
adults near nests, or with juveniles less than a year old. Thus the *Maiasaura* material provides a complete hadrosaur growth record from hatchling to adult, and
details of the nesting site and the construction of the nests themselves provide an

uncanny insight into the animals' day-to-day behavior.

Most of the eggs found on Egg Mountain and Egg Island were *Orodromeus* eggs. About thirteen millimeters by five centimeters in diameter, the eggs appear to be smooth but are actually made up of a series of longitudinal striations or grooves, as if each egg were wrapped tightly in string from end to end. Most of them had hatched, and so only the bottom halves were intact, stuck upright in the calcareous siltstone stratum surrounded by extremely perturbated bits of mud chips, broken bone, and root casts, as if the ground in which the eggs were laid had been churned up by thousands of feet. The eggs themselves were in clutches, arranged in a spiral pattern, like snail shells; they were about five centimeters apart, each egg tipped in toward the center of the nest. The number of eggs in a clutch varied from three to twenty-four, with the average at an even dozen. Horner reasoned that the clutches with more than twelve eggs represented nests shared by two or more animals, and the even spacing and uniform tipping pattern indicated to him that the eggs had been arranged by the female, using either her beak or her forelimbs, after they were laid.

The *Maiasaura* eggs were much larger, measuring nearly twenty centimeters in length, and were found in huge nests, each containing an average of twenty to twenty-four eggs. The nests were made of mud shaped into mounds about seven or eight meters apart — the approximate length of an adult female. Within the nests, besides eggshell fragments, there were also the skeletal remains of *Maiasaura* young, ranging from 35-cm hatchlings to 150-cm yearlings, suggesting that *Maiasaura* — unlike their hypsilophodont neighbors, whose young appear to have left their nests immediately after hatching — remained in the nest for the first few months or so of their lives and must therefore have been cared for by the females, who were "good mothers." Horner interprets the evidence to arrive at an enticing picture of Montana life 80 million years ago. "*Maiasaura* mothers," he wrote, "seem to have constructed a roomy mud nest and to have placed an insulating layer of vegetation over the eggs. (The one-and-a-half-ton adults could not have sat on the clutch.) Some modern birds do the same. Also, like birds that are altricial, or helpless upon hatching, the rather limp baby maiasaurs stayed in the nest and were fed regurgitated foliage and berries by a parent until their bones were strong enough to allow walking or running. [Probably the latter, since the area was also rife with carnivorous *Troodon*.] They grew rapidly, more than doubling their considerable size as nestlings. When they were about five feet long, they were finally able to leave the nest and forage with adults."

Dale calculates that a brood of twenty *Maiasaura* hatchlings would require twenty-two kilograms of foliage a day in order to grow at the rate of forty-six centimeters a month. "At this rate," he says, "the parents comprising a breeding colony would be unable to find energy-rich fruit in sufficient quantity." Less nourishing leaves and twigs would be substituted, and in a breeding colony comprising more than 2,500 adults, the environmental damage caused by stripping all available trees of foliage would be considerable. Parents would have to travel further and further from the nests in order to find food, which meant that one parent would have to stay to guard the nest from predators while the other foraged. One out of every four nests excavated contained dead hatchlings, which suggests that predation of the foraging parent was high. When a foraging parent failed to return to the nest, the guarding parent was forced to abandon the nestlings to forage for himself or herself, leaving the young to die of starvation.

Even with a 25-percent predation rate, however, the *Maiasaura* herds prospered. The bones of the great herd that was caught in a Mount St. Helens-like volcanic fall-out included skeletal parts of an estimated 135,000 individuals. The size of such a herd is reminiscent of the great herds of buffalo that, 80 million years later, roamed the same part of North America. The amount of food needed to support a herd of that size could not be found in a single area, so the urge to travel to where the food was must have been strong. In fact, in evolutionary terms, it must have been vital. "No environment could have supported a stationary group of this many large, warm-blooded herbivores," writes Dale. "These are the remains of a migrating herd of dinosaurs."

It seems likely, then, that some dinosaurs gathered in herds and returned to the same place every year to lay their eggs in communal ground, like puffins and other large marine birds do today. In the case of *Maiasaura*, the communal ground consisted of a high, arid plain on the shore of an inland lake (Egg Mountain), with an island just over half a kilometer offshore with similarly arid conditions (Egg Island). The lake shore would have supplied the vegetation needed for food as well as water for drinking and cooling, and the plain would have provided ideal nesting grounds for a herd of such tremendous proportions. Dale estimates that the average nesting site would have required room for 1,350 nests. The bonebed, on the other hand, gives some indication of the size of the herds. Using modern herding herbivores as models, it is fair to say that such large herds of relatively passive plant eaters attracted predacious carnosaurs, and pressure from marauding tyrannosaurs and packs of sniping *Troodon* would have made successful breeding imperative for the hapless hadrosaurs. It would also have helped to keep them on the move and healthy.

Babies in Eggs!

WHILE JACK HORNER AND HIS CREW WERE DIGGING FOR DINOSAUR EGGS IN THE badlands of Montana, Phil Currie and his three Tyrrell technicians began prospecting the Milk River Valley with Wendy Sloboda as a guide. Phil was curious about the absence of egg sites in Alberta. Dinosaur Park could be divided into two kinds of sequences: those that had been poorly drained during the Cretaceous and those that had been slightly better drained. David Eberth, the Tyrrell's sedimentologist and a future Dinosaur Project member, had found eggshell fragments in the slightly better drained areas. These were splay deposits, where rivers had flooded their banks seasonally, leaving wide marginal sedimentation. The water had drowned the eggs, then retreated, leaving them to dry out, break up, and eventually fossilize. Theoretically, the Milk River area had been better drained than the splay deposits, so it was possible that whole eggs had survived. Horner certainly thought so. He told Phil that if the Canadians didn't find eggs that summer, he would bring his team up and find some for him.

Geologically speaking, the Milk River Valley is like a layer cake. The upper strata is the Bearpaw Formation, the ancient inland seaway bed rich in ammonites — fossilized mollusc shells from the Mesozoic — so common in farmers' fields that they are collected and sold as "the Alberta gemstone." The Bearpaw is underlain by the Judith River, Pakowki, and Milk River formations, deposited more or less at the same time as the Two Medicine Formation south of the border. "What we were looking for," says Kevin Aulenback, "was a stable environment, drier upland areas where hadrosaurs were supposed to lay their eggs."

Throughout June, Phil and his crew prospected along the southern border of the province. Altogether, they found thirteen eggshell sites, places where sifting through the talus at the bottom of washed-out cliff faces in the badlands yielded lots of tiny gray triangular shell fragments but no nests or whole eggs. Phil began to wonder if perhaps the problem was perceptual: the eggs were there, but because no one had seen them before, no one knew what to look for. One day he took his team across the border to Jack Horner's camp in Montana and told them to take a good look at the eggs the American team had found.

Horner sent them out into the hills to see what they could find. After a half hour of prospecting, Kevin came upon a hill that had "tons of eggshell coming down it." Ignoring the shards at the bottom, he climbed up to the top of the hill and, looking down at the gravelly surface, made out oblong shapes in the rock. They looked like dark baguettes of bread, or the toes of old boots with the tops sheered off. "You don't actually see whole eggs," he says. "No one ever sees a round egg in the ground. What you see is a curved surface all crushed and warped and black, the bottoms of eggs with the tops worn off and the insides scoured by erosion and filled with sediment."

The eggs were in a huge piece of hardpan that encased the fragile shells like concrete. Kevin yelled, "Hey, look — eggs!" and the others came running and began to scour the outcrop for more. Before long they had found not only eggs but also dozens of tiny bones. Kevin grabbed a handful of these and ran back to Horner, who became very excited — he had not been able to find anything younger than yearlings before. These were the smallest *Orodromeus* bones he had ever seen. From their size, he thought that they were from the skeletons of hatchlings. He later determined that they were the bones of embryos; the eggs had not hatched, but had been broken open either by scavengers or by 78 million years of weather.

When the Tyrrell team returned to Alberta that evening, they knew what eggs looked like in the ground. All they had to do was find the right ground. The egg site in Montana had reminded Wendy of a section of the Milk River Ridge where she used to play as a child, and for lack of any more scientific ideas the team went there. It was a beautiful stretch of the river valley, full of hoodoos and high, soft bluffs. As soon as Kevin saw it, he "felt that there was bound to be something here." After asking the Hutterite colony that owned the land for permission to

The nest of dinosaur eggs found by Kevin Aulenback in Devil's Coulee, Alberta. They were laid by the duckbilled *Hypacrosaurus*, a dinosaur not known in nearby Dinosaur Park. These eggs contained fossilized embryos, providing a complete growth series for that animal.

prospect, Phil and his team started looking. Time was running out: it was the first week in August and Phil was scheduled to leave for China on the tenth. Dave Eberth came down and told them that the site had three separate horizons: braided river sediments at the bottom of the valley; stacked flood plain above that, created by flooding of the rivers, "flooding event after flooding event," he said, "for hundreds of thousands of years"; and, on top, more fluvial deposits. Dave said there was no point in looking for eggs in the lower horizon; the place to look was in the stacked flood plain, which was better drained. "Look up," he said, and pointed to a layer of caliche.

"So Phil just walked up the ridge about fifteen or twenty feet," Kevin recalls, "and there, about three feet below prairie level, he found the first dinosaur eggs in Alberta."

It was technically the last day of the field season. Still working on a hunch that there were more eggs in the area, Phil shifted the search down-canyon in the

Skull of an *Hypacrosaurus* embryo found in Devil's Coulee in 1987; Phil, Kevin, and Gerhard Maier found Canada's first egg nesting site and one of the few instances of embryonic bones in the world. The teeth are better preserved because enamel is harder than bone.

afternoon. Almost immediately, Gerhard Maier found a scree of eggshell fragments, this time with small bones associated with them. They worked the microsite extensively, but could not definitely associate the bones with the eggs. In other words, they could not say with scientific certainty that the bones had *come out* of the eggs. Still, the find was significant enough to convince Phil to stay one more day.

The next morning, Phil and Gerhard returned to the microsite and began collecting the bones. Kevin helped for a while, then, bored with bone picking, wandered off into a new coulee. He walked up and down the coulee slopes for a while, his eyes checking the sandstone as he climbed, and found three fifteen-centimeter clams, which he decided were "no big deal."

Just before noon he told himself he would walk up and down the scree one last time before the crew headed back to Drumheller. This time he didn't even see a clam, so he sat down with his back against the coulee wall and let the sun beat

Hypacrosaurus hatchlings were born with teeth, but without the large head crest
found on the adults, and were able to move swiftly almost immediately.
Mark Hallett's painting illustrates the duck-like beak of all hadrosaurs,
and the crest shows it was related to *Corythosaurus*.

down on him. Then he looked down at the ground in front of his feet. What he saw were huge chunks of eggshell, about the size of his palm, and when he reached down to pick them up he also found a section of tibia about six centimeters long. A closer search turned up all sorts of limb bones, heads of femurs, shanks of tibias, all very tiny and delicate, like a small bird's. They looked very like the small bones he had found in Montana.

The shell fragments and bones seemed to have washed down from somewhere in the bank above his head. He looked up. "And right there," he says, "right above my head, sticking out of the cliff face, I saw five whole eggs. I remained calm. I remembered not to run straight up the cliff face but to go around and come at it from the top. It was a long climb, but when I got there I saw a femur sticking out of one of the eggs. I had found an egg with an embryo still inside it!"

Kevin does not remember exactly what he did then. Phil says he saw him come running down the valley like a demented idiot, shouting "Babies in eggs! Babies in eggs!" Phil and Gerhard were already walking back to the truck, ready to pack up and leave, but when they heard Kevin shouting excitedly, they stopped and turned around. "Phil thought I was yelling 'Babies *and* eggs,'" says Kevin, "which we'd already found, so it took him a while to understand why I was so excited."

When Kevin explained what he had found, all three of them went running back to the coulee. Phil looked into the egg with the embryo and found a skull with teeth in it: "He was shaking so much he dropped the thing," says Kevin, "and had to get down on his hands and knees and find it again. Gerhard found another egg with articulated ribs still in it. Pretty soon we were all dancing around and shaking hands about forty times, saying 'Pinch me, pinch me — no, don't pinch me!'"

At first, Phil thought the eggs from Devil's Coulee — the local name for it, possibly because the end of the canyon forked off into three smaller canyons, like a devil's trident — belonged to a non-crested, duckbilled member of the subfamily Hadrosaurinae. All juvenile hadrosaurs were non-crested, however, and he later began to suspect that the Devil's Coulee specimens were actually Lambeosaurine eggs. After pooling the finds with Jack Horner's juvenile and adult specimens from Montana, however, he realized that the Devil's Coulee eggs and embryos were those of a new species of *Hypacrosaurus*. Hypacrosaurs were smallish, bipedal hadrosaurs, measuring about six meters long, with high crested foreheads —

although not as high and rounded as those of the related *Corythosaurus*. The find emphasized the great diversity that must have existed in Cretaceous times. No *Hypacrosaurus* was known from Dinosaur Provincial Park, a bare 160 kilometers away, but here they were in abundance. In modern times it is rare to find a genus inhabiting a location so far north that is not found generally across the continent. Such diversity and specialization is associated with more tropical climates, where a square kilometer of rain forest might contain every member of a species of orchid or insect. "It's beginning to appear," says Phil, "that even though dinosaurs could move great distances across any environment, they still seem to be fairly environmentally specific, and that's quite interesting."

But *Hypacrosaurus* also indicates that some kind of link might have existed between China and North America in the Late Cretaceous. *Jaxartosaurus*, a later relative of *Hypacrosaurus*, is known from Xinjiang. "The similarities are quite remarkable," Phil says. Although *Saurolophus* — a hadrosaur known from both the Horseshoe Canyon Formation in Alberta and the Nemegt Formation in Outer Mongolia — remains the best evidence of a connection, *Hypacrosaurus* and its crested relatives strengthen the tie. The real importance of the Devil's Coulee find, however, apart from the information it contained about dinosaur embryonic development and growth, is in the fact that the eggs were found in a drier environment contemporaneous with Dinosaur Park. They were the eggs of different dinosaurs from those found in the low, wet, coastal regions of the park. Other dinosaurs, mammals, and lizards found near the hypacrosaur eggs also indicated a fauna closer in many ways to Asian assemblages than to those of Dinosaur Park. Did the similarities result from migration or dispersal? Or were they examples of convergent evolution? These questions were running through Phil's mind as he boarded the airplane a few days later and headed for China.

CHAPTER 5

The Gobi Desert
Phil Currie's baby Ankylosaurs *and dinosaur nesting*

BEFORE THE START OF THE 1988 FIELD SEASON, MEMBERS OF THE DINOSAUR Project underwent some intensive soul searching. "In my estimation," Gilles Danis had written in his field notes toward the end of the previous year, "the expedition to the Gobi has been only marginally successful." Gilles felt that more preparation in quarrying techniques would have been valuable — "Technically we worked like amateurs" — and a better understanding between Chinese and Canadian workers would also have helped. "The people on either side of the Dinosaur Project did not know enough about the skills of the other side." There were very skillful technicians on both the Canadian and Chinese teams, adds Linda. "What was lacking, perhaps, was an understanding of the way each of us did things, and why we did them that way. But a lack of communication was to be expected, I guess, given two such different cultures."

More disconcerting than the lack of communication, which could be ironed out, was the enormous rift that had developed between Brian Noble and Dong Zhiming. "Oil and water," says Dale. "They just didn't get along at all."

The focus of the difficulties between Brian and the rest of the Project team was, of course, the Tipi-Yurt Exchange. In the end, the ceremony had taken place and everyone who participated in it had enjoyed it, but there remained a bitter aftertaste. James Rusk, a Canadian journalist with the *Globe and Mail*, called it "a spectacular backfire of a public-relations gimmick." Rusk had traveled all the way to Urumqi to report on the expedition but was unable to secure a travel permit to Jimsar because of the official ill will surrounding the exchange. "The press is sore," he wrote, "because it missed the dinosaur story when it was hottest, the first year of exploration. The Chinese are puzzled by Ex Terra's insensitivity. And Canada has lost a good chance to show off some of its best scientists to the world." Little wonder, then, that at a meeting between Chuck Gruchy and Brian Noble in Ottawa in December 1987, Gruchy informed Brian that if the Tipi-Yurt Exchange was to be part of the 1988 expedition, then the National Museum would not be.

Plans for the second instalment of the exchange went ahead nonetheless. No firm date or site was selected, but the event would take place somewhere in Inner Mongolia. Some team members were changed in order to give as many Canadian paleontologists as possible a chance to work in China. The previous year, Emlyn Koster had proven the value of having a sedimentologist on hand to work out the depositional histories of the various sites, so that the paleontologists could know what kind of environments they were dealing with. The new sites in Inner Mongolia and the Ordos Basin chosen by Phil, Dale, and Dong Zhiming were predominantly redbeds, and, as Dennis had predicted, they were not rich in pollen samples. Red indicates that a lot of oxidization has occurred in the sand before it became sandstone, and oxidation works against the preservation of organic material such as pollen. Two technicians — Kevin Aulenback and Jim McCabe — and Paul Johnston, a specialist in invertebrates, were added to the team, as was Tom Jerzykiewicz, a Polish-born sedimentologist with the Canadian Geological Survey in Calgary who was an adjunct research scientist at the Tyrrell. He had participated in the Polish-Mongolian Expedition to the Flaming Cliffs in Outer Mongolia in 1971, and the Canadians suspected that the geological formation that formed the Flaming Cliffs — where Roy Chapman Andrews had also worked — extended into Inner Mongolia to turn up at Bayan Mandahu. They needed Tom to tell them if they were right.

Brian Noble was to go, along with two others from Ex Terra: Bai Jing, whose father was Mongolian and who would be the Project's official interpreter; and Brenda Belokrinicev. The film crew — Alan Bibby and Tom Radford — were scheduled to join the scientists partway through the summer.

On the Chinese side, Zhao Xijin was to continue work in Jiangjunmiao with Don Brinkman and Jim McCabe from the Tyrrell; and the IVPP's Zheng Jiajian would preside over the field camp in Bayan Mandahu where Phil Currie and the

IVPP dinosaur specialist Zheng Jiajian (left) was in charge of the Dinosaur Project's first trip to Bayan Mandahu in 1988. Unlike Xinjiang, the exposures at Bayan Mandahu were similar in age to those in Alberta, although the dinosaurs in them turned out to be different. Don Brinkman, the Royal Tyrrell Museum's turtle specialist, returned to Jiangjunmiao in 1988 to work on the sauropod quarry with Zhao Xijin and Jim McCabe. He bought the violin on his way through Urumqi.

rest of the Tyrrell crew would work until July, at which time everyone would convene in Erenhot for the final few weeks of work. Dale and the National Museum crew would go to the Ordos later in the summer, after a short trip to the Arctic in June, and would then join the others in Erenhot. Dong Zhiming was in England during the early part of the summer, opening an exhibit of Chinese dinosaurs, but would join the Dinosaur Project team later.

The Tyrrell Museum team left Calgary on May 31 and arrived in Beijing on June 2, where they checked into the Western-style Friendship Hotel. For the next few days they spent most of their time at the IVPP, looking at specimens, arranging travel documents, and waiting for airplane and train tickets. Jim McCabe, in China for the first time, noted that the food at the welcoming banquet represented four phyla: Echinodermata (fried sea cucumbers), Vertebrata (sliced pig's bladder and baked fish eyes), Coelentrata (fried jellyfish), Arthropoda (shrimps), as well as plants (mostly green peppers), and a "vile liquor and lots of beer and wine."

Don and Jim flew to Urumqi on June 5 and were met at the airport by Wang Daifu and taken to the Academia Sinica hotel for lunch. The weather was cooler and less humid than it had been in Beijing, and the city was quieter; there were birds instead of cicadas, and the only street sounds were made by women sweeping the gutters with enormous twig brooms. They spent four days in Urumqi, shopping in the open markets, eating in the noodle houses. Don bought soap and a fiddle with a case for 200 yuan and visited a jade factory and a carpet factory.

They left Urumqi on June 9, spent that night in Qitai, and arrived in Jiangjunmiao at seven o'clock on the night of the tenth. Zhao Xijin and Tang Zhilu met them and distributed armloads of blankets, clothing, and cloth sun caps. There was now a total of seventeen people in camp. The temperature was 38 degrees, but the sky was clear and the air was very still. Don handed out Tyrrell Museum T-shirts, sorted out a work schedule with Zhao Xijin (up at seven, work in quarries until ten, breakfast from ten to ten-thirty, work until noon, "siesta" from noon until five, work from five to nine-thirty, break for supper, Chinese lessons from ten to eleven, then lights out). Neither Don nor Jim was happy with the five-hour siesta in the middle of the day. In Dinosaur Park, they worked from seven in the morning until four in the afternoon, then knocked off for the day. Here in the Gobi, where the midday temperature was not much higher than in Alberta, taking such a long break and then working four and a half hours at the end of the day seemed unnecessarily cautious. But they accepted the Chinese way, and after dinner the two Canadians set up their tents in the sand and went to sleep.

Work began the next morning in the theropod and sauropod quarries from the year before. The first thing Jim discovered was that the wrong bits had been sent for the jackhammer; the second was that the compressor to run the whackers would not start; the third was that, even if they could modify the jackhammer bits with a file, there was no container in which to measure the gasoline/oil mixture to fuel it, and without the right mixture its motor would race like a Beijing jeep with a slipped clutch. That evening the wind blew up so strongly they had to quit early and go back to camp. The next day it rained. A rivulet of brown run-off ran through the camp, into tents, and under the kitchen truck. The day after that, Tang Zhilu uncrated the dynamite.

The Road to Bayan Mandahu

THE DAY DON AND JIM LEFT FOR XINJIANG, PAUL JOHNSTON, BRIAN NOBLE, AND Tom Jerzykiewicz boarded the train for Linhe en route to Bayan Mandahu. Phil, meanwhile, went to the IVPP and examined the huge theropod skull that Gilles had found at Jiangjunmiao in 1987 — "Beautiful!" — and made careful measurements and extensive notes of it in his field book. It was definitely not that of the adult megalosaur they were tentatively calling "Jiangjunmiaosaurus," and which had been first found in Xinjiang in 1983. This animal lacked the megalosaur's typically crested skull. Neither was it an allosaur or tyrannosaur. The whole skull was more than eighty centimeters long and thirty centimeters across at the widest point. The roof and braincase were partially articulated, more or less the way nature had made them, and Phil could clearly see differences between this theropod and the North American *Allosaurus* and *Tyrannosaurus*: the narial or nostril holes were smaller, for one thing. The premaxillary teeth had "blood grooves" along them, as most theropod teeth did, but there were fewer of them. He thought he could detect a pair of pneumatic openings at the back, where a portion of the cap was broken off, and he could also see the skull's sutures — cracks across the crown, like a baby's fontanelle, that allow the head to grow as the animal matures — which told him that this theropod was a juvenile. Could it be a juvenile "Jiangjunmiaosaurus," with an as-yet undeveloped skull crest? Or was it a juvenile of a new type of theropod?

Pondering these matters, he stepped out to visit the world's largest Kentucky Fried Chicken restaurant, near Tienanmen Square. He had eaten a lot of chicken in China — lots of heads and feet and skin-covered bone — and he was curious to see if the Colonel had managed to find any chicken meat. He had. But it came with mashed potatoes instead of fries. None of the Chinese patrons knew what to do with the little plastic knives and forks: they watched Phil. He picked up his chicken and ate it with his fingers, as any allosaurid might do under similar circumstances. The Chinese around him sighed with relief and did likewise.

On June 7, he and Wu Guang Zhong, the IVPP's film technician, boarded the train for the twelve-hour ride to Linhe. This was not the infamous Iron Rooster; it was a modern, comfortable train with sleeping berths and a relatively clean

The field camp at Bayan Mandahu was built as winter quarters for nomadic Mongolian shepherds and was made from bricks originally belonging to a Buddhist lamasery. Dinosaur Project members slept in tents or in the motel-like units of the compound. The white building far left is the cook house.

dining car if they did not look too closely at the floor. Their route followed a broad, green valley north, through the Great Wall, then proceeded through Datong, Jining, and Hohhot, where they were joined by Brian Noble and Bai Jing. They arrived in Linhe at six o'clock the next morning. Li Rong and Zheng Jiajian took them to the same hotel in which they'd stayed the year before. There they joined Kevin, Paul, and Tom in time for a noon-hour banquet with the governor of Bayannur banner, the vast desert territory that stretches all the way from the Yellow River north to the Outer Mongolian border, including Linhe and Bayan Mandahu. Of the banner's 1.6 million people, Linhe accounted for about half and Bayan Mandahu for three — a Mongolian shepherd, his wife, and his wife's mother.

A seventeenth-century Buddhist temple once stood at Bayan Mandahu, but it was knocked down in the 1970s by the Red Guard, and the bricks from it were used to build a meeting hall for the local shepherds' commune. The meeting hall was long and low, a series of separate rooms each with a door giving out onto bare desert, like a midwestern motel. The large room in the middle was the actual meeting room — red banners slung across the end proclaiming the longevity of friendship between the Chinese and Mongolian peoples — and this was flanked by several smaller rooms in which sleeping platforms took up half the floor space. Here commune members and their families from the farther reaches of the Gobi could spend the night or the winter.

The Dinosaur People were borrowing these accommodations in the summer, when the nomadic Mongols were out on the desert with their yurts and flocks of fat-tailed sheep. There were three or four other buildings in the compound — a second, shorter series of rooms, one of which was a kitchen, and another was a kind of general store that opened every Tuesday afternoon for about half an hour and dispensed such items as rubber boots and slippers, harmonicas and farming implements — all of dubious use in a desert — as well as jars of pickled quail eggs and cans of peanuts imported from Xinjiang. The store was operated by the Mongolian shepherd, a small, dark-haired, sunbaked man with bright black eyes and deep creases in his face. His wife and her mother both wore large, starched, impeccably white head scarves, like bakers.

The exposures were a half-hour drive from these quarters along a twisting desert trail that crossed gravel beds and sand drifts and climbed laboriously over two far northern versions of the Great Wall. Built during the Han Dynasty, around 200 B.C., the walls are now little more than raised ridges of gravel stretching from horizon to horizon. A little over eight kilometers from Bayan Mandahu the road took a sudden plunge into a wide, dry riverbed lined with high red sandstone cliffs. The narrow canyon where the road cut through the lip of the gorge was called the Gate by the Canadians; in Mongolian it was Nu Qi Daba — the place where sunshine ends.

From their first day in the Gate, they knew they had struck it rich. Within minutes of leaving the jeeps, Kevin found a nest of *Protoceratops* eggs. A few minutes after that, Li Rong found another nest close to the first. Then Kevin found what looked like a small mammal skull — a tiny but complete skull about the size of a walnut — but which upon closer examination turned out to be that of an embryonic dinosaur.

On the first day of field work, Kevin Aulenback and Li Rong found two nests of the same kind of eggs Roy Chapman Andrews had identified as *Proto-ceratops*. From their size and location, however, Phil was beginning to think that Andrews's eggs were in fact those of an ankylosaur.

Larger *Protoceratops* material was everywhere, much of it simply lying on top of sandstone hillocks, as if already on display in a museum. The soft sandstone had eroded under the hard fossil skulls to form hoodoos. In one area, called Dune Sayr — a deep cut through solid sandstone cliffs nearly eighteen meters high — bones literally poked out through the cliff walls, a kind of dinosaur supermarket. Out on the flats, away from the cliffs, Brian and Bai Jing found a bonebed that contained the isolated teeth and vertebrae of a large tyrannosaurid, scattered bones of a smaller theropod, and a large number of things that even Phil couldn't identify. When Kevin began collecting his eggs, he found a *Protoceratops* skull beneath them. Almost everywhere they looked, their eyes fell on bone. On the evening of their second day in the field, Phil wrote in his logbook: "I'm feeling very good about the field season so far. We've already found more specimens, with a greater variety, than we did all last summer in the Junggar Basin. Our relationship with the Chinese is excellent, the cooks are good: what else could one ask for!"

Tom Jerzykiewicz and Paul Johnston were studying the sedimentation, trying to reconstruct the area as it might have been 85 million years ago. Geologists with the American Museum expeditions in the 1920s had described this part of Cretaceous China as an arid desert, very similar to the way it is today. But subsequent reports from Polish and Russian geologists suggested that the area was in fact lacustrine — composed of sediment deposited on a paleo lake bed. In order to know what kind of animals could be expected from the site, it was important for the Dinosaur Project to determine who was right. By examining the layers of sandstone in which most of the fossils were being found, Tom and Paul discerned four distinct levels. The lower layer, dominated by wind-blown deposits of red sandstone suggesting an arid environment, corresponded nicely with the distant Djadokhta Formation of the Flaming Cliffs in Outer Mongolia. The second, higher (and therefore later) layer appeared to be fluvial in nature — pools of water collecting between high, sloped sand dunes, as might be found at the mouth of a great river, where relatively lush vegetation grew and many of the smaller skeletons, including lizards and early mammals, were turning up. The two layers were then repeated in the same order, making four layers like the four lines of a poem with an ABAB rhyme scheme. All of this made sense; Phil felt it might explain why the dinosaurs found there appeared to be adapted to different environments,

In 1988, the first *Pinacosaurus* quarry in Bayan Mandahu was found to contain
five baby dinosaurs: Phil and Kevin painstakingly remove the skeletons (top). Back at
the field camp, Kevin further prepares the juvenile skull. Two years later,
a second quarry, a few meters from the first, was discovered by Phil (lower left).
Each young skull was barely sixteen centimeters across at the forehead.

**The second *Pinacosaurus* quarry contained seven juveniles, including
four complete skeletons. Phil speculates that the twelve dinosaurs died during**

violent sandstorms, but unlike the five in the first quarry, these do not appear
to have struggled. All seem to be lying peacefully side by side.

The five baby pinacosaurs from the first quarry (upper left), as imagined by paleoartist Vladimir Krb. A pedestaled pair (upper right) from quarry two (bottom) are ready to be jacketed in plaster-of-paris casts for safe transport to the IVPP laboratory in Beijing.

even though they had been found very close together. Both types of deposition were known in Outer Mongolia, but nowhere was the zone of contact between them so well preserved.

Paul began collecting trace fossils similar to those Dale had found in the Canadian Arctic. These look so much like fossilized tree roots that they have often been mistaken for them, and vice versa. In fact, they are the fossilized burrows of invertebrates, probably insects; as the insects worked their way down into the earth, backfilling their holes as they went, they left their tube-like traces in the horizontally structured soil. Over the millenia, these tubes fossilized in different ways from the rock that surrounded them. Imagine an insect colony in which all the holes have been filled with cement. They are quite wonderful; they shoot out of cliff faces and dart back in; they pile up like spaghetti; they zoom around like freeway overpasses. The size and shape of each tube is unique to a specific kind of animal, so that studying them reveals what kind of creature traveled through them. Sometimes it does not, though. *Scoyenia*, for example, are trace fossils that are about eight millimeters in diameter; Paul found lots of these, but he also found thicker traces that he could not readily identify. He thought they might be the work of arthropods at various stages of maturity. He found tubes that were elliptical in cross-section, and others that were thicker at one end than they were at the other. He found examples of anastomosis, the union of many branches into a single network. Collecting them was extremely difficult; merely touching one could cause it to crumble into sand. Paul had to gently infuse Glyptal into them and then try to remove the block of sandstone in which they were encased.

One day he and Brenda Belokrinicev were standing beside a high sandstone cliff that curved gently above them to form part of an inverted bowl. Jutting down from the bowl, hanging in midair above their heads and lining the cliff face itself, trace fossils twisted and gyrated. Paul realized with amazement that they were standing inside an ancient sand dune, looking up at the dune's surface. The angle the cliff face made with the ground was the angle of repose of sand. The wind had scoured away the dune itself, leaving the harder trace fossils to hang like frayed wires from the cliff. Together they soaked the samples in glue — about a liter for every meter of fossil. Then they carried them back to the jeep, knees bent, backs stooped, cradling their precious and fragile cargo in the crooks of their arms. On the way, Paul spotted a fan-shaped trace fossil on the side of a gently sloping dune. He shook his head. He had never seen anything like the riches offered by Bayan Mandahu.

The Chinese team found something that looked like a fossil fish. This worried Tom considerably, since he was convinced that the layer in which the specimen had been found was aeolian (deposited by wind) and not fluvial (deposited by water). What was a fish doing in the middle of a sand dune? Could it have been carried there by a fish-eating carnisaur? Or was it a lungfish — one of the most ancient of fish, dating from the Devonian — that could breathe out of water? More modern versions have been known to "walk" overland from one lake to another. Could this be an ancestor of those? But when Paul Johnston looked at the specimen under a magnifying glass, he declared it to be not a fish but a small armored lizard. Tom sighed with relief.

Kevin was staying up nights preparing a theropod foot that turned out to be more or less complete — the tibia, astragalus, and four metatarsals of a *Saurornithoides*. The bones hadn't come whole out of the quarry — held in place for millenia by their rocky matrix, they had disintegrated into bone chips when the matrix was scraped away. Kevin had to glue it back together, which he did with the aid of a candle and a darning needle. The foot had been found in a bonebed in an area which Brian called Nigerndeg, which means "one egg" in Mongolian.

The same site yielded Brian a baby *Protoceratops* skull. *Protoceratops* specimens were not eliciting the same excitement they had earlier. There were too many of them, and in all stages of development, from embryos and addled eggs to adults. Adults reached a usual length of about 180 cm, not including the tail — although one skull found by Hou Lianhai was nearly 120 cm long — and weighed up to a tonne, about the size and shape of a rhinoceros. Though they lived at the same time as more advanced ceratopsians, *Protoceratops* had retained some fairly primitive features — they had claws instead of hooves, and their foreheads had bumps that in other ceratopsians had become horns.

What was beginning to intrigue Phil was *why* there were so many *Protoceratops* in this area. All in all, the team eventually found more than sixty fully articulated skeletons along a four- or five-kilometer stretch of cliffs. Even a suspected iguanodon skull turned out to be that of a particularly large *Protoceratops* (which was another

A *Protoceratops* skull partly removed from its sandstone matrix. Like the Andrews Expedition in Outer Mongolia, the Dinosaur Project found great numbers of *Protoceratops* fossils in these red Late Cretaceous beds.

relief, since iguanodons were supposed to have become extinct during the Early Cretaceous). About three kilometers north of the Gate, Zheng Zhong, one of the IVPP's graduate students, made the most intriguing discovery of the expedition so far: a cluster of five *Protoceratops* skeletons on a sloped bedding plane, all facing in the same direction. Phil speculated that a small herd of the animals had taken shelter from a windstorm behind a high sand dune — in fact, a violent windstorm was in progress as he viewed the site — and the animals had all been buried and suffocated. But what could account for the deaths of sixty animals? They realized they were looking at many years of accumulation, but even so, the presence of so many skeletons suggested that the area had been unusually well populated. Was it a kind of protoceratopsian graveyard? The presence of shed theropod teeth among many of the skeletons, and tooth marks on some of the bones themselves, suggested that the carcasses had been scavenged. But that didn't tell them anything about the deaths. The more evidence they unearthed, the deeper the mystery became.

**Kevin Aulenback is jacketing a
Protoceratops skull in preparation
for removal and transport.**

On June 20, Phil, Paul, Kevin, and Zheng Zhong drove north from the Gate along the parched riverbed. Wang Ping was driving. They jounced along a hillocked floodplain for four kilometers, until the flat deltoid terrain plunged into a deep canyon, and for the next six kilometers they made their way between the red striated cliffs of the formation they were still calling Djado-khta. They were finally stopped by a huge dune that had drifted across the canyon, its fine sand as soft as white sugar. They got out of the jeep, climbed over the dune, and entered a wide coulee running west off the main canyon at more or less right angles. It was like entering a lost valley. The sun had disappeared behind a high bluff, and the heat was less intense. Owls watched them from the tops of hoodoos, just as in the Alberta badlands. Cranes cast their S-shaped shadows against sandstone cliffs the color of tomato soup. They passed a small herd of camels, grazing placidly on nothing. Suddenly, Kevin shouted to Phil just as he was about to bring his boot down on a large nest of *Protoceratops* eggs. They looked around them. Dinosaur bones protruded from the cliffs, from the ground, seemingly from the very air itself. They made a note of the place on Paul's map: they called it North Canyon. They decided to work there for the next week.

Northern Lights

Also on June 20, but back in Canada, Dale Russell and Clayton Kennedy were likewise looking north. They had left Ottawa that morning, a warm, hazy day, on an Air Canada flight heading for Pond Inlet, an ancient whaling station on

**Dale Russell and Clayton Kennedy prospect for dinosaur material on Bylot
Island, in the eastern Arctic, in 1988, before joining the rest of the
Dinosaur Project in China. An Arctic find would support Phil's theory that
dinosaurs migrated to northern feeding grounds during the Cretaceous.**

northern Baffin Island that now serves as a jumping-off point for scientists working in the eastern Arctic. In Pond Inlet they were going to meet up with a crew of
geologists from Memorial University in St. John's, Newfoundland, that had been
devoting the past few summers to mapping the stratigraphy of the Canadian Arctic.
The Memorial team was led by Elliot Burden, a young geologist who had been
trained at the University of Calgary. With him were Philip Benham, a graduate
student in palynology; a geography student, Bob Rowsell; Helen Gillespie, a
research assistant with a bachelor of science in geology; and Joshua Enookoolook,
their Inuit guide.

The previous year, the Memorial crew had been mapping the exposures along
the south coast of Bylot Island when Joshua walked into camp carrying a handful
of blackened rocks that he thought looked like bones. Burden looked them over
and agreed. They were bones, all right. What was more, he said, they were fossil
bones. From the airport in Ottawa that fall, Burden phoned Dale, whom he had

met a few years before in Alberta. "I've got thirty minutes until my next flight," he told Dale, "but I've got something here I think you might find interesting." Dale jumped into his car and raced out to the airport. He found Burden sitting in the departure lounge with a cardboard box on his lap. Burden handed the box to Dale, who pulled out a small black object wrapped in toilet paper. Dale recognized the object immediately. It was bone. It was fossil bone. It was dinosaur bone. In fact, it was a hadrosaur's metatarsal. Dale asked Burden where it had come from.

On June 22, 1988, Dale and Clayton stepped out of a helicopter on Bylot Island. It was a cold, raw afternoon, with the temperature slightly above zero; behind them, across the ice-choked bay, they could see Pond Inlet and the shimmering mountains of Baffin Island. They set up their tents on a gravel beach at the mouth of a small stream gurgling into the bay. The water in the stream was meltwater from the Sermilik Glacier, whose white, groaning tongues licked at the shoreline a few kilometers to the east.

On the morning of June 23, Burden and Benham, who were camped west of the stream, walked over to the National Museum camp, and the four men prospected a high mound that contained an almost infinite number of fossil shark teeth — they named it Shark Tooth Hill. They walked for another forty-five minutes along the shoreline and came to a spot where the island's stratigraphy took a sudden sweep up and then was even more suddenly sheared off, so that the landscape resembled a giant petrified wave, caught at the moment of uplift. In the trough a second small creek trickled toward the sea. The sharp side of the wave, above the creek, was a series of exposed sandstone layers about one hundred meters high. The upper striation, accessible only by climbing up from the creek, was where Joshua had found the hadrosaur toe bone the year before. Dale ran up it. The others followed at a more dignified pace. Before very long they had amassed an impressive collection of dinosaur and other material; Clayton found another metatarsal, possibly the third, and what looked to Dale like an ornithomimid tibia. Burden picked up a hadrosaur vertebra and a small theropod tooth. Dale found another vertebra and the leg bone of a Cretaceous bird known as *Hesperornis*. Everyone was very excited.

The next morning they returned to the outcrop and then spent the afternoon flying over the southern part of the island in the helicopter. The plateau above the beach was still covered in snow. Here and there more outcrops poked up above the uneven plain, but few of them were Cretaceous. Glacial action had scoured the island down to Devonian time, leaving only an occasional scarp of more recent rock exposed. The chopper put them down to investigate these, but Dale felt their first site was much superior, so they decided not to shift camp. Besides, he said, the little creek where they had pitched their tents was the most tropical site on the island.

They were prospecting in two formations, the Kanguk and the Mount Lawson. Both were marine deposits — the abundance of shark and rat-fish teeth confirmed this — composed of yellowish, sulfurous sandstone and dark gray shale. The two strata interlaced, like two decks of unmatched cards shuffled together. Dale and Clayton determined that the spot where the dinosaur bones were coming from had been just off shore, the soft bed of a shallow sea during the Late Cretaceous. This was true of almost all Cretaceous exposures in the Arctic with the single exception of Alaska's North Slope, which had been dry land when the dinosaurs died on it. The animals whose bones Clayton and Dale were finding had died on or near the shoreline, and their carcasses had drifted out to sea and sunk. Their bones were disarticulated and water washed, crunched by mosasaurs and gnawed by plesiosaurs; few of them were whole. Clayton called them "sea junk." The piece of theropod leg bone Clayton had found was a mere fragment, and it was impossible to tell from it how big the rest of the bone had been. It was like finding a pot shard, says Clayton, and trying to calculate the size of the pot it came from.

On their next to last day on the island, Dale and Clayton walked over to the Memorial camp for dinner. They ate caribou steaks, took each other's photographs, and then at midnight walked back to their own camp in the soft, warm light. The midnight sun was hidden by the mountains of Baffin Island. Dale made some hot chocolate and wrote up his notes on the day's prospecting while sitting in his tent with the flaps open, the bay churning with ice before him in the eerie phosphorescence of the Arctic summer. Bylot Island was a good spot, worth coming back to next year with the rest of the Dinosaur Project, he wrote. It was the most northerly location in the world to have yielded dinosaur bones, and there was more material to be found. But for now, it was time to return to Ottawa to prepare for China.

One of the five juvenile ankylosaur skeletons found in a single quarry in Bayan Mandahu's North Canyon. The quarry suggested to Phil that the five had died together in a single event, which lent even more support to his theories about dinosaur herding.

The North Canyon

ON JUNE 29, WHILE DALE AND CLAYTON WERE PACKING THEIR TENT IN THE Canadian Arctic, Phil and his crew were working on a skeleton in the North Canyon with mounting excitement. A few days before, Brian Noble had found the teeth of a baby ankylosaurid, a family of bird-hipped dinosaurs from the Late Cretaceous that was also known from Dinosaur Park. The quarry was on the side of a gently sloping sandstone dune formation about three kilometers from the mouth of the canyon. Kevin and Phil had not had time to investigate it until the twenty-eighth, but that evening they had walked down from the jeeps to take a look. The weather was unpromising; it had started to rain and the wind had picked up to nearly gale force, filling the air with wet sand and threatening to send everyone back to camp early. Kneeling over the exposed bone, wearing a pair of ski goggles to keep the blowing sand out of his eyes, Phil dug deeper into the area where

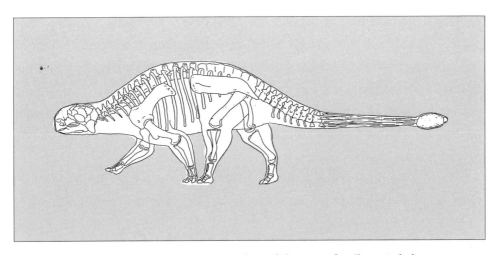

***Pinacosaurus* was a Mongolian member of the same family as Ankylosaur, found in Alberta. A small (five meters) herbivore with a back covered by bony scutes, the adults developed bi-global tail clubs that are believed to have functioned as sexual displays as well as weapons.**

the teeth had come from and saw that the top of the skull had eroded off, but the lower part — the nuchal plates and perhaps a few cervical vertebrae — were still there. Because more post-cranial material could be lurking in the sandstone, he decided to leave the skull alone until the next day, when the weather might be more accommodating.

So on the morning of June 29, under a clear blue sky and with the temperature already closing in on 40 degrees Celsius, Wang Ping, Paul, Kevin, Brenda, and Phil went back to the ankylosaur site. Paul went off to look for trace fossils, but the others began scratching away at the matrix around the skull and neck vertebrae. More bones began to appear and by noon they had uncovered the full length of the skeleton: the skull at one end, what looked like a fossil tail club at the other, and the tips of ribs and the thin lines of ossified tendons in between. Phil was puzzled; the skeleton was obviously that of a juvenile, and tail clubs do not usually appear on ankylosaurs until after adolescence — they were probably sexual displays as well as defensive weapons. He mulled the problem over during lunch back in Bayan Mandahu.

Ankylosaurs were heavily armored herbivores that looked like a cross between an elephant and an armadillo. Ankylosauridae ("fused lizards") is the family: *Ankylosaurus* is the genus known from Alberta and Montana; the Bayan Mandahu genus is *Pinacosaurus*. The backs of the adults were covered by a series of bony plates, some of them with sharp, hollow horns protruding from them. Their heads were armored as well, and hung low and hunkering, like a stegosaur's. When attacked by a carnivore, the ankylosaur probably hunkered down to the ground, something like a porcupine, and waited for the nuisance to go away. The end of its long tail, however, sported a huge, bi-global club that might have helped the predators make up their minds.

During the lunch break, another great windstorm began brewing over the Gobi. When Phil looked up from his tin bowl of eggplant and boiled mutton, he saw the sky to the northwest had turned yellow. Ten minutes later it began to rain, a cold, hard, driving rain that looked as though it intended to continue for days. It stopped at five-thirty, however, and Phil roused the others and they drove back to the ankylosaur site. He was glad he did, for in the two hours they worked that evening they solved the mystery of the juvenile tail club. It was not a tail club at all; it was a second skull. The baby ankylosaur had not died alone.

They continued to work on the quarry for the next week, stepping up the pace because it was their last week in Bayan Mandahu. On July 1, Kevin found a third skull, and Phil began finding teeth at the back wall of the quarry. Then he found a trail of vertebrae leading to them and guessed that there was a fourth skeleton inside the wall somewhere. They took off more overburden. Another trail of vertebrae appeared — the fifth. Phil noticed that the baby ankylosaur teeth looked amazingly like those on two skulls found earlier that had been tentatively identified as lizard, suggesting that the earlier skulls may have been embryonic ankylosaurs. In the afternoon, Li Rong found the fourth skull where Brenda had been digging and began working on it so vigorously that Phil had to slow him down; the bone was soft and easily broken. Tom came over, studied the matrix surrounding the quarry, and told Phil that it was possibly a dune created by wind; he found an inclined bedding surface that was about 30 degrees, close to the angle of repose for dry sand. Phil speculated that the five baby ankylosaurs had been caught in a windstorm and sought shelter from it behind a large dune. As the dune collected more windblown sand, it reached its angle of repose and slumped down on the group of young dinosaurs, suffocating them.

Paul Johnston was not convinced of this interpretation, however. He reasoned that if a slump had occurred, there would be evidence somewhere of contorted or wavy bedding, and though he and Tom searched hard for such contortions, they could find none.

Reconstructing the cause of death was fascinating to everyone, even if it was pure speculation; it was like following a mystery novel and re-creating the crime. But equally interesting to Phil was the picture of events leading up to the deaths that the scene represented. What were the five baby ankylosaurs doing together in the first place? Until then, there had been no real evidence that ankylosaurs stayed together in herds — specimens found in Alberta were always isolated. They could have been like turtles, spending most of their lives completely alone, but always returning to the same beach to lay their eggs. But baby turtles, when they hatch, head off immediately for the sea and go their separate ways. This quarry suggested that ankylosaur young stayed together. The babies were just over a meter long, so they were not hatchlings. But were they nestlings? Did ankylosaur young stay together in some sort of nest? Did the adults care for them, forage food for them? Did one parent guard the nest while the other went off in search of food? All these questions were raised by the existence of the five baby ankylosaurs.

Also intriguing to Phil was the absence of armored plates on the five skeletons. As ankylosaurs matured, the bony plates fused to the bones of the skull, making it almost impossible for paleontologists to examine the bones themselves. These ankylosaurs died before the fusing could take place. But there was more to it than that. Historically, it has been very difficult to establish growth patterns in dinosaurs. Young animals are hardly ever miniature replicas of adults, and skeletons of immature dinosaurs of one known species have in the past been inadvertently ascribed to a new species. The lack of osteoderms, or bony external plates, on the baby ankylosaurs told Phil that these defensive mechanisms developed in maturity, strengthening his hunch that young ankylosaurs were protected by their parents. A picture of ankylosaur behavior was beginning to emerge.

As Phil and the others extracted the blocks of sandstone containing the skeletons, Kevin worked on them back at camp, exposing enough of the bone to give Phil an idea of their size and position. The skulls were small — less than thirteen centimeters long and fifteen centimeters wide across the forehead. Phil made careful measurements of the quarry, pinpointing the exact location of the individual animals and their relationship to each other, their angle to the horizontal and vertical, the direction of their movement. The five ankylosaurs seemed to have been struggling to get out of the sand. The skeletons were twisted as if the animals had died writhing, stepping on each other to get a purchase for their feet. Their bodies were lying parallel to the dune surface, several centimeters from the top, and had remained petrified in their death throes for more than 80 million years. The top skeletons appeared to have been dug up and scavenged, possibly by *Velociraptors*. Rarely do mere bones provide such a graphic picture of the way death came to them, and the paleontologists who worked on them did so with a feeling almost of reverence.

The day before the group was scheduled to break camp and move on to Erenhot, Alan Bibby, soundman for the film crew, found a sixth ankylosaur skull, not in the main quarry but about three and a half meters east of it, poking out of another paleodune very similar to the first. Phil decided to leave it for next year. There was no time to take out another specimen. July 2 and 3 were spent jacketing and crating the Bayan Mandahu finds; when the truck left for the train station in Linhe, it was carrying sixty *Protoceratops* skulls and skeletons; nineteen rat-sized mammals; eight ankylosaurs; *Velociraptor* teeth and claws; two partial *Oviraptor* skeletons; five kinds of eggs (including five *Protoceratops* or possibly ankylosaur, and the rest unidentified) from eight different nests; one turtle and several varanid lizards; and 180 kg of trace fossils. The total was 125 specimens from forty-nine different quarries, many more than they had found the previous summer. Three of the baby ankylosaur skulls and the small theropod hind foot stayed behind; Phil and Kevin wanted to work on them in Erenhot. On July 4, at eight o'clock in the morning, they watched the truck disappear over the hill on its way to Linhe, where the crates would be loaded onto a train going to Beijing.

Those left behind in camp spent two days cleaning up the quarries and packing their personal effects. The sixth ankylosaur skull was re-buried and its position marked with fluorescent tape. Then they, too, climbed into the jeeps and headed for Linhe. Instead of continuing south to Beijing, however, they turned west, to Hohhot, and then north, to Erenhot.

Erenhot

AFTER A TWO-DAY BREAK IN HOHHOT — WITH VISITS TO THE INNER MONGOLIAN Museum, dinner at Li Rong's apartment, and a wobbly bicycle tour of the city — the caravan continued to Erenhot. It was the rainy season, and the jeeps seemed to be perpetually stuck in the Gobi sand, which, when wet, turns into a thick, sucking goop, like quicksand. Good for preserving dinosaur fossils, bad for preserving composure. The ninety-six kilometer trip took nearly nine hours. When they arrived at Erenhot, they found that they had been billeted in the small, crowded village near the soda mine that Phil had seen the year before. The compound was built on a man-made promontory jutting out into a salt lake at the center of the Iren Dabasu basin. No cattails grew around the shallow lake shore. Mildew hung from the walls; two dead rats floated in the well. When Paul went for a walk around the compound, he sank up to his knees in fungal mud. A meeting was hastily organized, and a decision to move into a hotel in Erenhot was reached without a word of dissent from the Canadians.

On July 16 work finally began in the field, and morale picked up almost immediately. Paul, poking around in the ruins of the Sino-Soviet Expedition's quarries from 1959, discovered what he and Phil tentatively identified as part of the metatarsus of a small bipedal dinosaur known as *Elmisaurus*. Phil was extremely excited, for this animal had also been found in Dinosaur Provincial Park. It had been a lightly built, bipedal creature (barely 180 cm long) with a whip-like tail and short, slender arms, probably a theropod very like *Saurornithoides* and *Troodon*. As no skull or teeth had been found, not much could be stated about its true affinities, but it was known that certain foot bones had fused together, as in modern birds. The Erenhot locality was Late Cretaceous, but Phil had thought it might be slightly earlier in age — perhaps 10 million years older than the Late Cretaceous exposures in Alberta. The possible presence of *Elmisaurus* made him think the two localities must in fact be very similar in age, although probably quite dissimilar in their environments. These speculations came to a halt, however, when upon closer examination the metatarsus turned out to be that of an *Avimimus*, a dinosaur that was even more bird-like than *Elmisaurus*, but is found only in Mongolia.

Work continued on the site during the next week. The quarries aroused mixed emotions among the Chinese researchers, especially Zheng Jiajian, who had been a young student on the Sino-Soviet Expedition. Relations between the Chinese and Russian scientists had been strained, and when diplomatic relations were cut off between Beijing and Moscow in 1960, the Russians had simply been pulled out. They had taken all the food, all the tents, all the specimens, climbed into the trucks, and driven off, leaving the Chinese stranded in the middle of the Gobi Desert to find their own way back to Beijing.

The Soviets had used bulldozers to strip off the top layers of desert, and the bulldozed mounds had eroded in the intervening years, exposing thousands of tiny bone fragments broken up by the dozer treads. Bulldozing is a fairly brutal quarrying technique; it makes dynamite and jackhammers seem positively finicky. However, as a way of finding out how many different species occupied a single chunk of landscape, it is very effective. On the same day as the *Avimimus* find, Kevin catalogued a total of fifty-two fragmented specimens, none of them bigger than five centimeters, including a lot of dromeosaur bone; some shark teeth and gar fish scales; the maxilla, braincase, and jaw of a *Bactrosaurus* (a small hadrosaur found only in Asia); several alligator teeth; Ziploc bags full of ornithomimid and hadrosaur unguals; some crocodile scutes and part of the hand of an *Archaeornithomimus*, another small dinosaur, about the size of an ostrich. Collecting was a matter of walking with a bag over the mounds and tread marks, still clearly visible in the mushy yellow loess, and picking the stuff up. It was like picking strawberries. In all, there were more than a dozen families of dinosaurs represented, and who knows how many genera and species. Iren Dabasu had been incredibly rich in biota 75 million years ago.

Dale and Clayton, who had had a two-week rest after their Arctic trip, and Francis Chan and Rick Day arrived with Dong Zhiming and Peng Jianghua on July 23. They had taken the train up from Beijing — a sixteen-hour adventure in a hot, humid train that became cooler only when it had climbed up onto the green Mongolian Plateau. Forty minutes before arriving in Erenhot the train had hit a camel, breaking its hind legs. At the Erenhot station, loudspeakers on the platform were blaring out the music to *Hair*. That afternoon the new arrivals toured the bulldozer site and Kevin showed them the ornithomimid eggs he was excavating: Dale wrote "ornithomimid" in quotation marks in his notebook because it is impossible to identify dinosaur eggs that positively unless they have embryos in them, and these did not.

Back at the hotel, the expedition leaders sat down to discuss the field schedule: on the twenty-sixth, the National Museum team would go with Dong Zhiming and Peng Jianghua to Qagan Nur, a desert location not far from Erenhot, where there were Early Cretaceous sauropods and stegosaurs. The Tyrrell group would work at Iren Dabasu for another day or two, then return to Hohhot to look at the specimens stored in Li Rong's laboratory at the Inner Mongolian Museum. After meeting up in Hohhot, the two groups would proceed to Dong Shen, in the Ordos Basin, for round two of the Tipi-Yurt Exchange; Zhao Xijin and the Xinjiang team would join them there. After the Tipi-Yurt, Zhao and Tom Jerzykiewicz would return to Bayan Mandahu to continue their stratigraphical investigations; the others would work in the Ordos for a week, then the Tyrrell Museum crew would leave for a tour of classical dinosaur localities in the south of China while the National Museum group moved to the Alashan region until the end of August.

The day after Dale and the others left for Qagan Nur, Phil and Paul made what turned out to be the most significant find of the week. Prospecting near the salt lake, at the base of a small outcrop, Phil discovered what appeared to be the disarticulated remains of an *Alectrosaurus*, one of the tyrannosaurs unique to Asia. The animal had first been discovered and named by the American expedition in the 1920s, and the type specimen — the skeleton that forms the base upon which all other specimens are identified — is now in New York. A second specimen is in the Outer Mongolian Museum in Ulaan Baator. Paul exposed a few ribs and what looked like a furcula, or collarbone — the Ulaan Baator specimen lacked a furcula, so this was an important discovery — but there was no time to take them out of the ground. Next year, they told themselves as they Glyptaled the bones and covered them with sand. The next morning they boarded the train for Hohhot.

Meanwhile, Dale and the National Museum crew were enjoying the cooler breezes of the Mongolian grasslands. Qagan Nur was a relaxed, three-hour drive from Erenhot. On the way, they stopped at a yurt to ask directions, and the Mongol shepherd who lived there offered them tea and horse-milk cheese. "Most pleasant," Dale wrote in his field book. The Qagan Nur exposure, however, was disappointing. The seven scientists prospected for three hours and came up with two small bone chips and part of an unidentifiable spine. Qagan Nur itself was a town barely two years old, built to provide housing for the workers at the soda mine nearby. Construction was proceeding at such a furious pace that dynamite blasts near the hotel continued well after dark. Rain during the night threatened to make the roads impassable. Their gear had been stowed on one of the trucks back in Erenhot, and all the Canadians had with them were the clothes they were wearing and their toothbrushes. On the morning of July 27, they decided to push on to a new locality to the southwest. They drove for four hours and arrived at Baiyinhuxao, a Mongolian yurt compound set up for tourists, most of whom were from Hong Kong and Japan. During their lunch stop, scattered showers became driving rain, and the downpour obliged them to stay in the yurt-hotel for the night. The next day they drove straight to Hohhot to meet up with the Tyrrell group and proceed to the Tipi-Yurt Exchange in the Ordos.

They arrived in Dong Shen, a city of about 100,000 people on the main road in the eastern end of the Ordos Basin, on July 30. Phil, Dale, and Dong Zhiming continued on to Hanggin Qi, about 160 kilometers farther into the basin, to do some prospecting in the Early Cretaceous beds before the Tipi-Yurt Exchange, but the others remained in Dong Shen to await the ceremony on August 1. Rain dogged the Hanggin Qi group as they poked around in the badlands for an hour or so, finding nothing more than a turtle, an ornithopod tooth, and what seemed to be unidentified theropod bones. On their way back to Dong Shen, they came upon a convoy of two trucks and a few jeeps parked by the side of the road. The vehicles looked familiar; it was the crew from Xinjiang, including Zhao Xijin, Don Brinkman, and Jim McCabe. After an animated reunion, they started up the vehicles and began driving through the rain back to Dong Shen. They had not gone a kilometer when they were stopped by the Chinese police and fined 500 yuan for driving on a clay-topped road during a rainstorm. They had to sneak into Dong Shen along winding back roads made of sand that did not turn into gumbo in the rain, and they did not get back to the hotel until eleven-thirty that night.

Don, Jim, and Zhao Xijin had been traveling from Xinjiang for twelve days. They had finished up the quarries on July 13. Earlier, they had divided the camp into two groups: one, including Don, Jim, and Zhao Xijin, had worked on the theropod quarry; the other, under Cao Qiang, had continued to blast away at the sauropod. The hard rock, the winds, and the rain hampered them nearly every day — once they looked up from the sauropod quarry to see a tent flying by from the camp. By late June it was already obvious that they would be able to get out only a few more neck vertebrae from the sauropod before the end of the season. Jim called this "very good progress," considering the size of the bones and the hardness of the matrix. The vertebrae were more than a meter long, not solid bone, but rather hollow tubes (at least in life) supported by buttresses and ribs. The fretwork made the vertebrae lighter, an adaptation that benefited the dinosaur, but the hollows now were all filled in with stone. Fragile bone and extremely hard matrix slowed the work: if there was a skull farther in the cliff, it would have to wait until next year.

The theropod quarry had gone more smoothly; a huge block encasing the skeleton had been carved out, and the work consisted mainly in reducing the size of the block and removing whatever bones came to the surface. They had originally thought that the animal was lying stretched out, with its head disappearing into the cliff, and so they had spent an enormous amount of time removing tonnes of overburden. After all that work, they found that it was actually curled up in a ball. Don took out a femur and parts of a hand. The matrix came away from the bone more easily than in the sauropod quarry. Officials from Qitai visited often, finding yet another problem with permits and staying for yet another round of *bai-jo*.

Because of the steady rains, Zhao Xijin set Jim to digging a drainage trench around the theropod block. He said he had once lost an entire turtle skeleton in a flash flood; he had gone to the quarry in the morning and found nothing there but a few scattered bones. The only thing that holds the bones in position is the soft sandstone that surrounds them, and when that washes away the bones go with it. So he was practicing some healthy paranoia with this theropod specimen.

Jim used the jackhammer and trenched around the block for two days while the others shaved away sandstone from the top. As it was, the block was much too big to take out in one piece. It would have to be broken up into two or possibly three smaller blocks. The trick was in finding places to make the breaks where the skeleton could be separated cleanly without snapping ribs or leg bones. Cui Gui Hai, one of the IVPP researchers, started "swiss-cheesing" the block from the side — boring holes through it laterally with his geo hammer and awl to check for bones in an attempt to find sections where only vertebrae would be disturbed. The work went very slowly.

Meanwhile, the sauropod quarry was closed down on June 25. Five new blocks, all encased in burlap and plaster-of-paris jackets, were ready and waiting to be hauled down the sandy slope to the trucks. That morning everyone lent a hand as burlap slings were maneuvered underneath the huge jacketed blocks. The weather had cooled considerably — it was sweater weather — but the work and the dust made everyone hot and thirsty. At lunch, the cook passed around ice-cold oranges: ice-cold anything is a rare treat in the desert.

In the afternoon, they all moved to the theropod quarry to speed things up there. The theropod was still encased in its monolith, with various bones sticking out of it at odd angles where some of the stone had been chiseled away. They decided to take it out as a single block rather than risk breaking it into smaller chunks. The Chinese technicians calmly set about coating the whole thing with a thin layer of plaster of paris, followed by a single layer of plaster-soaked burlap. Then more plaster of paris. Then they made a box for it. The box was 180 cm long, 90 cm wide, and 90 cm high. This was topped up with more plaster, and the lid was nailed down. It looked like a coffin.

In order to flip the coffin over so they could plaster and nail on the bottom, a huge hole was dug in the ground beside it with the jackhammer. The block had been well pedestaled underneath, and when a come-along — a sort of block-and-tackle with a crank handle — was attached to the box, the whole thing tumbled easily into the pit. Getting it out was less easy. Lying in the pit upside down, the box was filled again with plaster and the bottom nailed to the sides. No one could guess how much it weighed. No one could lift even a corner of it. Steel bars had to be slung from the back of the truck into the pit, and a winch from one of the Beijing jeeps was passed over the truck cab and attached to the coffin. Don and Jim stepped way back, but the coffin was hoisted onto the truck bed without incident. Packing all the smaller specimens into crates and loading them and the larger jackets onto the trucks took four days.

On July 4, the camp packed up and started out to a new location in Wucaiwan Station. To get there, they had to drive south to Qitai and Jimsar, where they were caught and entertained for three days by the local officials. On the seventh, they headed north again into the oil-bearing portion of the Junggar. The new camp, in an area called Pingfengshan, was surrounded by oil rigs and a landscape churned up by heavy vehicles and crisscrossed by tire tracks. The exposures nearest the campsite were Early Cretaceous (the Tugulu Group) and Jurassic (Shishugou). Both yielded turtles. Don found three the first day prospecting; only the back half of the plastron had been preserved on two of them; the third was more complete but disarticulated. In the Tugulu, Jim found a turtle skull with a "nice braincase," as well as what looked like a pterosaur jaw fragment.

They spent three days weaving north and south across the formations that had been prospected the year before: Tugulu, Wucaiwan, Shishugou. In the microsites they found crocodile teeth and bits of broken turtle shell. Jim found the foot and forelimb of a small dinosaur and the tail of another that, Don thought, might be complete, but there was no time to take it out. They covered the exposed bones with preservative until they could return the following year. The rain was not letting up; creek beds normally dry were running with water. On July 13, sodden and cold, they packed up their tents and headed east to meet up with the rest of the Dinosaur Project in the Ordos. They did not want to be late for the Tipi-Yurt Exchange.

The Tipi-Yurt Exchange

THE ORDOS BASIN IS BETTER KNOWN TO WESTERNERS AS XANADU, FOR IT WAS HERE that Kublai Khan built his stately pleasure dome during the Yuan Dynasty, which began in A.D. 1272. The Khan's rule was humane and generous, marked by advances in China's relationship with the Western world as well as by an understandable improvement in policies affecting the country's minority peoples. Mongolian rule in China lasted only ninety-seven years, barely surviving Kublai Khan's three sons, but the memory of it was so distasteful to the succeeding Han Chinese that they moved the capital south to Nanjing and extended the Great Wall westward to protect all of southern China from any further incursions of Mongols. No ruling dynasty since has welcomed Western influences so warmly, and problems with China's minorities have continued to plague the descendants of the Han.

When Genghis Khan died in A.D. 1227, he was said to have been buried in Erjin Na League, in the Ordos Basin. In Mongolian mythology, the Ordos is the

The Genghis Khan Mausoleum at Erjin Na League, in the Ordos Basin. When Genghis Khan died in A.D.1227, four hundred Mongolian families were named to guard his tomb. The Chinese government restored this historic site in the 1980s, and the traditional Mongolian families still attend the shrine.

Omphalos, the center of the universe: still part of the Gobi Desert, but south of the Yellow River. Four hundred Mongol families were assigned to guard his tomb, presumably forever. They are still guarding it. The mausoleum is actually a crescent-shaped building, built in the Chinese style by the Han government in the 1950s. The site was chosen not because of any solid evidence that Genghis Khan was buried there, but because it was near a sacred obo, or rock cairn, where Mongols have been holding Buddhist ceremonies for centuries. It was as good a place as any. It was also near some Early Cretaceous exposures that Dale examined on the way to the Exchange. The building doubles as a Genghis Khan museum and is very popular with Chinese tourists. Inside are ancient Mongolian artifacts — stirrups and saddles, for Genghis Khan's army was famous for its horsemanship; long bows and fiercely tipped arrows; yurts furnished with Buddhist chests and tables. A huge modern mural on one wall depicts the Khan welcoming delegates from each of China's minorities.

Nearby, a Japanese film company had built a set for a movie they were making about Genghis Khan. The set comprised a central wooden pagoda, round with a pointed roof and many small windows, built in the Japanese style, surrounded by three or four canvas yurts. There were also two reconstructed yurts on wheels — Genghis Khan's innovative design that allowed him to move his army great distances in record time, the secret of most great army leaders. The two Peigan tipis were set up here, on this Japanese movie set, at one end of the enclosed grassy field. Near it, a small Mongolian pony, about the size of a Shetland, was tethered to a post. Tourists could rent authentic Mongolian costumes in the pagoda and have their photographs taken astride the little pony. There were sample Polaroids on the wall of the pagoda; the Japanese Genghis Khan samurais glared fiercely at the camera while the little pony gazed sadly at his feet. On the other side of the fence, the vast green grassland dipped beautifully down to a shallow valley, and a huge herd of semi-wild Mongolian ponies grazed placidly beside a small river.

The mausoleum is approached from the parking lot by a steep, wide, flag-stoned walkway flanked by irrigated poplar trees and souvenir shops. Sari Ledai, a short, dark distinguished-looking man in his fifties, is a descendant of the Four Hundred Families and the current chief of the Erjin Na League. He welcomed Reg Crowshoe and his wife Rose as they stepped out of their red Toyota Land Cruiser in the parking lot and began the long climb to the mausoleum. The Toyota had been accompanied for the last few kilometers by twenty Mongolian horsemen. The paved courtyard in front of the mausoleum was spread with a red carpet. On it was a low, red table laid with a set of silver welcome cups, a sharp knife, and a tub containing a whole, roasted sheep. The sheep's head, with a pat of butter on its forehead, was positioned so that it looked down the stair-way as Reg and Rose approached it. When they arrived, Sari Ledai placed his right hand across his chest and bowed deeply. Then he presented the sheep's head to them along with a meter-long strip of white silk called a *hada*. Reg licked the pat of butter from the sheep's forehead and tossed back a welcome-cupful of *bai-jo* without batting an eye. Then Sari Ledai took a bottle of snuff from under his robe and handed it to Reg. Reg expressed his deep appreciation for the gift and handed it back to Sari Ledai without taking any snuff from it. Sari Ledai thanked Reg for holding his snuff bottle for him and took a great pinch of snuff

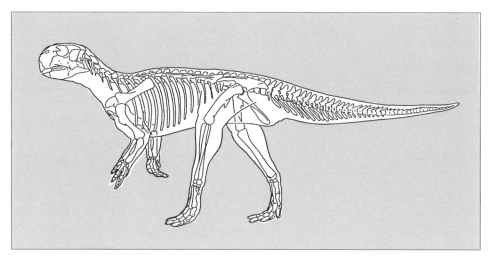

**Psittacosaurs are the most common dinosaur found in China's Ordos Basin
and are the type fossil for Asia's Lower Cretaceous period. Small,
bipedal herbivores with parrot-like beaks, they were distant cousins
of the ceratopsians, such as *Protoceratops* and Alberta's *Leptoceratops*.**

to show his respect for his guests. The ceremony was over.

The focus of activity then shifted to the Japanese movie set, where Reg dedicated the tipi. There followed the traditional banquet, this time with lots of *bai-jo*; Jim McCabe's field book records that he hoisted fifteen *gan-bays*, a Chinese toast best translated as "Bottoms up!" During the dancing and singing after the banquet, Don Brinkman played his fiddle. At the end of it all, a lively discussion took place between Brian and Dong Zhiming as to who was to pay for the banquet; there was some confusion as to who was the host and who was the guest. The film crew left early the next morning. The Dinosaur Project crew were anxious to get back to work; it had been ten days since anyone had been on an outcrop.

The morning of August 2 was gray and unseasonably drizzly, but fortunately not wet enough to prevent passage on the clay roadbeds. By lunchtime, the entire team had checked into a sort of motel at a place called Abuchaideng, about sixty-five kilometers west of Dong Shen. The rooms were damp and dark; compared to the Xinjiang and Erenhot localities farther north, the Ordos was almost tropically humid. The gravely desert floor was covered with short, prickly vegetation, a kind of wormwood called *Artemisia ordosica*. Camels munched on it without any discernible enjoyment. There were more geckos and ground squirrels. There were

A juvenile *Psittacosaurus* skull exposed in the sandstone of the Ordos Basin.

rumors of vipers. While prospecting an Early Cretaceous outcrop in the afternoon, Hou found a weathered skeleton and Paul discovered a series of bones that turned out to be a pair of hands. The next day, when Kevin, Clayton, Paul, and Hou went back to collect the hands after a violent rainstorm in the morning, they also found a string of small vertebrae with a possible skull at the end of it. They took out everything, but were unable to jacket the specimens because it was too wet for plaster of paris to dry. Back at the motel, Phil and Dale looked at the bones. They were *Psittacosaurus.*

It was the Dinosaur Project's first encounter with a psittacosaur, and it was a fine moment. The animal was discovered in 1923 by the American Museum expedition, and named *Psittacosaurus,* or "parrot lizard," by Henry Fairfield Osborn. The bones lying on the table in Dale's room were thus a direct link to Roy Chapman Andrews as well as to the ancient past. Psittacosaurs were small, primitive members of the Ceratopsia, which also includes the protoceratopsids and ceratopsids.

Except for their parrot-like beaks, psittacosaurids did not look like ceratopsians at all. Ceratopsians were the last great family of ornithischians to develop toward the end of the dinosaur era. Psittacosaurs were the earliest known members of the family, and they raise some interesting evolutionary questions.

They had no neck frills, for starters. And they were bipedal. As humans, we like to think of bipedality as an evolutionary advance, that animals walking on their hind legs are more evolved than animals still walking on all fours. Ceratopsians more "advanced" than *Psittacosaurus*, however, from *Protoceratops* in Asia to *Triceratops* in North America were quadrupeds. The ceratopsians seem to have "reverted" from walking erect to walking on four legs. And curiously, psittacosaur hands were more developed than those of the later ceratopsians. The hands Paul and Hou brought back that night had only three digits, while *Protoceratops* had four distinct fingers. Evolutionary theory — supported by the fossil record — has it that vertebrates started out with five digits, and those that had fewer must have lost some along the way. *Psittacosaurus*'s digit count is a clear indication that the animal is not an ancestor of *Protoceratops* but makes up a family of its own and is one of the most interesting to come to light in China. It is also so common that it is the most typical vertebrate fossil for the Lower Cretaceous in Asia; find a psittacosaur and you can assume you are in a Lower Cretaceous exposure somewhere in Asia.

Not that the Dinosaur Project crew were in any doubt about where they were. Abuchaideng, to which they were confined by a persistent rainstorm that lasted off and on for ten days, was a muddy compound surrounded by flat adobe buildings in the middle of a vast gray basin. The clay roads stayed wet for two weeks, but the crew members were able to walk to nearby exposures. There were very few to walk to — the name Abuchaideng means "no mountains" in Mongolian. One exposure was in a stretch of very recent badlands visible from the motel. As a relief from the boredom of confinement to camp, Phil, Jim, and Kevin walked to them on the third day. They found a kind of compost heap of relatively modern fossilized bones — lizard, bird, mammal, frog, sheep, and human. On August 6, Phil, Paul, Jim, and Kevin left for Dong Shen, where they caught the train back to Beijing to prepare for their trip south. Don Brinkman stayed on with Dale and the rest of the National Museum crew. They made friends with the animals belonging to the cook. One was the most immense white pig anyone had ever seen. At least twice as big as a

Psittacosaur, it wandered at will about the courtyard, into the dining room, into individual guest's rooms. Brian named it Wonder Bread. Three smaller pigs, black and quick and obviously destined for the soup pot, were named Bacon, Lettuce, and Tomato by Clayton. There was also a small herd of goats kept in a fenced-off area of the compound. After a week of constant dampness, the goats developed a kind of barking cough. The Canadians did not name the goats anything.

The situation improved on the seventh, which brought relatively fair weather and a return to prospecting. The crew drove to an outcrop near a village named Yujiachuan, about thirty kilometers from the motel, and spread out across a long cliff of gray-green sandstone. By noon they had amassed three psittacosaur specimens, something that looked like a protoceratopsid muzzle, three pterosaurs, and three teeth that Dale identified as being from a *Chiayusaurus*, a large sauropod tentatively assigned to the same family as *Camarasaurus*. This Early Cretaceous animal is known only from teeth — enamel is much more durable than bone — which are long and chisel-shaped, like ivory wood-carving tools — and in light of Dale's interest in sauropods from China and their connection with those from North America, these were treasurable items.

Rick Day found a skeleton that contributed to the psittacosaur mysteries; obviously ceratopsian, from its parrot-like beak and lower jaw, the new skeleton was not the same species as the psittacosaurs already known to science. It was older, it had a narrower beak, and it was smaller. Once again, this small creature from Asia was forcing project members to rethink the way species develop.

As the clouds gathered above the outcrop in the evening, Lao Liu, one of the senior Chinese paleontologists, made another important discovery. At the base of the cliff, he found parts of a skeleton just beginning to wash out of the soft sandstone that could only be that of a stegosaur. But what a weird stegosaur it was! Its pelvic structure was very wide, the ilium fanning out toward the front into a broad funnel. This usually indicates a more evolved structure, which made sense, since the beds were Lower Cretaceous, and North American stegosaurs were all Late Jurassic. It was known that China had the earliest stegosaurs; it now seems to have had the latest ones as well. And the smallest: the North American *Stegosaurus* reached an average length of eight meters; this whole skeleton was only three meters long — there was, of course, no skull, and most of the tail was missing, but even at that this was a peculiarly small stegosaur. The bony plates that ran down the back and tail of all stegosaurs were present on this one, but these, too, were different: they were long and slender, like palm fronds, rather than short and triangular, and some of them seemed to have lain flat on the animal's rump. "I don't know what it is," Dale frankly confessed to his field book. "Dong Zhiming and Zhao Xijin are puzzled, too."

On August 13, they finally said goodbye to Wonder Bread and the barking goats and moved camp to Ahlingbola, stopping at two turtle localities along the way — the reason Don Brinkman had stayed behind. China, especially in the Ordos Basin, has an exceptional record, perhaps the best in the world, of freshwater vertebrates. A great number of fish, crocodile, champsosaur (a crocodile-like reptile that resembled the modern gavial of India), and turtle specimens turn up in its loosely consolidated sandstones. Especially turtle. After two days' prospecting in several outcrops of the Yijingholo Formation — a low, undulating series of hills and ravines barely deep enough for a camel to hide in — Don and Peng Jianghua brought in enough pieces of turtle to keep them busy reassembling and describing for years.

Don is "a turtle person." What others call the Age of Dinosaurs, Don calls the Age of Reptiles. He might call it the Age of Turtles, except that that would be too non-specific; as far as Don is concerned, we're still in the Age of Turtles.

He has not always been a turtle person. Born near Drumheller in 1953, he studied biology at the University of Alberta and paleontology at McGill under Robert Carroll, one of the world's foremost experts in vertebrate evolution. He specialized in reptile locomotion: how various skeletal structures would have affected the way the reptiles moved. From Montreal he went to Boston, where he spent three years at Harvard University's Museum of Comparative Zoology, still studying pelvic configurations. Then, in 1982, he was hired by Phil to work at the Tyrrell Museum. When he got there he found there were a lot of people studying dinosaurs in Dinosaur Park, and only one person — Dr. Elisabeth Nicholls — studying the park's excellent fossil turtle material. "There was," he says, "a kind of turtle vacuum, and I was drawn into it."

Unlike dinosaurs, turtles did not suddenly become extinct 65 million years ago; many of the turtle families that were around during the time of the dinosaurs are still around today. No one knows why. Turtle survival has become a thorn in the side of those who believe in the Big Bang theory of dinosaur extinction: if the bang was so big, why did it not wipe out the turtles as well as the dinosaurs? So Don became interested in turtles. He felt that figuring out why they did not become extinct might help to explain why the dinosaurs did.

The fragments he was finding in the Ordos turned out to represent two entirely new types — a new species and a new genus. Don would later name one of them *Ordosemys leios*, from the Greek word *leios* meaning "smooth": the shell of the new turtle lacked any sort of ornamentation. It differed from other specimens of its kind by having

Don Brinkman works on a dinosaur egg near Erenhot, probing with an awl for signs of embryonic bone. The Erenhot eggs were round, like those from Milk River in Alberta, but smaller, and tentatively identified as those of *Avimimus*, a small, swift theropod of the Late Cretaceous.

retained its fenestra — literally, window-like openings between the upper shell and the lower plastron — long after they disappear in most turtles, whose windows slam shut after puberty. The presence in this specimen of fenestra after puberty made it a kind of teenage mutant.

The new species of *Sinemys* was much more unusual; Don found only the back quarter of the shell, but was able to reconstruct it to about the size and shape of an inverted twenty-centimeter dinner plate, with a pair of "wings" extending aft from the posterior corners. These wings, Don hypothesized, might have acted as stabilizers when the turtle was gliding and grazing along the bottom of ancient Ordos streams, like ailerons on an aircraft. The wings — they are actually adapted spines — were not exactly unique, but the only other species known to have had them was a much smaller turtle named *Sinemys lens*, specimens of which had been found in China's Shandong Province. The question confronting Don was whether *Sinemys lens* was (a) a juvenile version of a spineless turtle, (b) an ancestor of his turtle, or (c) a "sister-taxon" — a related but distinct species dating from the same era. Because of some peculiar aspects in the carapace — again, the presence of fenestrae in a relatively mature individual — Don opted for a combination of (a) and (b); he thought the new specimen was a descendant of *Sinemys lens*, but had retained into adulthood some of its ancestor's juvenile characteristics. This phenomenon, called paedomorphosis, or sometimes neoteny, is not uncommon. Adult humans, for example, retain features found in juvenile chimpanzees, such as large brains (relative to our body size), small jaws, and selective hairy patches on our bodies. Don named his new specimen *Sinemys gamera*, after a flying turtle he had seen in a Japanese monster movie. The name and the retained juvenile characteristics made it a kind of teenage mutant Ninja turtle.

The presence of so much aquatic material confirmed Dale's analysis of the Yijingholo Formation; composed of strongly cross-bedded sandstone full of tiny flecks of mica that glinted in the welcome sun, the sediments suggested to him a fluvial environment, with seasonal streams cutting deep channels in the soft substrate that eventually filled with coarse-grained gravel. The depth of the channels and the coarseness of the grains meant the streams were very fast-flowing; the diversity of the faunal assemblage showed that the water was teeming with life.

The expedition moved camp again on the eighteenth. En route to the Alashan, they stopped to regroup at Dengkou, a town deeper in the Ordos and large enough to boast a bookstore, a movie theater, and a department store, where, under the curious gaze of half the town's population, Dale bought a pair of "old man's shoes," those black cloth slippers that are ubiquitous in China. In the afternoon, a dust storm blew in from the interior, dark swirling clouds that turned the sky a dirty yellow, followed by a cold, splattering rain. They stayed in Dengkou for three days without visiting a locality, then left for Linhe on August 21. Don stayed on until the next day. He was taking his annual vacation, and on the twenty-second, a Monday, he simply boarded a train for Langzhao, and after some strenuous dealings with Chinese officialdom he managed to secure a train ticket *and* an airline ticket to Shanghai. He took the plane.

The National Museum crew, meanwhile, continued on their way to the Alashan, a section of the Gobi west of Dengkou and up on the Mongolian Plateau. They spent a short time in the Maortu Formation, a stream-bed stratum of heavy sand and gravel with very little aquatic material. There were, however, plenty of dinosaur bones. Dale found a sauropod humerus, a theropod ischium and caudal vertebra, and many disarticulated *Probactrosaurus* bones. *Probactrosaurus* was an early Late Cretaceous iguanodont, known only in Asia. The site had been visited in 1960 by the Sino-Soviet Expedition; seventy people had camped there, with two bulldozers, eight trucks, and a half-dozen smaller vehicles. The bulldozer tracks were still faintly visible in the gravel.

On August 23, the crew moved on to Hanwulasuma, a village near the Dashui-gou Formation, which proved disappointingly unfossiliferous. What bone there was — a turtle chip, a few small ankylosaur scutes — were widely scattered. The next day they moved again, this time to the village of Tukumu, and prospected in three locations in the Bayin Gobi Formation. This site proved to be much more rewarding; Rick Day found parts of what looked like a deinonychosaur — one of a group of small theropods that include the dromeosaurids — which they collected; Da Cui found another theropod, smaller than Rick's; and Dong Zhiming found a *Psittacosaurus*, which identified the exposure as Early Cretaceous. There was also much aquatic material: champsosaurs, turtles, and fish vertebrae and scales.

They spent several days in this locality, driving back and forth between the quarries and Tukumu, a distance of sixty kilometers, working on three articulated theropod skeletons. The weather was becoming cooler; they finished jacketing the major theropod in strong, gusting winds and a fine rain on August 30. As they drove back to camp a thunderstorm closed in that lasted for two days; the road they had taken from Linhe was washed out and Zhao Xijin and Wang Ping had to take one of the jeeps to scout a new route back to the south. Dale and the others spent the time sightseeing in Tukumu. On the first of September the trucks were finally loaded with jacketed specimens, and the caravan left for Linhe on a course that took them through Alashanzuoqi, a town of 40,000 people and a surprising blend of the ancient and modern. The hotel was the cleanest they had been in since Hohhot and had been almost entirely reconstructed over the past five years. Marco Polo had passed through the town, recording that the inhabitants heated their homes by burning black rocks. They still do.

They arrived in Linhe on September 3, and the next day boarded a train that took them to Hohhot, where they changed trains for Beijing. "Beijing," Dale wrote in his field book when they arrived on the fifth, "is beautiful."

The Canadians remained in the capital for ten days, examining the specimens from Xinjiang in Dong Zhiming's office at the IVPP. Dale was particularly interested in the small sauropod caudal vertebrae from Jiangjunmiao. "I am amazed at how solidly constructed they are," he wrote in his field book. He also made a series of close measurements of the Jiangjunmiao theropod, and again "was amazed to note how much the cervical vertebrae resemble those of *Carnotaurus* from South America." The Canadians then left Beijing for a two-week sweep of museums and classic quarries in the south of China, especially Sichuan and the huge museum and bonebed in Zigong. They were back in Beijing on September 25 and flew home to Canada on October 2.

It had been an extremely successful field season. More localities had been explored, and more specimens collected, than in any other year of the Dinosaur Project so far. So many crates had come back to Beijing from Xinjiang, Bayan Mandahu, the Ordos, and Erenhot that the IVPP had no room to store them. Some ended up being trucked down to an old IVPP warehouse sixty kilometers south of Beijing. The warehouse was on the grounds of the old Chou K'ou Tien caves, where, in 1926, Davidson Black and his colleagues had found the first evidence of Peking Man.

It had also been a relatively peaceful field season. The Tipi-Yurt Exchange had come as a welcome relief from a hectic work schedule, and personal conflicts had either been smoothed over or avoided. Work in the field in 1988 had been productive and unclouded by politics.

That, of course, was about to change in 1989.

CHAPTER 6

Reunion

Dale Russell's Hadrosaurus *and dinosaur migration*

O N MAY 4, 1989, SIX CANADIAN MEMBERS OF THE DINOSAUR PROJECT LANDED
at Beijing International Airport. The timing could not have been more ominous; it was the seventieth anniversary of the May Fourth Movement, the student-
led protest of 1919 still celebrated in China as the dawn of the new revolutionary
era.

During the fourteen-hour flight, Dale had read an article in *Discover* magazine about the gradual evolution of the human species from *Australopithecus
africanus* (3 million years ago) to *Homo erectus* (1.7 million years ago) — the species
that included Peking and Java Man — to the relatively modern Cro-Magnons, who
had mysteriously ousted the Neanderthals from Europe about 35,000 years ago.
Cro-Magnons, according to Jared Diamond, the author of the article, had been able
to outcompete their burlier neighbors because they had possessed a "magic twist,"
an evolutionary edge: the anatomical basis for complex spoken language, otherwise known as a larynx. Dale was aware that he was on his way to a China that,
since the middle of April, had seemed to be gearing up for another student revolt,
and the article's title had intrigued him: it was called "The Great Leap Forward."

In Beijing, the air was cool and moist; the Lombardy poplars that lined the
arrow-straight boulevard from the airport to the city were just beginning to leaf
out. The Canadians checked in at the Da Du Hotel — three thousand delegates to
a conference of the Asian Development Bank had taken up most of the rooms in
the larger hotels — and after dinner had gone walking along the hushed streets.
They watched a large group of students from Beijing Teachers College returning

A corner of Beijing's Tienanmen Square in May 1989, days before the rioting. By the end of the month, the square would be home to nearly 1 million student and worker protesters. The building in the background is Mao Zedong's tomb, in which Mao's body is displayed in a glass coffin.

from a massive demonstration in Tienanmen Square. Carrying banners painted with pro-democracy slogans, the students marched arm in arm, five or six abreast, using the wide bicycle paths beside the road. Even this far from the square, crowds of people turned out on the sidewalks to watch silently, obviously supporting the marchers. It was, after all, May 4. Nevertheless, the softly lit streets, the polite restraint of the marchers, and the sympathetic silence of the crowds charged the night with a sense of unreality and danger. To the Canadians, it was as though they were watching an illicit foreign newsreel. The next night, Dale wrote in his field book that he felt like a spectator at "the huge drama that is China."

Although Dale and Clayton, Linda Strong-Watson — now director of science for Ex Terra and the Canadian field-work coordinator — photographer Mike Todor from Ex Terra, and Don Brinkman from the Tyrrell Museum were supposed to proceed directly to Xinjiang, a delay in scheduling obliged them to wait in the cap-

While waiting to leave Beijing, Dinosaur Project members looked at specimens in the IVPP's work rooms. Here (from left) Linda Strong-Watson, Chang Meeman, Kevin Taft, and Dong Zhiming discuss a *Bellusaurus* vertebral column from the Junggar Basin.

ital until May 12. They spent most of the time at the IVPP, photographing and examining the specimens Dale and Zhao Xijin had collected the year before in the Alashan Desert. One of these, the "deinonychosaur" that Rick Day had found near Tukumu, turned out to be "a very odd dinosaur." Dale thought it looked more like a segnosaur: it had teeth like those of a theropod and elongated cervical vertebrae like those of a sauropod. In China, when you find a fossil that has characters total-ly at odds with anything you have seen before, you call it a segnosaur.

Segnosaurs were extremely peculiar dinosaurs. They had four toes on each hind foot with large, sharp claws, and therapod-like teeth, although they do not appear to have been carnivorous. They differed from all other dinosaurs by virtue of certain specializations of the skull and pelvis: the pubis had turned back to lie parallel with the ischium, as in ornithischians, but the ilium was extremely short and wide, like those of the early sauropods. Although segnosaurs have been found in Upper Cretaceous beds, some of their characteristics are more typical of Upper

Triassic dinosaurs; the broad foot, for example, resembles that of *Plateosaurus*, a quasi-bipedal prosauropod from Europe and South America, and was much more primitive than that of any theropod. American paleo-artist Gregory Paul suggests that the segnosaurs' combination of saurischian and ornithischian traits points to a common ancestor of both orders later than the usually quoted thecodonts. Bob Carroll classifies them as "Theropoda Incertae sedis," carnivores of unknown affiliations, and notes that "the large number of derived characters that are shared by prosauropods, segnosaurs, and ornithischians suggests that all the herbivorous dinosaurs may belong to a single, monophyletic assemblage." Prosauropods are usually thought to have been ancestral to the later sauropods; Phil Currie's guess is that primitive prosauropods were the ancestors of segnosaurs. The latter are usually found in areas where there were permanent, freshwater lakes, suggesting that they were fish eaters, although they did not have fish eaters' teeth. In fact they had no teeth at all at the front of their jaws, and some scientists have speculated that their mouths ended in sharp, bony beaks, like those of such early ceratopsians as *Psittacosaurus*. With samples of both, the Dinosaur Project team might be able to make more revealing comparisons.

Dong Zhiming, who described the first segnosaur ever found in Asia, *Nanshiungosaurus*, believes that they should be classified as a separate order of dinosaur altogether, making three instead of two major groups; in his system, there would be saurischians, ornithischians, and segnosaurians. "Two reasons," he says. "One, because the material is not like either of the other two. They are very strange animals — big claws, I've never seen claws like that on a herbivore — big arms, and a very wide pelvis. The second reason: because three is a much stabler number than two in Chinese philosophy. If a table has only two legs, it won't stand up."

Dale was reserving judgment; like Phil, he tended to think of segnosaurs as theropods, but, working in the dusty, darkened offices of the IVPP while China's internal politics seethed around him, he noted that their anatomy was "very difficult." With calipers and magnifying glass, he set about measuring each individual part of the skeleton; if he couldn't classify it, at least he would be able to describe it. The absence of the midshafts of the long leg bones bothered him; he couldn't tell how big the animal had been. He noted that the specimen showed "seg-

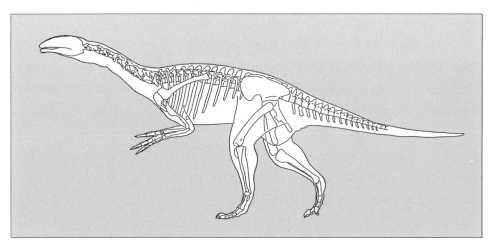

Segnosaurs, says Dale, are "a very odd dinosaur." Late Cretaceous in age, they exhibit characters more usually found in the Triassic. Some think they were the ancestors of sauropods, others that they evolved into theropods. Dong Zhiming wants to classify them as a separate Order.

nosaurian suggestions," but in the end decided it "cannot be assigned to the segnosauridae."

Don was occupied with fifteen turtle specimens from Xinjiang and the Ordos Basin. Some of these had been fine-prepped by IVPP technicians, and for the first time Don was able to get a good look at what had been found. During the winter, he had thought a lot about the wing-backed *Sinemys gamera* that Zhao Xijin had found in the Ordos. Talks with hydrodynamics experts had confirmed his guess that the wings would have greatly increased the turtle's ability to stay underwater in fast-moving streams. Its shell was flat on top and the plastron was curved underneath, exactly the opposite of most aquatic turtles; water flowing over the *gamera*'s back would actually push it down rather than buoy it up. The normal shell shape was an advantage for swimming in still ponds, but in swift-moving water the *gamera* design would provide a competitive edge.

The Dinosaur Project's stay in Beijing coincided with a brief lull in the political turmoil that was shaking the country. The May Fourth demonstration had not been as large as authorities had feared and was thought to have ended the three-week series of peaceful confrontations between students and leaders of the Communist Party that had begun as a show of mourning for Party Secretary Hu Yaobang, who had died on April 15. The police did not prevent the students from entering and occupying the forty-hectare Tienanmen Square.

Encouraged by the lack of interference, however, the next night four thousand students, all wearing white arm bands — white is the color of mourning in China — once again marched the sixteen kilometers from Beijing University to the square, chanting slogans such as "Long live democracy, down with dictatorship," and "Hu was the spirit of democracy." When they reached the square, they listened to speeches from their student leaders: Deng Xiaoping, the eighty-four-year-old Party chairman, was too old to govern wisely; he was also against scholarship and was anti-Western. Deng's given name — Xiaoping — is a homonym for the Chinese words meaning "small bottle," and thousands of small glass bottles were smashed in protest on the flat concrete paving stones of Tienanmen Square. Still the authorities did not step in; the police actually aided the marchers by continuing to direct traffic at intersections.

On April 22, the day of Hu's funeral, students again marched on Tienanmen Square. This time there were 200,000 of them from Beijing's sixty colleges and universities. Again, they were not prevented from entering the square. Three of their leaders were even allowed into the Great Hall of the People, the Chinese Communist Party headquarters that faces the west side of the square, to present a petition to the government. Deng Xiaoping was not there. Zhao Ziyang, Hu's successor as Party secretary and a soft-liner when it came to dealing with the student uprising, was. In the subtle world of Chinese politics, Zhao's presence was taken by the students as a sign that the Party's unofficial attitude toward the students' demands and actions was to be one of tolerance. They were wrong.

The marches and occupation of Tienanmen Square continued sporadically throughout the week. More students and supporters arrived — estimates place the total number of people occupying the square at 1 million. On May 3, the day before the Dinosaur Project people arrived in Beijing, Zhao Ziyang talked to a group of three thousand students from the platform of a commandeered bus. He begged them not to threaten the country's political stability. "If stability is destroyed," he said, "what can be achieved? Can science and democracy be achieved? They cannot. All that will result is turmoil."

The linking of science and democracy in Zhao Ziyang's speech casts an interesting light on the Dinosaur Project. Working with Canadian scientists was an opportunity for Chinese students and scientists to learn Western techniques and use Western equipment. The IVPP, in other words, was already engaged in the kind of cooperative venture that the students in Tienanmen Square were demanding. Unfortunately, as Zhao Ziyang's speech made clear, Western science had become entangled with Western democracy, and in order to discourage movement toward the latter, Deng Xiaoping was prepared to sacrifice the former; on May 23, he would say to the 27th Army, "Do not be afraid to spill blood."

The summer field schedule in place, Kevin Taft flew back to Canada while the rest of the Canadians waited in Beijing. For the next few days, Tienanmen Square was quiet, and would remain so until May 13, the day Mikhail Gorbachev was scheduled to arrive in Beijing to mark the reinstatement of relations between the Soviet Union and China that had been broken off in 1960. The members of the Dinosaur Project drove out to Beijing Airport on the twelfth through a city charged with tension. Zhao Xijin, a middle-ranking member of the Communist Party, was accompanying them to Xinjiang, and the night before they all left he invited everyone to his apartment for a farewell dinner. The atmosphere was friendly but subdued. Chinese members of the expedition had mixed feelings about leaving friends and family in Beijing.

The trip to the airport the next day was a refreshing example of how easily high drama in China can tumble into low farce. After they had all been deposited with their luggage at the main terminal and the IVPP bus had left, they learned that the terminal was under construction, and the departure lounge for domestic flights had been moved to a different building. No one knew which one. There was nothing they could do but pick up their bags and crates and make the rounds of the possibilities on foot. Halfway to the first building, the IVPP bus returned and picked them up, and they sat in the parking lot while Zhao Xijin walked around trying to find the departure lounge. Five minutes before their departure time, they were told to return to the main terminal; when they arrived there, they found that their flight to Urumqi had been delayed by half an hour. Clayton said that he had heard that because of recent crashes, Air China had quit using the Russian-built Tupalov jets; when their flight was finally announced, they all trooped gratefully aboard — a Tupalov jet.

Urumqi was cooler than Beijing. The crew spent two days there, staying at the Academia Sinica hostel and touring the markets and carpet factories while Zhao Xijin made the rounds of the government offices making arrangements for the field camp. They were still in Urumqi on May 15 when news reached them of Gorbachev's arrival in Beijing. The television report was brief and noncommittal; there was no mention of the student demonstrations in front of the Great Hall of the People, where Deng Xiaoping and Gorbachev were holding their summit. The silence was ominous.

They left Urumqi early on the sixteenth, driving in two jeeps through light rain along the now-familiar northeast route through Jimsar and Qitai, and arrived at the Wucaiwan oil station at three in the afternoon. The station was less populous than it had been two years before, when they had been entertained by local dancers and singers. After lunch they drove north along a newly paved road to Pingfengshan, where Don and Jim McCabe had found dinosaur and turtle material in 1988 — including a small ornithopod of particular interest to Dale — and set up camp about ten minutes from a seismic installation where they could get water. The weather was warming up for summer: by two-thirty the next afternoon, the temperature in Dale's tent was 43 degrees Celsius.

The rock section in which the ornithopod had been found was in an exposure to the east of camp, a thirty-three-meter layer of sandstone that was peach-colored at the bottom (Late Jurassic Shishugou Formation) and graduated up into reddish, oxidized conglomerates (Early Cretaceous Tugulu Group) at the top. Ripple marks in the higher sandstone suggested that there had been shallow water flowing over the sand when the sediments were deposited; scattered turtle and crocodile fragments confirmed the presence of water. Don almost immediately discovered a rich seam of fossils in the Tugulu strata, and the crew decided to leave the ornithopod for the moment and look around to establish an overall picture of the paleo-environment. There were many turtles, mostly of the species *Sinemys wuerhoensis*, and the pterosaur *Dsungaripterus*, but very few larger animals; Peng Jianghua found the caudal (tail) vertebra of what looked like an ornithomimid, but this could have been carried downstream from a higher inland region, or dropped from the beak of a scavenging pterosaur. The absence of larger animals intrigued the scientists since the same formation farther north, in the Jiangjunmiao region, had yielded primarily large land-based dinosaurs.

The camp at Pingfengshan, in Xinjiang's Junggar Basin, in 1989. The camp was very near localities where, the year before, Project members had found a small ornithopod, a suborder that included the iguanodonts and hadrosaurs, which was of particular interest to Dale.

On the afternoon of May 17, four Chinese geologists from the seismic camp came over with news from Beijing, where the situation was worsening: student demonstrators joined by thousands of steelworkers had prevented Gorbachev from laying a wreath on the Monument to the People's Heroes, and the Soviet leader had left China without making a public appearance. Since this was the first meeting between Soviet and Chinese leaders since the détente, and was to have been Deng Xiaoping's crowning achievement, many thought the students had caused the Chinese leader to lose face. There were now a million people, including students and workers, occupying Tienanmen Square, some of them conducting a hunger strike, all of them demanding Deng Xiaoping's retirement.

The next day, while Zhao Xijin went to Jimsar for more news, the scientists returned to the ornithopod quarry, where Don found turtle and pterosaur bits, and Dale found deep channel structures in the solid rock, below the paleo lake bed, evidence that the environment had been one of fast-moving rivers before becoming a large, freshwater lake. Almost all the turtle and pterosaur bones were found in oxidized, cross-bedded sandstone, which meant they had probably been deposited on the sandy stream banks. Clayton noted plant and algal structures in the stone as well, further signs of a wet habitat.

That evening, Zhao Xijin brought back a box of cups from Jimsar, but no news from the IVPP. During a discussion of the field schedule, the team decided to speed things up. They would leave Pingfengshan on the twentieth, spend a day in Qitai, and then move on to Jiangjunmiao on the twenty-second to work on the *Mamenchisaurus* neck. So much of this animal had been exposed already that they thought it only a matter of days before they would reach the skull, or at least the place where the skull ought to be. However, the political situation was making all movement difficult to predict. Martial law had been declared in the entire country and traveling in to Urumqi could pose a problem. They could be detained in the provincial capital indefinitely, allowed neither to go back into the field nor to return to Beijing.

Despite worries about developments in Beijing, they all poured their energies into the field work. Dale began to be concerned about the lack of diversity in the Tugulu fauna they were unearthing. Apart from the one ornithopod and some petrified wood, everything they turned up was turtle or crocodile or pterosaur. He and Don discussed the food-chain implications; had the pterosaurs been feeding on the turtles? On May 20, Don found a deposit of fossil fish scales, all grouped together, but no bones: had the scales been regurgitated? Dale tried to relate the paleo picture to the contemporary one, since he believed the climate had not changed very much. He noted that, on average, he saw five or six skeletal fragments of gazelles each day, but only about one good, articulated skeleton. Something was messing with the carcasses, just as had been the case with the fossil turtles. One day he came across the carcass of an eagle, the first carnivore he had seen. Avian raptors (eagles, pterosaurs), he speculated, may be more efficient predators than terrestrial ones (ornithomimids), and so have taken over the dinosaurian niche.

On May 21, still in Pingfengshan — schedules in China at the best of times are notoriously loose — they decided to look for the quarry that the Chinese had begun in 1983, in which there was thought to be a member of the titanosaurid family. Titanosaurs were sauropods, about half the size of *Mamenchisaurus*, despite their name. The interesting thing about the family is that it is found on nearly every continent — South America, India, Asia, Europe, and North America. Dale suspects this to be a case of parallel evolution rather than species migration, but the jury is still out. Holed up in the IVPP building in Beijing, he had made a careful study of the 1983 titanosaurid specimen. Spread out on the floor of Dong Zhiming's office, it consisted of twenty-one caudal vertebrae forming a 1.17-meter line tapering toward one end like the ribless skeleton of a snake; eight dorsal or back vertebrae; then five cervical vertebrae, which fit together in such a way as to suggest the neck was not curved; fragments of the scapula and pelvic girdle; some of the right side of the lower jaw with about thirty teeth; and a few incomplete, badly preserved ribs, mostly from the left side of the body. Dale thought it was a juvenile; adults grew to about seven and a half meters.

When they found the old quarry, they saw that the cliff above it had collapsed and completely filled the hole, and five years of wind and rain had consolidated the sand to a hard, almost rocky consistency. Dale jumped into the pit and began attacking the rock with his geo hammer "like a human earth-moving machine," Don noted in his field book. He turned up another cervical vertebra and kept digging, this time with a pick. Before long, he began to feel unwell but kept working until lunch. He suspected a mild infection from a tick bite he had received on his chest two days before.

Back at camp, however, he felt cold. He had stopped sweating and could not eat, and even wrapped in his sleeping bag in his tent, with the temperature over 37 degrees Celsius, he could not stop shivering. Huang Daifu, the camp doctor, was in Urumqi, and Linda and a driver, Wu Rong Gei, were about to leave camp to join him; Linda insisted that Dale go with them. As soon as they set out on the five-hour trip, Dale, reclining on the front seat beside the driver, began to feel his arms and legs going numb. He soon lost all feeling in them and was unable to move them. He had to fight to stay awake. Linda searched frantically in her field pack and found a jar of plums; she opened it and poured the juice into Dale, telling the driver to step on it. Some feeling began to return to Dale's hands. When they reached the Wucaiwan oil station, she ran inside to ask for a box of salt and a glass

Huang Daifu (*daifu* is Chinese for doctor), who with Linda Strong-Watson helped Dale Russell through a nearly fatal case of heat prostration. Dale had collapsed while removing overburden from a titanosaurid quarry near the Pingfengshan camp, with the temperature above 45 degrees Celsius.

of water, dumped a few chunks of the salt into the water, and brought it out to Dale. He was barely able to drink. She wrapped his head and chest with wet towels and placed another wet towel on his lap. They hurried on to Urumqi, where Huang Daifu immediately took Dale into his care. He had been displaying the classic symptoms of heat exhaustion; the doctor told Linda that if she had not got salt into him when she did, Dale would have been dead by the time they reached the city.

The next day Dale was almost completely recovered; he spent the morning "loafing," as he called it, reading a translation of a popular Chinese historical novel that was making the rounds of the camp — *A Dream of Red Mansions* — and in the evening he was able to walk with Linda to the telegraph office, where she sent a cable to Edmonton to let Ex Terra know she was in Urumqi and that everyone in the field camp was all right. They also did some shopping; Huang Daifu had forbidden Dale to return to camp unless he bought a proper sun hat and some long trousers. It was May 23. Linda had heard the BBC broadcasts, and assumed that people in Canada were worried.

She was right. Four days earlier, on May 19, Zhao Ziyang had again gone into Tienanmen Square to reason with the student demonstrators. "The problems you have raised will be resolved," he told the hunger strikers. "Live to see the modernization of China." Communist Party president Yang Shangkun, however, had already called in the 27th Army. Newspapers in the West were reporting that the people of Beijing welcomed Yang Shangkun's decision; in fact, hundreds of thousands of ordinary citizens were filling the streets leading to Tienanmen Square to prevent the army from reaching the students. The square itself was still clogged with people. Buses and trolley cars — made available to the students by the Beijing Transit Authority for hospitals and shelters — were positioned sideways across the streets and set on fire to stop army vehicles from getting through. Zhao Ziyang had disappeared. When reporters asked for him, they were told the Party secretary was "on vacation."

Driving into Urumqi the day before Dale's bout with heat exhaustion, Huang Daifu had seen the body of a man lying in the ditch. Four days later, returning to camp with Dale, he had seen the body again, and this time they stopped at the Wucaiwan oil station to radio the police. The next day two police officers came to the camp to tell Huang Daifu that they had found the body and not to worry. The officers stayed for lunch. The body, they said, had had no identification on it, so they had simply buried it by the side of the road. He was probably just an escaped prisoner, they said, or a vagrant.

Linda did not go back to camp with Dale; she flew to Beijing on May 25 with no idea what to expect. She found the city alive and excited, groups of people talking and reading posters, "thousands of them," she says, "riding their bikes, marching arm in arm around Tienanmen Square, continually on the move and watching, waiting." The hunger strikes were on, and the square itself was filled with makeshift tents and donated buses. Truckloads of soldiers roared along the main streets. More students had arrived by train from universities outside Beijing. Linda met Bai Jing at the Xijuan Hotel, near the IVPP. At night, students slept on the roads to prevent tanks and armored personnel carriers from reaching Tienanmen Square. Sympathetic citizens were giving them food. Once Linda and Bai Jing heard what sounded like gunfire in the distance. On the twenty-eighth, worried and apprehensive, they flew back to Canada.

The rest of the Canadians and Chinese remained in the Pingfengshan camp until June 3. They had collected a large crocodile and the ornithopod from the Shishugou Formation and loaded them onto the Jie Fang truck along with a dozen turtle specimens to be shipped to Beijing. That was on May 31. The weather was hot and windy; at night they could see storm clouds passing high overhead, but no rain reached the ground. The titanosaurid quarry had progressed in Dale's absence, yielding three more dorsals and two more caudals. The wind changed direction from northwest to east. At night, tents billowed and flapped loudly.

A group of Chinese field technicians flip a partially jacketed crocodile specimen in order to apply burlap and plaster of paris to the bottom of the block. The Pingfeng-shan region of Xinjiang contained fossil turtles and crocodiles as well as dinosaurs.

Clayton awakened at two-thirty one morning and looked outside; the wind was so strong that grains of sand striking each other were setting off millions of tiny blue sparks that lit up the desert at ground level. As he watched, the wind knocked over the coal-fired water boiler, spilling red-hot embers and blowing them against the wooden wall of the cook shack, where they shattered into orange and yellow explosions of light and were hurled away across the eerily luminous desert.

On the morning of June 4, a Sunday, they were in Qitai. The four Canadians, Zheng Zhong, and Peng Jianghua explored the market and residential section of the city and visited a Moslem mosque, where they were invited inside by the imam, an old, thin, white-bearded man with hands the color of polished chestnuts, to attend a funeral service and to have lunch. Later that day, Zheng Zhong and Peng Jianghua returned to the hotel and Dale, Don, Clayton, and Mike continued to explore the old part of town. They followed narrow, twisting adobe-walled alleys, like badlands canyons, and came upon a tall, thick-walled building that looked like an ancient fortress. They walked around the perimeter looking for an entrance; finding none, they headed off along a narrow alley that gave into a huge private courtyard filled with women and small children. Mike took a roll of photographs while Don passed out balloons with "Tyrrell Museum of Paleontology" printed on them. Although they had no language in common, they were invited to stay for tea. The oldest woman laughingly took a silver ring off Clayton's toe and put it on her finger. More balloons and Tyrrell Museum lapel pins were passed around. After tea the four Canadians left the courtyard and retraced their steps toward the fortress, followed by a phalanx of small children, and to their surprise came immediately upon the gate they had been seeking earlier; it was a very formidable-looking entrance, and Don took a photograph of the Chinese characters painted on the wall beside it, hoping that he could later have it translated.

That night the Qitai government hosted a banquet for their Canadian guests, followed by Uygur dancing and an acrobatic show. All through dinner they heard the static from a dozen radios in the banquet hall as people listened for news from Beijing. When it came, it was shocking in its simplicity: "special measures" had been taken to put down a reactionary riot in Tienanmen Square, the broadcasters reported. One thousand soldiers were dead or wounded. That was all. Attempts to communicate with the capital were unsuccessful; not even Zhao Xijin could get through. The next day they learned that all internal Air China flights had been canceled. There was nothing they could do but continue on to Jiangjunmiao to complete the field schedule.

They drove from Qitai north into the Junggar Basin on June 5. At the military checkpoint, their travel documents were examined with unusual thoroughness. They continued north along a deteriorating road. Two gazelles raced beside them for several minutes, their feet seeming barely to touch the sand, then cut suicidally across the road, narrowly missing the front of the lead jeep. Farther on, an eagle glided straight toward them not a meter and a half above the ground, as if intent on a head-on collision, then landed suddenly on the road between the tracks, staring into Clayton's eyes. The driver cursed and swerved, and just as the jeep was about to close over it the eagle spread its enormous white-tipped wings and took flight.

After some searching, they found the old campsite at Jiangjunmiao, the tent rings of petrified wood and broken beer bottles, the dismantled bricks from the kitchen stove. The paths to the old quarries were still visible on the wind-scoured stone, noticeably feebler than they had been in 1987. Everything, the old camp, the old quarries, seemed empty and futile. Mortal. Dale envisioned Brian Noble and General Jiang toasting each other with *bai-jo*, and young men becoming old and returning to this site year after year to dig for relics from an unimaginably distant past. "Traces of the camp are dissipating," he wrote in his field book; "when they're gone, I will be too."

They set up a new camp on a paleo lake bed, in a flat-bottomed coulee nearer the sauropod quarry. The walls of the coulee had been dug out of the cliff face, and the floor was slightly lower than that of the lake bed, as if the coulee had been meant as a man-made reservoir to catch water after major rainstorms. But torrential downpours were infrequent enough that they decided to take their chances. The walls sheltered the tents and the cook shack from the strong winds that swirled around them, creating miniature tornadoes called dust-devils. Dale's spirits rose in the evening; there were no biting insects, the temperature was in the low twenties, the breeze was light, and, at dusk, the snow-covered Tien Shan Mountains were visible on the southern horizon. After dinner, the sky was black and filled with stars and a crescent moon. Radio reception was greatly improved; for the first time in weeks they could pick up the BBC from Taiwan on their shortwave set. The news was of Beijing, of course, and it was not good.

On the night of June 3, they learned, tanks and armored personnel carriers belonging to the 27th Army had rolled into Beijing from the west in an attempt to wrest Tienanmen Square from the students. Fighting between soldiers and demonstrators had gone on all night, with soldiers firing indiscriminately into crowds of students from the backs of trucks, and students retaliating with paving stones and baseball bats. A group of students from Beijing Teachers College — perhaps the same singing students the Canadians had seen on the night of their arrival in Beijing — had lain down on the street in front of a row of tanks, and two hundred of them had been killed. In all, five thousand students had died, their bodies stacked in hospital corridors or thrown onto huge bonfires along Chang'an, the Avenue of Eternal Peace. On the morning of the fourth, with Tienanmen Square cleared, soldiers had begun making the rounds of the universities, drag-

The Dinosaur Project team were in Jiangjunmiao on June 3, anxiously listening to the BBC evening news on shortwave radio. In Beijing, steelworkers had joined students in occupying Tienanmen Square, and truckloads of soldiers were patrolling the streets.

ging students out of their dormitories and either shooting them on the spot or taking them away for interrogation.

No work was done in the Dinosaur Project camp the next day. The Chinese students posted a notice on the wall of the cook shack declaring that they were on strike for the day to honor their dead colleagues in Beijing. Zhao Xijin fumed at them, lectured them for an hour, but was unable to change their minds. Everyone in camp was glued to a radio. Wu, the head driver, had a son at Beijing University; Wang Yu's father drove a bus that passed beside Tienanmen Square, and his sister went to a school in the same district. Peng Jianghua was worried about his wife, a student at Beijing Agricultural College. Everyone knew someone who might be in danger. Dale and Zhao Xijin and two of the older crew members went halfheartedly to the sauropod quarry, but after one blast of dynamite they decided to call it quits. "Not a good day," Dale wrote.

That afternoon, three policemen from Qitai arrived in camp in a Beijing jeep

**Dale Russell takes measurements of a fossil tree stump from Middle
Jurassic beds near Jiangjunmiao. He found the petrified forest
"more impressive" than similar sites in California and on Ellesmere Island.
Altogether, he measured thirty-six giant metasequoia stumps and logs.**

with red flags on the hood and a red light on the roof. A few days ago, they said, someone had taken photographs of a secret military installation in Qitai, and could they please have the film. Don remembered the adobe-walled compound, the children with balloons and lapel pins with the Tyrrell Museum name emblazoned on them, and handed over his film. Then the Canadians decorated the policemen's uniforms with Canadian flag pins as they left.

Dale spent the next morning measuring fossil logs in the stump field near the old campsite. It was the best fossil forest he'd ever seen, on a scale with the Petrified Forest in Arizona and more impressive, he wrote in his field book, than the hundred-stump log field on Ellesmere Island. He measured thirty-six individual logs and stumps. Most of the logs were fourteen to eighteen meters long, and their average diameter was just under a meter; one stump was 185 cm across. Another rose a meter and a half above the desert floor. It was an eerie sight, stone trees rising from the sand like tombstones, or like the terra-cotta figures in Xi'an but from a far more ancient army. They were Middle to Late Jurassic, huge conifers, giant metasequoias, or dawn redwoods, whose feathery leaves had hung thirty meters above the swampy ground; a British scientist had visited the site a few years earlier and determined that they had grown on a delta; during the Late Jurassic, there had been a river there, flowing down into a freshwater lake. The fossil forest and Jiangjunmiao were at the mouth of the river; Wucaiwan Station and Pingfengshan were near the middle of the lake bed. Lying at crazy angles on the desert floor, half-buried in sand, they looked exactly like driftwood on an ocean beach. The wood had been silicified, deep blue and orange rock veined with ivory, and was very beautiful when polished. They learned that during the winter a businessman from Hong Kong had come to the site and tried to remove some of the logs with a bulldozer. He had loaded several of the bigger specimens onto a truck and was hauling them south when he was arrested and jailed in Urumqi. According to their report, he was still there.

At the sauropod quarry after lunch, the technicians let off two blasts of dynamite, but when the dust settled there were no discernible results. No skull gleamed at them from the collapsed overburden. The wind died and the temperature shot up to 48 degrees Celsius. No one's heart was in digging. Dale was wondering whether the events in Beijing would cut their field work short or extend it indefinitely. One of the drivers, Wang Shoutian, had gone to Urumqi to find out if Air China flights had been resumed, but just before supper a second driver, from the Academia Sinica in Urumqi, arrived with two telexes. One, from the Canadian Department of External Affairs, said that the situation in Beijing was very serious and to get out of China immediately by the quickest possible route; the other, from Ex Terra, contained news that Dale's mother-in-law had died suddenly.

The Canadians lost no time getting ready to leave; within an hour their personal belongings were stowed in the jeeps and arrangements had been made with the Chinese to store Ex Terra's equipment and the specimens they had collected in China for the winter. Then they said goodbye to their colleagues, who were more worried than ever. The inevitable bottles of *bai-jo* were produced, however, and the Canadians brought out the last of their whisky, and a brief but emotional farewell party ensued, with many toasts. They were on the road by seven in the evening, the alcohol making the road seem smoother and the drive to Urumqi shorter.

Urumqi was quiet. Air China service had been resumed, but the situation in the rest of the country was alarming. The first telex had advised them to leave China through Guanzhou or Shanghai, but there were reports of clashes between students and soldiers in both cities. Ironically, the safest route out of China was through Beijing; Academia Sinica told them that international flights were leaving more or less on schedule. Dale desperately wanted to talk to his wife, Jan, but it was impossible to place a call through to Canada; he finally gave up after a morning of fruitless attempts. That night they watched an official news report on Chinese television; when the broadcaster reached a description of the Beijing citizens joyfully welcoming the People's Liberation Army into the city, she stopped, looked up at the camera, then looked back down and continued reading, visibly trembling.

Accompanied by Peng Jianghua, the group left Urumqi on June 9; as if to underscore just how chaotic things had become, the flight to Beijing left ten minutes ahead of schedule. At the Beijing airport, Air France and Continental jets were taking on passengers, mostly Japanese and Americans. Zheng Jiajian met them at the arrival gate and took them to the Friendship Hotel — the Da Du was being used by the army. On the way they passed the burned-out hulks of army vehicles. They found the business section disturbingly calm. Most of the shops were closed, but the buses and trolley cars were running. At the Friendship Hotel, which had room for 2,400 guests, there were only eight others: an American; two Egyptians; an Italian, who said his embassy was not answering the telephone; a Mexican engineer, who was chatty and friendly; two Romanians, who said that democracy was not for everyone; and a German television journalist, who told them that all television broadcasts were under the control of the army and that many of the photographs shown on television had been confiscated from departing Japanese tourists.

Calls to the Canadian Embassy were guarded: rooms in foreign hotels were almost certainly bugged. But the embassy suggested it would be prudent to move to a hotel closer to the airport, say the Lido Holiday Inn. The Friendship Hotel was very close to several universities; the agricultural college was only a few blocks away, and when the Canadians went for a walk they could see the front gate of the People's University strewn with white flowers, mourning the dead students. Posters and banners hung like bunting from the residence windows. That night, they heard sporadic firing all around the hotel.

June 9 was a Friday; the next — in fact the last — Canadian Airlines flight out of Beijing would be on Monday. The city was still under martial law; there was a curfew at dusk, and taking photographs or even notes was illegal. At the IVPP, they learned that Chang Meeman had left China on May 27 to do research in Europe. Sun Ailing said she was afraid that arrests and reprisals would soon begin; someone from the institute had sent the student protesters cases of soft drinks, and they had been delivered to Tienanmen Square in an IVPP bus with anti-government slogans painted on the side in huge Chinese characters: "Peking Man and Dinosaurs Cry for Beijing Students." The sign had appeared on television. On the night of June 5, a Chinese television newscaster, prevented by law from referring to the events in Tienanmen Square, had found a way to get around the censors. Every newscast ended with a short English lesson. That night, in obvious support of student claims that China's leaders were too old and out-of-date to speak for the country's youth, the broadcaster had picked three words for the lesson: "dinosaur," "monster," and "extinct."

On Saturday morning, the four took the Friendship Hotel's only remaining taxi and headed toward Tienanmen Square. On the way they saw much evidence of the past week's mayhem. "Our driver knew where the trouble had been," says Mike Todor. "He would point to a spot and say 'Tank-tanka' or 'tuka-tuka-tuka,' and we would know that either a tank or a machine gun emplacement had been there." Soldiers controlled every major intersection. Tienanmen Square was a parking lot for tanks, its concrete flagstones broken and churned by tank treads. When their taxi tried to approach the square from the south, it was stopped by barbed wire barricades and troops with AK-47s aimed at their windshield. They retreated to Wangfujing Street — the main shopping street that ran off Chang'an beside the Beijing Hotel — which, incredibly, was open for business although there were no other Westerners in sight. The clerks were surprised to see the two Canadians; they were friendly but a bit nervous. One of them told Don that he and Clayton would probably be the last Westerners they would see for quite some time.

The group moved to the Lido on the eleventh. The Canadian Embassy called and advised Mike to bring his eighty rolls of film down to be shipped out by diplomatic pouch. At the embassy, they had a long talk with the ambassador, Earl G. Drake, and his wife, who told them that the building had been hit by stray bullets and the children had been evacuated, but that everyone felt more or less safe. At the airport the next day, moments before they boarded their flight to Japan, Don was quietly approached by a CBC reporter and asked if he would carry two video cassettes back to Canada. He agreed to do so, and then sweated blood as he passed through the security checkpoints. Twelve hours later they landed in Vancouver, where they were met by hundreds of journalists anxious for stories of great escapes. A group from the CBC, looking for their tapes, asked Don if he was one of the Dinosaur People. He said no, he was a turtle person. But he gave them their tapes anyway.

The View from Home

AT THE END OF MAY, TWO WEEKS BEFORE THE INCIDENTS IN TIENANMEN SQUARE, Phil Currie was in the American Museum of Natural History archives in New York, reading Roy Chapman Andrews's unpublished field notes for 1928. Phil still thought he was going to China in mid-June, and he wanted to compare Andrews's notes from Iren Dabasu with what he had learned about the locality in 1988.

The Americans, it seemed, had also been caught in China during some very turbulent times. Chiang Kai Shek's Nationalist Party was wrestling China from the grasp of a dozen powerful warlords, and Mao Zedong's small but determined band of Communists was waiting in the mountains for the other armies to destroy one other. Andrews was decidedly uneasy about being in the middle. Phil copied out his notes from Iren Dabasu for June 3, 1928:

> *Fine day, warm but not hot, bright sun. I hunted badlands for fossils — no bone....Buckshot found remains of large sauropod dinosaur like Brontosaurus in P.M. — bad condition — puts formation in Cretaceous — strange — we thought it Pliocene....At 10 p.m. we got time perfectly over the radio from Manila, 2,200 miles away. Then a little later they picked up our call letter from the legation in Peking and the message began to issue in slowly so that even in my tent I could hear its dots and dashes. Shack, Horvath and Hill took it down and then began the translation, for they were sending in code in which "o" = "a". Walt and Shack squabbled like crows over the translation while I lay in my bed on the qui vive with*

anticipation. The message finally read:

"Gen. Chang Tsao-ling retreated yesterday to Manchuria — the southerners are expected in Peking very soon. Everything normal in Peking and no trouble is expected — all are well — it is rumored that you are returning next week."

This news threw me into a fever of excitement for it changes the entire situation for us. It is well that the trouble has occurred so early in the spring, because the situation will probably have adjusted itself before we are ready to return. Certainly we could not get back now if we wanted to. All our permits, etc., are worthless now....How rumors that we are returning so soon could have got about, I can't imagine, except that anything is possible in Peking!

Phil also made notes on the egg specimens brought back by the Andrews expeditions. He had always been suspicious of these. Andrews brought back four different types of eggs — large eggs with thick shells and longitudinal lines; smaller, smoother eggs with thinner shells; even smaller eggs with very thin shells, egg-shaped rather than elongated; and a few tiny round eggs called simply "reptile," i.e., non-dinosaurian. A label on the third type read: "AMNH 2905. The first dinosaur eggs found, collected in September 1922 and supposed at that time to be the egg of a bird."

Andrews — or more likely Granger — identified the first three types as *Protoceratops* eggs, attributing their different sizes and shapes to acceptable variations within the species. Phil doubted that any single species could lay such widely divergent eggs. And since many different types of dinosaurs had been found in Inner Mongolia, why should there not be different types of dinosaur eggs as well? Phil suspected that the elongated eggs measuring about twenty centimeters in length were in fact ankylosaur eggs. The second, smaller than the first but similar in shape, were the best candidates for *Protoceratops*. And the third type might be the same as the round eggs the Dinosaur Project had found in Bayan Mandahu and tentatively identified as theropod eggs. If Phil were right, Andrews's egg finds might have been much more significant scientifically than anyone at the time realized. But he would have to go back to Bayan Mandahu to find out for sure.

On May 26, Phil flew to Toronto, taking one of the American Museum's possible ankylosaur eggs with him. He was met by Andrew Leitch of the Royal Ontario

Museum, and the two of them took the egg and Tang Zhilu's *Troodon* braincase to Sunnybrook Medical Centre to be CAT-scanned; the images appeared immediately on the screen: the egg contained some mineralized material that looked as though it might have been bone, but it was in the middle of the egg, rather than at the bottom. Phil decided it was not an embryo. The CAT-scan of the braincase was more rewarding: it clearly showed the pneumatic openings and the semi-circular structure of the inner ear, confirming Phil's suspicions that *Troodon*'s anatomy had much in common with the larger theropods. He then caught an Air Canada flight home.

Dong Zhiming arrived in Edmonton on June 1. He had been in Sweden, setting up an exhibition of Chinese dinosaurs at the University of Uppsala. He was planning to spend some time in Dinosaur Park and other localities. Like Phil, he was aware that things were heating up in Tienanmen Square, but he could not find out much more than that because phone lines to Beijing were either jammed or shut down. No word had arrived from the IVPP. When he learned from Ex Terra that Dale and the others would be returning as soon as possible, he decided to travel down to Drumheller to visit Phil at the Tyrrell and wait for more news.

Phil took him around to the various fossil sites in Alberta. The Devil's Coulee field camp had been set up, with half a dozen volunteers — including Wendy Sloboda, who was working at the Tyrrell for the summer — renting a farmhouse in the Milk River Valley and working on Kevin Aulenback's egg site. A cluster of "feathery pink eggs" had been found very close to the original nest. On June 15, Phil found three *Troodon* teeth and Dong Zhiming found what looked like three dinosaur footprints. On the nineteenth they set out on a day trip to Grand Prairie to have a look at a large *Pachyrhinosaurus* bonebed. But because of the political situation in China, everything had an air of unreality.

Phil and Dong Zhiming drove to Edmonton for a meeting with Linda and Kevin Taft at the Ex Terra offices on the twenty-second. During the meeting they discussed the events in China and their possible effects on future field work there. Dale and his team had just returned, safe but shaken, but Phil, Dong Zhiming, and the rest of the Tyrrell crew were scheduled to fly to Beijing on August 15, after spending a month on Bylot Island in the Arctic. For now, the China trip was on hold — no one knew if even the IVPP crew would be able to get to Bayan

Mandahu, as scheduled — but the Arctic leg was still on. They would leave for Pond Inlet on July 7; in the meantime, Dong Zhiming would go to Ottawa to see Dale, who was back at the National Museum, and from there they would join the others in the Arctic. Linda had intended to go to the Arctic as well, but in the end decided to send Mike Todor instead. She and Kevin were to return to Beijing in August, to "check on the status of the Dinosaur Project," she says, "and to try to iron out any problems."

Bylot Island

BYLOT ISLAND WAS NOT BALMY. THE TEMPERATURE WAS 5 DEGREES CELSIUS UNDER broken clouds and there were snow flurries for most of the day. It was July 10. The Dinosaur Project team had been on the island for three days, and rain and snow squalls had kept them in camp, in fact in bed, for most of the time. But on the tenth a break in the weather allowed everyone to spend at least part of the day prospecting for bone.

Phil walked halfway up Dinosaur Valley and began working his way back toward the coast, systematically covering each exposure along the southern side. He had his lunch with him — pastrami sandwiches and a thermos of tea — and ate it sitting on a lump of frozen sandstone staring across the thirty-two kilometers of Eureka Sound at the scattered buildings of Pond Inlet. At around three-thirty in the afternoon he saw Dale and Rick Day measuring distant sections of the valley walls, but otherwise he was completely alone. Dong Zhiming, Clayton, and Mike Todor were on Shark Tooth Hill. Back in camp by six o'clock, Phil counted the day's finds: nearly a hundred specimens, all broken scraps of bone but much of it identifiable. As usual in the Arctic, most of the material was marine — bits of mosasaur and plesiosaur, fragments of a ratfish skull — but some of it looked terrestrial. He labeled one "a hadrosaur posterior zygopophysis (cervical)"; another "hadrosaur (?) radius." And two days earlier Clayton had found parts of a *Hesperornis* backbone, so that beasts of all three realms were represented.

Dale's measurements gave him a sense of the sedimentary history of the valley. It was, he felt, all alluvial — the delta of a vast, north-flowing river that had emptied into the Arctic Ocean 78 million years ago. Bylot Island itself had been

The field camp on Bylot Island in July 1989, looking south across ice-filled Pond Inlet to the northern edge of Baffin Island. Phil and Dale believe the Arctic is waiting to be opened up, paleontologically speaking: "There are so many badlands here," says Phil, "so much potential."

off-shore, a spot where bones, carried out to sea by the force of the river's current, were deposited. The top section was a layer of yellow sandstone 173 m thick, over-lying a thinner indistinct zone of more massive sandstone. The size of the grains of sand in the stone was evidence of fast water. Under this was a 161.5-m zone of gray sandstone streaked with yellow, then more yellow sandstone, then a 152-m section of whitish rock. Not until near the bottom of the slope — almost a thou-sand meters from the top — did the sediments become more finely bedded, indi-cating that at one time the area had been under relatively quiet water.

On July 14, they shifted camp to Ellesmere Island to search for a chimera. They were accompanied this time by Randall Oshevsky, whom Dale had met in Ottawa while jogging. Oshevsky was a northern environmental specialist — he tested equipment for the armed forces — and an Arctic buff who collected books about the far north. He had told Dale about a book called *Tracks in the Snow*, writ-ten by David Haig-Thomas. In 1938, Haig-Thomas had heard about a previous expedition to Ellesmere Island from his Inuit guide, a man named Nookap. It had been, in fact, an illegal hunting trip for musk oxen led by an RCMP staff-sergeant named Joy. Nookap told Haig-Thomas about a curious thing they had found on the trip: a strange round mound on the side of a small, dried-up stream. Inside the mound they found the fossilized bones of "a large animal, six meters or more long. Its tail was hanging into the valley; its head and feet were still underground. Some of the bones were clearly showing; and in places parts of the body could be seen, though turned to stone."

Excited by their find, the hunters had taken one of the vertebrae from the tail and lashed it to the sledge. But Joy stopped them. "If we take this back to Canada," he had told them, "many men will come to see these remains, then they will see the skulls of the dead musk oxen, and we shall get into trouble." They had thrown the vertebrae in the snow, and no one had mentioned the find (or the trip) again until Nookap told Haig-Thomas about it eleven years later.

The story intrigued Dale. Ellesmere Island was known to have Late Cretaceous deposits. Plesiosaurs can reach up to six meters long, but so can hadrosaurs. The mention of feet was interesting — plesiosaurs had flipper-like paddles, the internal bone structure of which could be mistaken for that of feet — and if it was true that the head and feet were still buried in the hillside, they might still be salvageable. In any event, Dale thought it possible that Joy's monster was a terrestrial dinosaur, and he decided it was worth checking out.

They set up camp in a little hollow filled with goose droppings and feathers beside a small lake near the dried stream bed mentioned by Haig-Thomas, at 78 degrees 47 minutes N, 83 degrees 55 minutes W. The rain closed in as they waited for the helicopter to bring in the last of their gear, and they didn't get the tents pitched and Oshevsky's bear alarms rigged until half past midnight. After a good night's sleep and a breakfast of pancakes, they all went prospecting in the rain. Dale found three musk-ox skeletons almost immediately and thought they might be the ones shot by Joy and his party in 1927. Over the course of the day, however, they found at least a dozen more, evidence that the area had remained a favorite hunting spot long after Joy's visit. The camp was in the Kanguk Formation, and they walked eight or nine kilometers south to exposures of the Isachsen Formation without finding any fossils at all. The wind was so strong that, leaning into it, they

Clayton Kennedy prospecting on Bylot Island, ready for an unscheduled visit from a polar bear. This hadrosaur vertebra found on Bylot Island probably washed down from the south during the Late Cretaceous. Everything else found on the island was marine.

could walk upright down steep hills. Back in camp, the ice sheet on their little pond had been blown to the other side, and the air was filled with the sound of needle ice tinkling like chimes in the wind.

Dong Zhiming found some bone on July 17 — indeterminate scraps that might have been dinosaur, or at least might not have been marine, but there was no sign of a six-meter monster. On the nineteenth, Phil found a second bone fragment above the spot where Dong Zhiming had found his, and the coincidence suggested a possible line of further investigation. They were halfway up the side of a butte between two stream beds — possibly the "round mound" — at the point of contact between the Kanguk and Mount Bell formations, greenish-yellow sandstone sitting on black conglomerates beneath a wide belt of brownish shale. On the opposite side of the butte, but at about the same level, Dong Zhiming found a plesiosaur, nearly complete, but so soft and rotten that Clayton said it was like wet sawdust, and they didn't even try to take it out. It was bitterly cold working in the wind, exposed on the side of the butte. The temperature was just above freezing in camp, but much lower in the wet southerly wind at the quarry.

When they woke on July 20, it was snowing, but the sky cleared after breakfast and they walked to another small lake several kilometers to the east, prospecting several more Kanguk and Mount Bell outcrops along the way but finding nothing. They did, however, meet a herd of ten musk oxen, which dampened their enthusiasm for reaching the lake. Dong Zhiming, who had stayed back to prospect near the camp, found the partial skeleton of an elasmosaur — another marine vertebrate — which Phil and Clayton collected after lunch. That evening the wind stopped, which was nice, and the mosquitoes came back out in force, which was not. They dined on pastrami and instant scalloped potatoes, made their seven o'clock radio report to Resolute, then went to bed.

On the twenty-first, they decided to spread out. Dale and Clayton walked north through a raw, snow-squally wind to a set of high hills overlooking Bay Fiord, then turned east and circled back to camp without finding any bone except for a number of seal skulls at the tops of several hills. Had they been left by gulls? Dale wondered. Owls? Dong Zhiming, Phil, and Rick Day, meanwhile, followed the creek bed north, intending to stay with it until it dumped into Bay Fiord. Halfway there, they were stopped by a large bull musk ox that decided to charge rather than retreat. They ran down into a gully, the bull snorting behind them, but when they reached the bottom the bull stopped and made itself comfortable on a ledge some nine meters above them. They decided their safest option was to prospect where they were, in a shallow cleft of the Mount Lawson Formation. Above a thin coal seam they found leaf impressions of *Metasequoia*. Still watched suspiciously by the musk ox, they sat down in the shelter of the gully to eat their lunch. The sun was warm on their faces. The air was still. Eventually the musk ox settled down too and closed its eyes, and they eased their way along the gully without disturbing its rest. Everyone had saved face.

They continued to Bay Fiord, searching through Kanguk, Mount Bell, and more Mount Lawson exposures without success. Back in camp that evening, each group estimated it had covered more than twenty kilometers without finding a single bone. Phil was reminded of Axel-Heiberg in 1986.

The next day they radioed for a helicopter to move their gear to a new camp about five kilometers west, on the other side of the major stream bed closer to Bay Fiord. They set up their tents beside a slightly larger lake, far enough inland to be between the wind of the fiord and the mosquitoes. Over the next few days they found abundant plesiosaur material and one large mosasaur, but no terrestrial fossils. One day they walked a twenty-four-kilometer loop without finding anything but fossilized wood and plant impressions. It was beginning to look as though Joy's monster was a plesiosaur after all. But at least the weather had improved: on the afternoon of July 24 the thermometer reached 29 degrees Celsius. They added two more formations to their collection — the Christopher and the Hassel — but no new specimens.

When the wind shifted from northwest to south it became cooler, because it blew over the glaciers on Ellesmere Island rather than over open water. That happened on the twenty-sixth, soon after the sun came out from behind a bank of clouds after midnight. Cold gusts persisted throughout the day, and by afternoon the temperature had dropped to 4 degrees. Sunspots played havoc with radio reception, and the team was unable to make its morning contact with Resolute. More circular sorties proved unfruitful; they found plesiosaurs, but all were eroded beyond worth. Rick walked once more along the stream bed that Joy's party had used and found what he felt must have been the monster described by Nookap: it was a plesiosaur, no more complete or spectacular than the dozens they had already found. He didn't bother to collect it. The next day they packed up their gear and were airlifted back to Resolute.

Despite the paucity of their finds, they were still optimistic about the Arctic. Alaska had yielded ceratopsians, hadrosaurs, and several types of carnivores, and the Canadian islands had proven that hadrosaurs wandered farther east. Phil decided to widen the search to the Yukon. "I like the Arctic very much," he says. "I didn't have much hope of finding dinosaurs in 1989, but I went back anyway because I loved it. There are so many badlands there, so much potential."

While they were eating dinner in the Polar Continental Shelf Project dining room in Resolute, they met a Chinese geographer from Langzhou. Dong Zhiming and the geographer talked for hours — neither of them had been in China since May. The geographer, however, mentioned that at the time of Tienanmen Square eight Chinese graduate students had been in Resolute; when they had learned about the events of June 4 on satellite television, they had gone out to the airstrip, climbed a hill, and written a message in the snow using rocks from the gravel hillside: "Chinese students for democracy" in English and Chinese.

After dinner, Clayton, Dale, and Phil walked out to the airstrip. The rain was still strong, a cold, penetrating wetness that made talking difficult. They found the hill easily and climbed to the top. Rain and wind had melted the snow; the rocks that had formed the Chinese students' message were still there, but the words were no longer legible.

MEANWHILE, KEVIN TAFT AND LINDA STRONG-WATSON HAD RETURNED TO BEIJING to try to salvage the Project. The original arrangement with the IVPP had been for four field seasons (1986 to 1989); this time was now up, but because of the interruptions caused by Tienanmen Square, the final two legs of the 1989 season had not been accomplished. Linda and Kevin wanted to meet with representatives from Academia Sinica to arrange for the continuation and completion of the 1989 field season, even if it had to take place in 1990.

"The Dinosaur Project was not a political project," says Linda. "It was a scientific project that dealt with issues common to all of us. We were concerned about our Chinese colleagues, not knowing how they had been affected by the political happenings at that time. They were affected, however, in the sense that their own emotional upset and a new governmental interest in ensuring that Chinese academics remained committed to the policies of the government left little time for concentration and research."

The Canadians met with Li Chuankui, who was acting director of the IVPP during Chang Meeman's absence, and with the scientific directors of Academia Sinica's programs in Western Europe, North America, and Oceania. Since Linda and Kevin were among the first Westerners to enter China after the uprising, there was some initial concern about the effect that Tienanmen Square would have on the Canadians' willingness to go on with the project. "The Chinese scientists," Linda says, "were very concerned that the Western world, including us, would abandon them." Once assurances were made that that was not the case, however, "it was gratifying for all of us to see that the commitment and interest in the project was still there."

Outside the Academia Sinica offices, however, it was obvious that China had undergone some profound internal changes. "It was a sinister, angry, and hopeless time in Beijing," Linda recalls. "One day I tried to go downtown in a taxi, to some of the shops I had visited on earlier trips just off Tienanmen Square. When we got close to them, the street was blocked by people, and we had to drive very slowly through them. Suddenly we found ourselves face to face with a line of soldiers with machine guns, stretching from one side of the street to the other, moving toward us and sweeping everyone before them. My driver turned the cab around and got us out of there in a hurry, and when I asked him what was going on, he said the soldiers were searching for weapons that had gone missing during the uprising in June.

"Another time, I visited the Canada-China Trade Council offices, which were located in a tall office tower just down from Tienanmen Square. Their offices were on the twenty-sixth floor, and yet there were bullet holes in the ceiling, and the windows had just been replaced."

Still, the meetings went well. Linda and Kevin spent time at the IVPP talking to Sun Ailing and Zhao Xijin. Once it was clear that everyone wanted to complete the Dinosaur Project in 1990, it remained only to work out a possible schedule and to hope for the best.

CHAPTER 7

The Ordos Basin
Li Rong's trackway and dinosaur herding

THE FIRST THING THE CANADIANS DID AFTER CHECKING INTO THE DA DU ON June 11, 1990, was walk over to the IVPP. The team included the Tyrrell Museum crew, Phil, Don, and Dave Eberth; the National Museum group, Dale, Clayton, and Kieran Shepherd; and Linda Strong-Watson and Mike Todor from Ex Terra. At the IVPP there was much hand-shaking and an unstated feeling of relief that everyone had made it through the past year. No one mentioned Tienanmen Square, but the events of June 4 were still fresh in the minds of the Canadians who had gone through it, and of the Chinese scientists who had survived its aftermath.

After greeting Chang Meeman, who had returned the previous week after more than a year out of China, and catching up on personal news — Tang Zhilu and his wife had had a baby daughter; Peng Jianghua and his wife were still living at the agricultural college, but had their names on a list for an apartment in the city; Dong Zhiming's ulcers were still acting up — Dale asked about the sauropod quarry in Xinjiang. Chang Meeman told him she had just received a telephone call from Tang Zhilu, who was at the quarry, saying that he and his workers had removed the last cervical vertebra and were beginning to find fragmented pieces of skull.

This was great news, and everyone was elated. It looked as though the quest for a *Mamenchisaurus* skull was about to come to a successful conclusion. Dale had all but given up hope for an intact skull, but Zhao Xijin had been determined and had kept his crew at work. Three days later, when Chang Meeman received a second call from Tang Zhilu saying they had found five teeth, a mandible, and more skull fragments, Dale could hardly contain his excitement.

"What were the teeth like?" Dale asked.

"Spatulate," said Meeman.

"*Mamenchisaurus*," he said triumphantly. "That's great!"

Great for Dale's theory of Asian isolation during the Early Cretaceous, and great for the Dinosaur Project in general. The Xinjiang quarry had yielded the first *Mamenchisaurus* teeth known to science, and they were different from the teeth of North American sauropods. It now seemed clear to Dale that Asia had been joined to Pangaea until about 170 million years ago, during which time it had shared similar dinosaurs. Then, about 150 million years ago, when Pangaea split into Laurasia and Gondwanaland, the Asian land mass had separated from both of them and drifted off on its own, physically as well as evolutionarily. Dinosaurs that had once been identical to those on Pangaea began to develop their own unique characteristics. For example, some as yet unidentified sauropodan group had evolved into the family Mamenchisauridae (spatulate teeth) in Asia and Diplodocidae (pointed teeth) in North America. With teeth available for diagnosis, it was now possible to say with some certainty that *Mamenchisaurus* was not a member of the Diplodocidae, although it must date from the time when Asia was just beginning to separate from Pangaea.

After the meeting, during which a tentative field schedule was worked out for the summer, the Canadians went downstairs to Dong Zhiming's office. The segnosaur humerus from Erenhot that Dale had examined the year before had been further prepared over the winter, and Dale hefted it in his hand and declared it to be extraordinarily heavy. Dong Zhiming then picked small metatarsals from various white boxes on his work table and handed some to Phil and some to Dale, who held them up to the light and identified them as ornithomimid, dromeosaur, or segnosaur.

After that they all trooped out to a small, brick building in the IVPP compound. In it were three crates of fossils from the Sino-Soviet Expedition of 1959-60, which Dong Zhiming had only recently begun to unpack. They had remained unopened in the basement of a Beijing apartment building for thirty years. Recently, the IVPP had been pressuring the Soviets for the rest of the Sino-Soviet

**Bylot Island, in the Canadian Arctic off the northern coast of Baffin Island,
was the scene of an intensive search for dinosaur material in 1989. Dinosaur Project
members found hadrosaur jaw and toe bones and vertebra, making
Bylot Island the world's most northerly site for dinosaur discovery.**

Three locations in the Bayan Mandahu area of Inner Mongolia: the
Gate (opposite page, top), where most of the *Protoceratops* were found; the North
Canyon (opposite page bottom), scene of the two juvenile *Pinacosaurus* quarries;
and Obo Mesa, south of the Gate, where many of the turtles and mammals were found.
The entire area was part of a vast deltaic floodplain during the Late Cretaceous.

Don Brinkman collected this *Xinjiangchelys* turtle shell (top) near
the *Mamenchisaurus* quarry in the Junggar Basin. A desert rainstorm closes in
on Iren Dabasu (bottom), near Erenhot, several kilometers from the Outer
Mongolian border. The mounds were made in 1960 by Soviet paleontologists,
who used bulldozers to clear away the upper layers to expose a variety of
dinosaur bones strikingly similar to those found in the badlands of Alberta.

**The Inner Mongolian Museum in Hohhot was visited in 1990 by
members of the Dinosaur Project en route to the Ordos Basin.**

material, so Dong Zhiming had decided it was time to see what was in the crates
they had. Various bones lay spread about the small room, lying on the floor or
propped up against the walls. Most of them were from the bulldozer site in
Erenhot, broken up and not particularly new to the Dinosaur Project members —
"Hadrosaurs galore," as Dale put it — but they did identify some rare dromeosaurid
and troodontid material, and it would obviously take years to uncrate, identify, and
prepare everything. "Maybe thirty more years," he said, smiling happily.

On June 15, the Tyrrell crew flew south for a week-long tour of China's museums before heading north to Bayan Mandahu to begin the field season; the
National Museum team, with Linda and Mike Todor, boarded a train to Hohhot
en route to the Ordos Basin.

Hohhot lay under a thick blanket of coal smoke when the train arrived at the
station early the next morning. Li Rong met the Canadians with the jeeps — drivers had driven up from Beijing overnight — and took them to the Inner

**Specimens on display at the IMM: the large dinosaur in the background
is a *Bactrosaurus*; mounted on the wall at right a complete
Psittacosaurus; and on the rug, parts of a small ornithomimid.**

Mongolian Hotel, a large, relatively modern establishment boasting hot water daily, a Western-style bar and restaurant, and a kind of mini-mall in the lobby. They were allowed an hour or so to rest after the trip, then Li Rong escorted them to his museum to meet various Inner Mongolian officials and to tour the exhibits.

The museum was a large, white, brick building, its entrance surmounted by a huge statue of Genghis Khan's leaping white stallion, the emblem of Mongolia. Beneath the statue, wide steps led up to a pair of massive wooden doors. The building's interior was vast and gloomy — poorly lit like every official building in China — with two wings spreading left and right from a central reception hall. The right wing housed the museum's modern collection — cultural artifacts of indigenous Mongolians that showed remarkable similarities to those of North American native peoples: deerhide gloves and jackets, bows and arrows in leather saddle quivers, beaded necklaces and headdresses, carved knives, even a birchbark canoe with a double-bladed paddle, like that of an Inuit kayak. The yurt that occupied one corner of the hall looked like a cross between a tipi and an igloo. The figures of animals carved on a wooden cradle were also eerily familiar: a broad-antlered moose, several reindeer, geese, and a squirrel. The ancient cultural links between Mongolia and North America seemed tangible and immediate, as if the exchange had been made only yesterday. In fact, some of them had: one of the Peigan tipis from the Tipi-Yurt Exchange was being stored here, and one of the Mongolian yurts had been sent to Canada.

In the left wing, where the fossils were kept, the links were more ancient but no less evident. The main room was dominated by the resurrected skeleton of a huge mammoth, its four-and-a-half-meter tusks curving up toward the vaulted ceiling as the animal lifted its skull in an exultant cry of triumph over death. Glass display cases lining the walls contained more fossils, all collected from Inner Mongolia, and most of them common to Asia and North America: turtles from Bayan Mandahu, lizards and theropods from Erenhot. Photographs of previous paleontological expeditions into Inner Mongolia showed Roy Chapman Andrews sporting a wide smile and a pistol, an elderly C.C. Young holding court in a room full of students, and the bulldozers of the Sino-Soviet Expedition boldly destroying specimens in the sands near Erenhot.

Facing the mastodon, mounted on a partition like a huge modernist sculpture, was a six-by-three-meter slab of gray rock. It was actually a cast of a slab of gray rock, painted to look like the real thing. Embedded in the rock were the footprints of dinosaurs — forty-five of them — collected by Li Rong in 1978 from Chabusumu, deep in the Ordos Basin.

Looking at dinosaur bones is exciting, certainly, but bones are, after all, the remains of animals that are dead; footprints were left by living, moving dinosaurs, and they tell more about dinosaur *behavior* than any other kind of fossil. Short of finding a living fossil in some lost mountain lake — there are speculations that the Loch Ness Monster might be a descendant of the marine reptile *Elasmosaurus* — looking at a footprint is as close as we can come to contact with an actual dinosaur.

Dinosaur tracks are much more common than bones, and have been known longer. The first was discovered in 1802 in the Connecticut River Valley by a young college student by the name of Pliny Moody, who turned up a piece of Triassic red sandstone while plowing on his father's farm in South Hadley, Massachusetts.

Embedded in the slab was what looked to Moody like the three-toed print of a huge turkey. The animal that made the print was dubbed "Noah's raven," since it was assumed that the impression could only have been made by the bird released by Noah toward the end of the Flood. The bird-like characteristics of the tracks were also noted by Edward Hitchcock, a clergyman and amateur paleontologist who, in 1836, published a description of the prints, naming them *Ornithichnites*, or "stony bird tracks." T.H. Huxley later pointed out that *Ornithichnites* were actually stony dinosaur tracks, and he deduced from them that some dinosaurs may not have stomped around on all fours, like elephants, but rather walked on their hind legs or may have *had* only two legs — like birds. "The important truth which these tracks reveal," Huxley argued, "is that at the commencement of the Mesozoic epoch, bipedal animals existed which had the feet of birds, and walked in the same erect or semi-erect fashion." Dinosaur footprints became part of the great dinosaur-bird debate.

Although thousands of dinosaur footprints have been found since Noah's raven, some have been more important than others, for — as every reader of detective fiction knows — a single print may tell what kind of animal made it, but it takes a sequence of prints to tell a story. A sequence of prints is called a trackway, and the ability of trackways to tell a story was recognized by Roland T. Bird in the 1940s. Bird examined a series of sauropod tracks in the bed of the Paluxy River near the town of Glen Rose, Texas. At the time, most paleontologists assumed that sauropods were semi-aquatic monsters, a sort of amphibious whale: they assumed that sauropods were far too heavy to walk on land and had to spend their entire lives at least partially buoyed up in water. Lake-bed or stream-bed tracks, however, would be very blurry, because the swirling about of the water after the animal's passing would partially fill in the print. Bird found twelve rows of four-toed tracks, each row consisting of prints ninety centimeters in diameter and 180 cm apart, so well preserved that the fact they were 100 million years old was barely credible. They had obviously been made by an adept terrestrial quadruped. As he uncovered the tracks, Bird also found the three-toed tracks of a carnosaur that ran along the left side of the sauropod's path. Perhaps it was the seeming freshness of the tracks that awakened Bird's imagination, but as he worked it became clear to him that the carnivore had been chasing down one of the sauropods, that he was in fact witnessing evidence of a hunting scene played out in Early Cretaceous times. The footprints clearly showed that when the sauropod veered to the left, the tyrannosaur veered with it, then closed in for the kill. The final scene of the drama was lost to Bird, however, as the tracks disappeared in tandem beneath a limestone cliff.

In the 1970s, paleontologists Bob Bakker and Martin Lockley went back to the Texas trackway site to fine-tune Bird's deductions. Bakker found evidence that the twenty-three sauropods that made the prints formed "a structured herd," with "the very largest footprints made only at the periphery of the herd; the very small-est...only in the center." Lockley made careful maps of each of the twenty-three trackways and disagreed with Bakker's version of herd structuring. "If we treat the whole group as a herd," he notes, "the largest track makers are... centrally locat-ed.... The herd appears to have consisted of several laterally spaced subgroups with individuals following in line. There is some indication both that the larger indi-viduals led the way followed by smaller ones, and that the speed of the individu-als in each subgroup was remarkably consistent." Far from Bakker's image of a herd of herbivores moving with their young carefully protected in the center by adults, Lockley's interpretation suggests a ragtag group of individuals lumbering along at about four and a half kilometers an hour, with the youngsters left trailing behind, exposed to attack by marauding theropods as they struggled to keep up with the fast-moving adults.

Dale Russell, in *An Odyssey in Time*, identifies the sauropods as *Pleurocoelus*, Early Cretaceous brachiosaurs that weighed more than forty tonnes, and the car-nivore as an *Acrocanthosaurus*, an allosaur-like theropod measuring about twelve meters in length and weighing more than three tonnes. *Acrocanthosaurus* differed from other theropods in that it sported a single row of very high, webbed spines along its backbone. Dale speculates that since theropods were highly active and lived in warm environments, these thin, membranous spines may have acted as heat dissipators, allowing the animal to cool off after running. He gives his own version of the encounter envisioned by Bird. The sauropod, he writes, "was mov-ing at a regular cadence at a normal walking speed of about four kilometers per hour. A large *Acrocanthosaurus*, whose hind limbs were over two and a half meters long, walked along the same trackway, and in every case where footprints from the two animals coincide, the one from the carnivore is superimposed over the print of the sauropod. Near the center of the excavated portion of the trackway, the carnivore's cadence seems irregular, and both animals appear to have veered to the left. Had it seized the moving herbivore, and was it pulled off balance by the powerful sauropod? It was moving twice as fast as the sauropod, but this was nevertheless a normal walking speed for a carnivore."

In 1922, the first dinosaur tracks discovered in Canada were found in the mid-Cretaceous sedimentary rocks of British Columbia's Peace River Canyon by F.H. McLearn, a geologist with the Geological Survey of Canada. The canyon is a deeply cut gorge, beginning just west of Hudson Hope and falling eighty-three meters over a distance of about nineteen kilometers. In the upper portion of the cliffs, the erosive force of the river has cut through the coal-bearing Gething Formation, and when the water is at its lowest in midsummer, the Gething strata are revealed as rock shelves at river level. It was on these rock shelves that McLearn found more than four hundred individual dinosaur tracks. The shelves had once been the bottoms of shallow flood-plain lakes, exposed as mud flats during times of low water.

Nothing much was done about the Peace River trackways until 1930, when Charles M. Sternberg — Charles Hazelius's son, who was then working for the National Museum of Canada — went to the Peace region and looked at the footprints himself. He determined that they included the prints of six entirely new genera and eight new species. He named one of the prints *Irenesauripus mclearni*, made by a three-toed carnivore that was "the most numerous of all those in the canyon." (Fossil footprints are given their own taxonomic names, which are quite different from the names of the dinosaurs that made them.)

More new prints were found upstream during the construction of a hydro dam on the Peace River during the energy-mad 1960s. In 1975, plans for a newer, bigger dam downstream from McLearn's site that would eventually turn the entire canyon into a reservoir spurred Phil, then with the Provincial Museum of Alberta, to go up with a crew to see what could be salvaged before the flooding. McLearn's original trackway site, near Ferro Point, was under water when Phil got there in 1976; nonetheless, he managed to make a spectacular discovery: a single bedding plane eleven meters long by four and a half meters wide, containing more than a hundred dinosaur prints.

Phil returned to the Peace every summer for four years (ironically, the expe-

Footprints of a herbivorous dinosaur (possibly an ankylosaur) near Grand Cache, Alberta, found in 1990 by the Dinosaur Project. Trackways are evidence of dinosaurs on the move: herbivores this far north were probably migrating to or from summer feeding grounds in what is now the Arctic.

ditions were funded in part by grants from British Columbia Hydro). During that time, he and his colleagues found more than 1,700 individual footprints, and ninety were cut out of the sandstone and shipped back to the Provincial Museum. Plaster casts of another two hundred were made, and more than a thousand prints in a hundred trackways were measured and mapped. Many more new prints of species first described by Sternberg were discovered, including those of *Amblydactylus* — the earliest known hadrosaur evidence in North America — as well as the earliest bird footprints anywhere.

Investigating dinosaur footprints is not easy, as Phil's account of his efforts to find the *Amblydactylus* print from which Sternberg had identified the species shows. Sternberg established the species in 1931 on the basis of a single footprint, and although he had made a cast of the print, he had been unable to cut the actual print out for preservation, and so it was extremely important for Phil to find that print and collect it before the whole canyon was flooded. Phil searched every sum-

The Royal Tyrrell's Darren Tanke catalogues dinosaur footprint casts at Grand Cache. In 1990, Dinosaur Project members found hundreds of prints in this area, and earlier Phil had collected others from the Peace River.

mer for four years and could not find it; then, in 1979, he spotted the print from a helicopter. It was under sixty centimeters of water. "Three attempts were made to produce a new and better cast of the holotype when the levels of the river were extremely low," Phil records, "but failed because the river level never stayed low enough for more than a few hours. Although it is an extremely important and well preserved specimen (comparison with Sternberg's photograph shows that there has been no significant erosion of the specimen after fifty years), the water levels and hardness of the rock prevented any attempt to excavate it. This specimen and most others in the canyon are now inundated by a reservoir behind the Peace Canyon Dam."

Phil and his crew did find other *Amblydactylus* prints, however. In fact, half of all the trackways discovered, and 90 percent of all the isolated footprints, belonged to this genus. In one site, the tracks were found in a gray, fine-grained sandstone containing rootlets and other vegetable materials, suggesting that the dinosaurs were walking on the weedy margin of a quiet body of fresh water. At another site, the sandstone is rippled: paleo mud covered by several centimeters of water. At Site 4, the trackway is in red sandstone, and the pattern of the tracks suggests that the animal was "partially floating when the trackway was made, and that the tracks were made in the muddy bottom of a quiet body of water that was at least two meters in depth." Hadrosaurs, it appears, were good swimmers. All in all, the fifteen hadrosaur trackway sites were found in every available type of environment: they were the tracks of herds on the move. Parallel tracks of two juveniles at Sites 7 and 3 further suggest "that the juveniles were gregarious and stayed together after hatching until they were large enough to join herds of more mature animals."

Trackways in which numerous animals of the same type are moving in one direction is strong evidence of herding. There are many such sites in the world, but Site 8 in the Peace River canyon may be the best anywhere, because it shows that the animals actually all changed direction at the same time. The rock shows nine or ten animals walking across a crevasse splay. "The more northerly footprints must have been made in very soft mud, because they were deeply impressed and there was considerable fluid mud flow after the dinosaurs walked on. The footprints are shallower and better defined towards the end of the series, suggesting the mud was firmer in this area." The hadrosaurs, it appears, were moving spread out on a wide front, walking side by side and seldom crossing paths. In one case, the track of a juvenile crosses that of an adult, suggesting that — as with the sauropods in Texas — the young followed behind. The hadrosaur herd in the Peace River also appears to have been stalked by predators — three theropod tracks, named *Irenesauripus acutus*, are mixed in with the *Amblydactylus* tracks and follow the herd into fairly deep water.

Trackways in Grande Cache, a second Peace River Valley site visited by Phil and Dong Zhiming in the spring of 1990, provide further insights into dinosaur behavior and spark tantalizing conjectures. The Grand Cache trackway was the same age as the Chabusumu trackway in the Ordos Basin and contained theropod tracks that were virtually identical — three toes and a "thumb" that had moved around to the back of the foot. Were herds of herbivorous dinosaurs migrating to summer feeding grounds in the Arctic, trailed by packs of theropods? The

Amblydactylus prints are identical to those found farther south, in Alberta and Utah. What kind of hadrosaurs made them, and what theropods made the *Irenesauripus* prints?

To Dale, examining the huge cast in the Inner Mongolian Museum, the similarities seemed remarkable. Most of the Ordos prints were of the three-digit theropod type, with deep heel- and toe-pad impressions and claw marks at the ends of each toe. The largest are thirty-eight centimeters long and thirty-five centimeters across. What kind of theropod made them is anybody's guess, but it was obviously a large allosaurid-like creature of the same overall dimensions as the maker of the *Irenesauripus* prints. The sheer number of prints in such a concentrated area was instructive; divided into four types of carnivore — a large theropod and a small theropod, possibly a juvenile of the first, and two ornithomimids — they seemed to represent an active theropod causeway. But, unlike the Peace River and Texas trackways, there were no herbivores. Phil might find the absence of tracks of a prey species — there must have been food around somewhere — intriguing. To Dale, the paucity of sauropod and hadrosaur evidence in western China was worrisome.

Ordeal in the Ordos

THE CANADIANS, LED BY ZHAO XIJIN, LEFT HOHHOT ON JUNE 18 AND DROVE WEST toward Baotou, dipping through Lower Cretaceous formations familiar from previous years — Lower and Upper Dong Shen, Lower, Middle, and Upper Yijingholo. Zhao Xijin explained that in the top two meters or so, at desert level, IVPP paleoanthropologists had found evidence of Neolithic man — pottery shards and chipped stone tools. This was also the area Teilhard de Chardin had passed through in 1922, on his way across the Ordos to Shui Tung Kou, on the western bank of the Yellow River. There he had found the remains of Paleolithic — Old Stone Age — people; quartz tools, bits of charcoal from campfires, even the remains of meals — shell fragments of ostrich eggs, bits of bone from the Mongolian desert wild ass, and even remains of rhinoceros, hyena, and antelope. Other sites had yielded a vast diversity of Pleistocene mammals: wild boars, red deer, big-horned sheep, aurochs, wolves, and badgers, none of which exist there now, even though geological evidence suggested that the area was as desertified then as it is today.

It was dark by the time they reached Dong Shen and twelve-thirty when they checked in to the Ordos Hotel. A thunderstorm raged through the night, flooding the roads and eliminating the possibility of field work for at least a day. In the morning, three crates were discovered in the truck that were supposed to have gone to Bayan Mandahu, and Zhao Xijin spent most of the day arranging for their transfer and organizing sightseeing excursions. At noon, everyone set out for the Genghis Khan Mausoleum, where the Tipi-Yurt Exchange had taken place in 1988.

Frustrated at being kept from the exposures, Dale contented himself with making geological observations from the back of the jeep, noting in his field book places where the redbeds of the Dong Shen Formation poked up through the yellow sand. He called these "*Troodon* beds," because in 1988, in just such a red sandstone outcrop in the Ordos, one of the most important specimens of the entire Dinosaur Project had been collected, although the significance of the find had become apparent only this year. While the scientists had been spread out over the outcrop, Wang Ping, one of the drivers, had noticed a small piece of bone sticking out of the ground near his vehicle. He called Dong Zhiming and Dale over. Thinking it to be yet another *Psittacosaurus* specimen, they had removed the small skeleton and left it almost entirely encased in matrix to ensure its survival during transport to the lab. The specimen had been sent back to the IVPP, its plaster-of-paris jacket marked "Psittacosaur"; there it had sat creating dust until it was included in a shipment of Dinosaur Project specimens sent to the National Museum lab in Ottawa.

Clayton had started preparing it more or less out of curiosity. But as he worked on the soft matrix, exposing the complex of bones encased within it, he realized immediately that the creature he was releasing was not a psittacosaur. The first complete bone he saw was a long, thin metatarsal, much too long and slender to be that of a chunky psittacosaur, even a juvenile. It looked, he says, like bird — by now a familiar enough initial reaction. He exposed a bit more of the foot and then called in Dale, who took one look at it and let out a whoop. It was a small theropod. Clayton went back to work, exposing the tail and part of the hand; there was now no doubt that they had found an Early Cretaceous troodontid, the earliest known ancestor of the Late Cretaceous *Saurornithoides*. Prevented from revisiting the site in 1989 because of Tienanmen Square, Dale was now determined to get

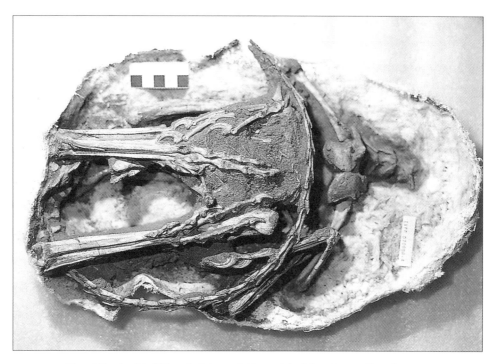

The delicate, bird-like skeleton of *Sinornithoides*, the earliest known member of the family Troodontidae, found in the Ordos Basin by Wang Ping, one of the Chinese drivers. When cleaned up in Ottawa by Clayton and Dale, this was seen to be one of the most important finds of the Project.

there this year; he wanted to be entirely certain of the age of the strata, and he wanted to see if the creature had died alone or with others of its kin.

But the rains continued. A glimpse of blue sky on June 21 lured them out toward Yong Po, ninety kilometers west of Dong Shen, to prospect at the site where, in 1988, Lao Liu had found the bizarre stegosaur skeleton. But when they were a few kilometers from the outcrop the clouds gathered overhead again, and the convoy had to stop, turn around, and flee back to Dong Shen along the rough, clay-topped roads, arriving in the city's paved outskirts with the downpour snapping at their heels. They tried again the next day with more success, making it almost to the stegosaur site before the jeeps became stuck in the soft sand; tantalizingly, the outcrop was visible on the horizon.

Dale was impatient. He wasn't particularly interested in stegosaurs, but in 1988, they had also found a possible sauropod site, and he did want to re-examine that quarry. Thanks to the weather and the sand, however, they would perhaps

Sinornithoides — "Chinese bird-like animal" — measured just over
a metre in length and possessed an unusually large brain.

have half a day at the site, and you do not find much in the desert in half a day
without being incredibly lucky. So far they had not been. When the drivers got out
of their jeeps to investigate the state of the road, Dale jumped out too. "Well, lads,"
he said, taking his camera and a small collecting bag, but not his water bottle, "I
think I'll go for a little walk." And he set off across the desert toward the outcrop.
Linda watched for a few moments, then, remembering Dale's brush with heat
exhaustion the year before, set out after him.

Twenty minutes later they were standing at the top of the exposure, looking
down into a sand valley with the village of Yong Po nestled in a curve of the dry
riverbed. Thin lines of green fuzz radiated from the village in irrigated fields of
sand — early crops of wheat. Above the hills on the opposite side of the valley,
high gray storm clouds were already gathering. Dale figured they had about an
hour before they would have to leave. Linda dropped over the brow of the hill and
made her way down to the old stegosaur quarry, while Dale worked along the out-

Even four-wheel-drive jeeps can get stuck in sand, as happened often in the Ordos Basin: here Li Rong (in the white suit) helps out near the dinosaur trackway site he discovered at Chabusumu.

crop toward the foot of a high escarpment to the west, noting conglomerate sizes and colors in his field book as he went. The outcrop was greenish-yellow sandstone, still Dong Shen Formation but not the redbeds associated with the troodontid. Were they older or younger? In Zhao Xijin's view the psittacosaurs found here in 1988 were more primitive than those found in the *Troodon* beds, and Dale was inclined to agree, so it was reasonable to assume that these green beds were older. The only formation older than Dong Shen was the Yijingholo, and so two years ago they had assigned these primitive psittacosaurs to that formation.

The day before, however, they had examined a road cut through a section that, on Zhao Xijin's map, was called Upper Dong Shen, and the rock had looked very much like this. If the psittacosaurs came from the Upper Dong Shen, then it was an interesting case of dinosaurs from one formation being more primitive than those from an older formation — not unusual but worth noting. Dale worked down the face, looking for signs of an underlying layer of red. Finding none, he concluded that either their previous estimate of this exposure's age had been out by nearly 30 million years or else these psittacosaurs had in fact been "living fossils."

That night they moved to a government hotel in Hanggin Qi, closer to the site where they had found the troodontid specimen, and Dale spent the evening working on his field notes. He was beginning to get a sense of the geology of the Ordos Basin and was able to draw up a rough chart of the region. The oldest beds they had examined were Yijingholo, and so far no fossils had been found in them at all. The stegosaur site was not Yijingholo. The formation was of unknown age, although it could not be more than 125 million years old because coal seams below it were clearly Late Jurassic. Above the Yijingholo was the Lower Dong Shen, the stegosaur beds with the primitive psittacosaurs. Above that were the predominantly red *Troodon* beds of the Middle Dong Shen. This was where things began to get confusing, because there were also some bluish-gray sandstone cliffs called Middle Dong Shen that contained fossils usually thought to be of the same age as those in the redbeds — turtles, another small theropod, and another stegosaur: could there be two faces of the Middle Dong Shen?

On June 23, the group visited the troodontid site, but found nothing new. Zhao Xijin rediscovered, embedded upside down on a nearby exposure, a psittacosaur maxillary but they did not bother to take it out. The next day they drove to another redbed locality where, in 1988, Zhao Xijin had discovered the jawbone of a new species of the theropod *Kelmayisaurus*. Again, they made no new discoveries except for the remains of what might, from its size, have been a sauropod femur, but it was so badly weathered that it looked like a splash of dried white paint on the red sandstone.

After two days of fruitless prospecting, they moved on to Allingbula, then to Otokoqi, more cadre hotels taking them farther into the Ordos Basin. From there they drove out to the trackway site at Chabusumu and then to a locality on the banks of the Hadatu River where they spent an hour splitting shale in search of fossil fish. Peng Jianghua and Linda found two, and Hou found what might have been a small lizard. But they visited no new locations and made no startling discoveries. When they joined the rest of the crew in Bayan Mandahu on July 14, they had almost no news to report: in a little over three weeks in the Ordos they had added only six psittacosaurs, two complete crocodile-like champsosaurs, two good turtles, and a crocodile skull to their collection.

But Dale was not as discouraged as he might have been; he at least had a better knowledge of the stratigraphy than almost anyone else on earth. When he returned to Canada, deciphered his notes, and conferred with Tom Jerzykiewicz, he would begin to be able to correlate the Ordos and North American formations and, hopefully, substantiate his isolation hypothesis. And in many ways, the absence of North American fauna in the Early Cretaceous beds of the Ordos Basin — no iguanodonts or hadrosaurs, no direct ancestors to the ceratopsians, no confirmed sauropods — told him as much as finding them would have.

Magnetic South

PHIL AND HIS CREW HAD BEEN IN BAYAN MANDAHU WITH DONG ZHIMING AND others from the IVPP since the middle of June. They had worked the old quarries in the Gate area first, finding four more turtles, a few more *Protoceratops* skulls, and an adult ankylosaur. On the flatland below the cliffs, Hou had found a nearly complete multituberculate mammal, about the size of a shrew, and he was extremely excited by it. Roy Chapman Andrews's expedition had found mammals in the Late Cretaceous Djadokhta Formation, across the border in Outer Mongolia, and comparing those with this new specimen would help to determine whether Bayan Mandahu was a southern extension of the Djadokhta.

By this time, the Dinosaur Project had turned up enough creatures in Bayan Mandahu to begin making comparisons with North American species, and accurate dating was becoming important. If two animals were from the same family, knowing which was older might help to determine where the family originated. But accurate dating is laboratory work, not field work, and even in the lab accuracy is a relative thing. By the argon-39/40 method, volcanic ash from the Judith River Formation in Montana — roughly equivalent in age to Dinosaur Provincial Park — had been dated at 78.2 to 78.5 million years before the present, with an error margin of plus or minus 0.2 million years. That is a 400,000-year gap, however, and evolutionary changes can take place in 400,000 years.

The best guess for the age of the Djadokhta Formation is that it is roughly equivalent to the Campanian in North America, a Late Cretaceous epoch stretching from 72 million years ago to 84 million years ago. Exactly where in the Campanian the Djadokhta is is not yet known. The Judith River Formation in Dinosaur Provincial Park, however, is Upper Campanian, so knowing whether the Djadokhta is early or late Campanian is crucial to determining whether look-alike dinosaurs traveled from Asia to North America or vice versa. But how to tell that? Not by the argon-39/40 method, because there are no known volcanic ash beds in Bayan Mandahu. Fortunately, there's another way.

It has to do with earth's magnetism. All rock contains minerals, and some minerals are magnetic; when they were laid down in the sediments, these magnetic particles aligned themselves

The skull of a varanid lizard, found in Bayan Mandahu. Although such tiny specimens are hard to spot, more than seventy were collected in this area, representing six families and two new genera. Varanid lizards are also known from Outer Mongolia and Montana's Judith River Formation.

in a north-south direction like the needles of a billion tiny compasses. In 1909, the French geophysicist Bernard Bruhnes discovered that in some volcanic rocks the north-seeking ends of magnetic minerals pointed toward the south, as if at one time the north pole had actually been in Antarctica. Two decades later, Motonari Matuyama, a young geophysicist from Japan, found the magnetic reversal occurring in the late Pliocene and early Pleistocene epochs, 2.4 to 0.7 million years ago — and he came to the somewhat startling conclusion that at that time in earth's history its magnetic field had in fact flipped around so that the positive and negative poles were reversed. Since then, other, deeper layers of magnetic reversals have shown up in the geologic record; it is now known that earth's north and south poles have reversed many times, causing magnetic particles in rock to point one way for several millions of years, and then the opposite way for another few-million-year period.

Using the spreading sea floor as a kind of horizontal chart, and taking the

Dave Eberth and Xiao Li coat a cliff face in Bayan Mandahu's North Canyon with white rubber latex: when peeled off, the latex will carry a layer of sand that will provide a record of the dune structure that formed the cliff 70 million years ago, which Dave will be able to study back home.

current orientation of "north" as "normal," geophysicists have established a magnetostratigraphic time scale of alternately "normal" and "reversed" periods of polarity, each lasting 2 to 15 million years and stretching all the way back to the Cretaceous. Give a geophysicist a series of rock samples taken forty-six centimeters apart from the bottom of a formation to the top, and he or she can tell you where the magnetic boundaries are and when the reversals took place; in other words, the approximate age of each sample.

Which is why Qiu Zhanxiang, the IVPP's senior mammalogist, and his Chinese colleagues at Bayan Mandahu could be seen carving small cubes of sandstone out of cliff faces and very, very carefully marking on them which side was up and which side was north. One great advantage that magnetostratigraphy has over other dating methods from a Chinese standpoint is that work done in North America is relevant to Asia; when those needles flipped, they flipped globally. "This is very useful," says Qiu. "The universal standard paleomagnetic scale has been established for the Cretaceous, but no one has ever checked it in China before." The Campanian, he says, is a special case; there was one long period of normality followed by rapid periods of normality and reversal. "Between 110 million and 80 million years ago, for example," says Qiu, "the paleomagnetic field was normal. Then there was a short reversal, then a short normal period, and so on." Now, 80 million years ago falls very neatly in the middle of the Campanian, so if the particles in Qiu's samples are reversed, he will know for certain that the rocks in Bayan Mandahu are late Campanian; if they are normal, there are still six chances out of eight that they're early Campanian. He and his assistants took three three-cubic-centimeter samples from each of fifteen horizons throughout the formation.

Qiu Zhanxiang himself was betting on normal because his gut feeling was that the mammals and lizards he and his crew were finding in Bayan Mandahu were more primitive than those Andrews and the later Polish expeditions had found in Outer Mongolia.

Looking for mammals and lizards is not like looking for dinosaurs. The scale is enormously reduced; an entire mammal skull can be hidden in a rock the size of a walnut. Mammalogists spend hours on their hands and knees scrutinizing less than a square meter of ground, trying to find something as hopelessly tiny as a shrew's toenail embedded in rock. Even their instruments are miniature. Where dinosaur specialists use dental picks, mammalogists use watchmakers' tools; Qiu's was the size of a darning needle, and it made Phil's awl look like a jackhammer.

On July 11, Qiu and his team of four spent all morning on the North Canyon floor, about a hundred meters down canyon from Phil's baby ankylosaur site, crawling over an area of concretionary sandstone about as big as a two-by-three-meter area rug. The temperature at head height was well over 48 degrees Celsius; at ground level, usually a few centimeters from their faces, the heat was all but unbearable. Hands and knees blistered first, then noses, then eyelids. At two in the afternoon, Qiu straightened his back painfully and said that he thought the site was exhausted. Just then Li Rong wandered over from the ankylosaur site, sat down on a rock to take a drink of water, looked between his feet and saw the upper and lower jaws of a varanid lizard gaping back up at him.

"Okay," said Qiu. "We'll give it another two hours."

Phil, meanwhile, was working on the baby ankylosaurs. Using shovels, a blunt pry bar and a gas-powered jackhammer, he and Mike Todor and Tang Zhilu had further opened the 1988 quarry. In two days they moved another five tonnes of overburden, all by hand, but when they got down to bone level there was nothing left but a few teeth and some broken phalanges. No more skulls. As they began to pack up at the end of the second day, feeling somewhat discouraged, Dong Zhiming came by and, squatting beside Phil, handed him what looked like a small, round piece of sandstone, about the size and shape of a Ping-Pong ball.

"A lizard egg?" said Phil.

Dong Zhiming shrugged. "Dangerous," he said. "The Russians call it *Gobipteryx*, a fossil bird they found in Outer Mongolia. I don't know. It may be a mammal egg, but I think it's a small theropod."

The next day Phil moved fifteen meters along the ridge to look for the sixth skull that Alan Bibby had found on the last day of the 1988 field season. At first he could not find it — two years of wind and rain had covered it over and removed the bright orange survey tape with which Alan had marked the spot. But after an hour of crawling over the dune face on his hands and knees, his eye was finally caught by a small white flash of bone against the red glaring sandstone. He began to uncover it with his awl and saw that it was a small, crushed ankylosaur skull. When he widened his trench he discovered a second skull, better preserved than the first. He called Mike over and got him working on the first while he exposed more of the second. While prodding around to the left of the first skull, Mike found a third, better preserved than any of the others. "It was a great afternoon," Phil wrote in his field book.

That night there was a feeling of elation in the camp. After a dinner of stir-fried green pepper, boiled mutton, and warm beer, everyone gathered in Dave Eberth and Mike's room to discuss the day's finds. They realized immediately that they had found a second *Pinacosaurus* grouping; the skulls were the same size as those in the first quarry, obviously juveniles, but in this case they were all more or less at the same level. Where the first five seemed to have been clambering over each other as if trying to crawl out of a hole filling up with sand, these three were lying horizontally, as if calmly accepting their collective fate. By the end of the week, four more specimens had been exposed, making a total of seven, six of which were lying almost uncannily parallel to one other. (The seventh was just a tail, the rest of the skeleton having eroded away, but it was on the same plane as the other six.)

Two groups of identical animals so close together increased the significance of each, raising speculations about a possible nesting or nurturing site. Where were the adults? Phil guessed that if a nest had been covered by a collapsed dune or sudden sandstorm, adults would have been strong enough to climb out. Having enough evidence to guess at the story behind a specimen is one of the purest pleasures in paleontology.

Dave Eberth studied the composition of the rock in which the ankylosaurs were found and determined that it was composed of fine to medium-sized grains that, unlike the layers above and below, lacked any obvious structure. This might be evidence that the sand that buried the seven juvenile ankylosaurs had been blown in, filling an area between two dunes, for example, and filling it in extremely quickly.

More interesting news came that afternoon. Mike Todor had been working for two days on a nest of eggs he had discovered high up on the cliff wall in the North Canyon: as he cleared away the overburden above the eggs, he discovered the skeleton of a dinosaur, about the size of a large cat, that seemed to be crouching over the nest. The site reminded Phil of the very similar find made by Roy Chapman Andrews at the Flaming Cliffs, in which Andrews had identified the eggs as *Protoceratops* and Osborn had named the crouching dinosaur, which seemed to have died while scavenging the eggs, *Oviraptor philoceratops*. Mike's find strengthened the links between Bayan Mandahu and the Flaming Cliffs, but it also raised an intriguing question. How likely was it, Phil wondered, that two *Oviraptors* had been caught in identical positions while raiding two *Protoceratops* nests? When he looked at Mike's quarry, the position of the skeleton made it seem much more likely that the theropod was protecting the eggs, crouching over them in a sandstorm, perhaps. Had *Oviraptor* been misnamed? Were these eggs not *Protoceratops* at all, but rather *Oviraptor*? The more he looked, the more certain Phil became that he was right.

That night Phil made a list of all the specimen sites in North Canyon, and it came to 103. Most of them were *Protoceratops*. Phil was convinced that Bayan Mandahu and the Djadokhta Formation were virtually identical in their environments. "There may be some discussion as to whether they're the same formation," he says, "but the evidence is strong that the environmental conditions were the same. The fauna are the same. Andrews found about one theropod for every sixty *Protoceratops*, and we're finding the same here. He found some sauropod material and we're finding only a few teeth. You can't get much closer."

Dave Eberth's job had been to determine what those environments were like, and on the last day of the field camp he took the entire crew on a walking tour of the localities and explained what they had been like during the Campanian. The whole area, he said, had been part of an alluvial fan, a wedge of sediment from the Lang Shan Mountains to the south. Below the Gate, the fan had been dominated by braided rivers; north of it, toward North Canyon, where dinosaurs were found in great abundance, the fan had met a dune field stretching off to the northwest, and the area had been primarily desert. At the Gate, which Dave called "No Man's Land," water absorbed by the alluvial fan resurfaced as ponds and oases among small dunes and sand flats. "I don't know why," he added, "but it seems to have been *Protoceratops* heaven."

Redbeds are red because the sediments have been oxidized and the iron-bearing minerals have rusted. Oxidation destroys organic material — "Oxidation is burning, after all" — but Dave believed the area had been relatively fertile. Areas of low vegetation tended to be associated with standing water, and there was little evidence of that at the Gate. "If you have standing water for a long time," Dave says, "you get gray clay lenses in the sandstone, and you don't get that here. Here, the water table was close to the surface — about thirty centimeters under it — and the animals we're finding were herbivorous. We know from modern examples that where an alluvial fan meets a dune field, ground water does come up and there is usually fairly lush growth."

Dale would love for all this to mean that Bayan Mandahu was earlier than Dinosaur Provincial Park — i.e., that the Djadokhta Formation predated the Judith River Formation — because that would help to account for the faunal differences between the two continents. If China was isolated during the Early Cretaceous and joined during the Late Cretaceous, it would be natural for the animals dispersing out of China and into North America to differ from the animals that had been evolving on their own in North America.

Phil, on the other hand, says it is enough that the two environments were so totally different: why should a semi-arid, desert-like alluvial area like Bayan

Dave Eberth (centre) gives Phil and Dale a lesson in paleogeology in Bayan Mandahu's Gate area, which he found to have been mostly wind-blown desert with groundwater surfacing in places as ponds and oases: "I don't know why," he says, "but it seems to have been *Protoceratops* heaven."

Mandahu have the same animals in it, he asks, as a subtropical estuarine region like Dinosaur Park? You do not find the same animals today in Inner Mongolia as you do on the east coast of India.

Erenhot was a different story. The dinosaurs there were very similar to those of Dinosaur Park, and yet the geologists with the Roy Chapman Andrews expedition had declared it to be a semi-arid basin very much like Bayan Mandahu. Why should that be so? Phil wondered. And as the Dinosaur Project left Bayan Mandahu for Linhe, where they would travel to Hohhot and then north to Erenhot, he looked forward to finding out.

Return to Erenhot

ON THE WAY TO LINHE THEY STOPPED TO SPEND A FEW HOURS PROSPECTING AN EARLY Cretaceous outcrop at Tebchi. The red sandstone hills were overlain by a crumbling layer of black volcanic basalt like dark icing on a ginger cake, and Dale and Dave gathered samples of it for dating back in Canada. Dale said he had never seen such red strata before, but an hour of prospecting turned up only fragmented bone. A fossil log was discovered, however — or possibly rediscovered, since fossil wood from this area had been mentioned in Sven Hedin's Sino-Swedish Expedition report in 1930. It was a beautiful piece of cycadophyte just over a meter long, looking like a gigantic pineapple and weighing nearly 150 kg. To collect it, one of the Chinese technicians took off his blue jeans and six of the crew used them as a sling to drag the log to the jeep.

They ate lunch at the cadre hotel in Urad Houqi, the local government town. After the meal, the Project members split up; Qiu and half a dozen of his IVPP colleagues headed for Tukumu in the Alashan; Dale, Clayton, and Kieran went with Zhao Xijin to Ongon Gol, an Early Cretaceous site worked by the American Museum expedition in 1928. Andrews's party had discovered what they thought was a sauropod, and Dale and Zhao were eager to have a look at it. Phil and the Tyrrell group were to continue on to Erenhot, traveling through to Linhe and Hohhot by jeep, then taking the Beijing-Moscow train to Erenhot. The three groups would meet up again in Beijing at the beginning of August.

The morning train to Erenhot was a string of ancient coaches pulled by one of the world's last remaining steam locomotives — China is the only country in the world still making them. The hard-seat cars, in which passengers sat on wooden benches if they were fortunate enough to sit at all, were full of Mongolians on their way to a nadam, a week-long sporting event that takes place once every five years in Inner Mongolia. The Tyrrell group, Peng Jianghua, and Li Rong shared a coach with a large group of Mongolian wrestlers until Jining, where a group of Communist Party cadres got off and the Dinosaur People were moved to the soft-seat car.

After Jining, the train swung north toward the Mongolian border. It pulled into the Erenhot station at seven-thirty that evening. As in 1988, accommodation proved to be the first hurdle. At the Erlian Hotel, the Canadians were given rooms on the ground floor. In the People's Republic, hotels improve from bottom to top; the higher floors, consisting of large suites of rooms with double beds, sofas, desks, and bathrooms that occasionally work, are reserved for high-ranking Party officials and army officers. The ground-floor rooms — two single beds to a room, sometimes with sheets, a single hard chair, and bathrooms that never work — are reserved for peasants and soldiers. These rooms had patched wallpaper walls, floors made of scraps of dirty blue linoleum, reading lamps placed about a meter and a half above the beds (for those who like to read standing up), and open transoms over the doors that admitted the stench from two public washrooms down the hall. Once again, a mild protest produced results; two days later, the Canadians were moved upstairs to join their Chinese colleagues.

The first item on Phil's agenda was to reopen the *Alectrosaurus* quarry that he and Paul Johnston had discovered on the last day of the 1988 field season. The angle at which the front end of the skeleton had gone into the level terrain had suggested to him that the skull might be lurking beneath the surface. On a visit to the Outer Mongolian Museum in Ulaan Baator in the fall of 1989, Phil had substantiated a claim made by two American paleontologists, Bryn Mader and Robert Bradley, that although the main part of the skeleton in the museum was definitely *Alectrosaurus*, the arms were those of a segnosaur. Other segnosaurian material in Moscow, found by the 1959 Sino-Soviet Expedition, enabled Phil to identify much of the scattered material the Dinosaur Project had found in 1988 as belonging to at least three species of segnosaur. But the *Alectrosaurus* remained a mystery; thought to be nearly complete, it was actually known by only a partial skeleton. There was a good chance that this quarry in Erenhot was the original one worked by Roy Chapman Andrews, and that the rest of the type specimen was still in it.

Alectrosaurus is a large, primitive tyrannosaurid, similar in size and shape to *Albertosaurus*. "If we want to understand the origins of *Tyrannosaurus rex*," says Phil, "we need to know more about *Alectrosaurus*." He compares the evolution of tyrannosaurids to a staircase, placing *Tyrannosaurus rex* on the top step, the Asian theropod *Tarbosaurus* next (so like a *Tyrannosaurus* the two genera might even be synonymous), followed by *Albertosaurus*, then an indeterminate number of blank steps, then *Alectrosaurus* two steps from the bottom. The very bottom step is *Aublysodon*, a Late Cretaceous theropod from Alberta "that we don't understand at all yet."

The *Alectrosaurus* quarry, however, proved to be disappointing. Two days' digging uncovered only a few meter-long ribs, two vertebrae, a shoulder blade, and

The scattered ribs of the theropod *Alectrosaurus*, from the beds near
Erenhot. *Alectrosaurus* had first been found in this area by Roy Chapman
Andrews, and Phil thought this might be the same quarry, enabling
him to complete the specimen now in the Outer Mongolian Museum.

some gastralia. Under the disarticulated remains, they found a flat, smooth bone
that they thought at first might be part of the skull, but which turned out to be the
plastron of a trionychid turtle. A few days later, a trionychid skull that differed
widely from any other that had been found in Asia was discovered a few hundred
meters from the plastron.

Dave Eberth, looking at the sedimentary history of the basin, determined that
the area had been one of fast-moving, intertwining streams, a braid-plain marked
by seasonal flooding, with the actual streams measuring up to three and a half
meters deep in places and changing positions as new channels were carved into
the soft sandy earth. "The positions of the streams were maintained for a fairly
long time," he says, "long enough to deposit three meters of channel sand, and
then there would come a shift." The result is a heterogeneous distribution of fossils; as the streams flooded their banks and spread out over their flood plains, they

would lift the carcasses of animals that had died on their banks, or farther upstream, and drop the bones here and there. "Exactly as in Dinosaur Park."

On July 24, Don Brinkman investigated a small scattering of eggshell to the west of the *Alectrosaurus* site, on the side of a small outcrop near the abandoned salt mine. The shell fragments were light gray and pockmarked, about the size of a fingernail, and seemed at first to have washed down from a higher level. But as he carefully picked away at them he realized that they were lying on the ground in four distinct piles. Gently brushing away the surface sand, he found that some of the shell shards were sticking upright out of the ground forming a series of small circles: the sheered-off tops of whole eggs. At lunch back at the hotel, he calmly announced to Phil that he had found four nests of eggs, and that he thought they might be theropod.

That afternoon, he, Phil, Li Rong, and Dong Zhiming crawled over the entire area and found five more clusters of eggs, enough evidence to convince Phil that they had stumbled on a huge nesting site, "definitely colonial," he said excitedly. Even if the eggs were not theropod, Erenhot was still the site of the only known egg colony in the world except for Jack Horner's *Troodon* egg site at Egg Mountain, Montana, and possibly the site of Devil's Coulee in Alberta. Horner's eggs are elongated, or egg-shaped, however, whereas these in Erenhot were almost perfectly round, more like the hadrosaur eggs from Devil's Coulee, only smaller. Round eggs had been found before — a quarry in Utah had yielded a single round egg, and the American Museum expedition had found a nest of possible ornithomimid eggs in Erenhot, on the other side of the lake, in 1925 — but this was by far the largest find, with the most nests. After a day of meticulous preparation, of inching down below the surface with awls and paintbrushes, they found that each nest contained up to a dozen perfectly preserved eggs spiraling down into the sand. Many of the eggs were still intact, but enough were broken to enable Phil and Dong Zhiming to determine that there were no embryos inside them.

"That's the curious thing about Asian eggs," Phil says. "At first, it was assumed that the eggs were sterile, because the shells were thin and low in calcium and no embryos were found in them. In Alberta, the eggs found toward the outside of the nest were crushed and had embryos, and those found toward the center of the nest were intact but empty."

A cluster of eggs from Erenhot, one of six nests in a single quarry that Phil believes was "definitely colonial." Such strong evidence for dinosaur congregation is rare: only one other nest colony is known in the world. These large, round eggs are believed to be ornithomimid.

Studies of modern bird-egg development have shown that as embryos develop inside the egg, they resorb calcium from the shell, so that by the time the chicks are ready to hatch the shells are thin and easily broken. Low calcium content in thin eggshell, then, is a sign of healthy hatchlings. Low calcium content in unhatched eggshell is a different matter. This suggests that the embryos developed normally for a time, resorbing some of the calcium from the shell, then died and rotted before hatching. When an egg drowns, water seeping through its porous shell combines with the sulfur contained in the embryonic material to form sulfuric acid, which dissolves away the embryo but leaves the shell intact. In areas of seasonal wetness, this process takes place during the wet season then halts when the dry weather comes, leaving the empty egg to dry out and remain intact long enough to fossilize. In areas of permanent wetness, the acid-eating process continues until there is no egg left at all.

Phil suspected that these eggs were ornithomimid, one of the Late Cretaceous theropods. If so, they represented another link with North American fauna, since the only other theropod nesting site known was the *Troodon* colony in Montana.

The Alashan

WHILE PHIL AND HIS CREW TIDIED THINGS UP IN ERENHOT, DALE AND THE National Museum team were touring another part of Inner Mongolia — the Alashan region northwest of the Ordos — with Zhao Xijin and half a dozen Chinese technicians. Usually hot and dry, the area around Chuanjin poured with rain for most of the week, and the scientists were able to spend only three days on outcrops. On July 20, they did collect from the Early Cretaceous redbeds near Zhangqi the proximal end of a sauropod humerus and pieces of a theropod fore-arm exposed by the rain. Two days later, Wang Haijin found a hadrosaur jaw in a bed of white sandstone grading upward into a layer of pink shale: a "point bar" deposit, originally a spit of sand extending out into a mud-bottomed river. They drove westward along the Xinjiang Trail, an ancient road that ran so close to the Outer Mongolian border that the Chinese military had placed it off limits to civil-ian traffic. Dale spent most of his time "doing geology," as he called it, from the back of his jeep, trying to correlate their route with that shown on American Museum maps from 1928, which indicated promising redbed exposures at Ongon Gol. In the evenings, with the aid of a protractor, he prepared a map of the champsosaur site in the Ordos for the benefit of those who would be going down later to collect the specimens.

By July 24, the rains were so persistent that the field trip was called off early, and after driving in a rather roundabout way back to Linhe to avoid the gumbo-clay roads and washed-out bridges, they boarded a train for Beijing, arriving near-ly a week before the team from Erenhot.

Beijing was a welcome change from the miseries of Chuanjin; even the Da Du had "glorious air conditioning," Dale wrote, and the dining room served club sandwiches and hamburgers "reminiscent of Western food." Dale worked at trans-ferring his road logs to a topographical map of the field sites in order to get a fix on where they had been and to pinpoint the locations where dinosaurs had been found. He also talked extensively with Zhao Xijin about the dinosaurs of Tibet, about which Zhao Xijin was preparing a paper.

He had finished his final leg of the Dinosaur Project. He was on his way home.

ON HIS LAST DAY IN ERENHOT, PHIL LEFT THE SMALL GROUP OF PROSPECTORS AT A location they had been calling New Lake — really a shallow catchment basin for rainwater — and walked by himself to the north, paralleling the Outer Mongolian border. It was a hot, sun-filled day, and he walked slowly for about three kilometers, passing the concrete foundations of several long-disappeared buildings and a sign that warned of armed border patrols. After half an hour he reached the spot he had been looking for, a low mound of rubble barely rising out of the green Gobi grassland. Strewn about the ground were dozens of glass insulators and rusted-out battery bodies, bits of metal, and piles of broken glass. Frogs croaked in stagnant pools littered with hoops of wire and bits of squared timbers. It was the site of the old telegraph station, once the main border crossing between Inner and Outer Mongolia.

Although this was the third time he had been here, Phil was still thrilled by the idea that he was walking in Andrews's footsteps, that he had first read a description of these hills when he was eleven years old and dreaming of becoming a paleontologist. The concrete foundations he passed on his way up the hill had been quarters for the Chinese soldiers during the long winter of 1921, but the buildings were gone. It was here that Andrews and his team had pitched their tents and made their most important discovery: the skeleton of a Cretaceous dinosaur, the first, they believed, to have been found in Asia north of Tibet. It was here that Walter Granger had spoken his famous words: "The stuff is here." And it was here that Phil and his colleagues in the Dinosaur Project had made their own contributions to the history of paleontology.

For a while, Phil kicked around in the debris. He found an old Mongolian coin dating from the beginning of the century, a beer bottle with "Made in the USA" embossed on its base, a remnant of earlier celebrations. He paced off the distance noted on Berkey's map to the exact location of Andrews's tents, "on the gravel plain above the telegraph station," and squinted west to the Tertiary exposures where, the geologists had noted, the "sediments are cross-bedded, and their structure seems to indicate that they were brought to their present position from the northwest rather than from the south."

After a while, the jeeps arrived with the rest of the Dinosaur Project crew — Don Brinkman, Dave Eberth, Mike Todor, Li Rong, Dong Zhiming, Peng Jianghua — as well as officials from the Erenhot Museum. Phil presented the officials with the coin he had found, and soon everyone was scouring the ground for artifacts, some whooping with excitement, others silent with wonder. For everyone present, this had been a special place.

CHAPTER 8

Epilogue
Don Brinkman's birthday and international cooperation

To study these little known areas, to reveal the history of their making, and interpret that history to the world of today; to learn what they can give in education, culture, and for human welfare — that is the exploration of the future.

Roy Chapman Andrews, *On the Trail of Ancient Man*, 1926.

DON BRINKMAN WAS THE LAST MEMBER OF THE DINOSAUR PROJECT LEFT IN Beijing on August 3, 1990. It was two days after his birthday. Dave Eberth, who had left the day before, had told Peng Jianghua, and he and his wife, Xiao Ma, had invited Don to their room at the agricultural college for dinner.

It was a hot, sultry night in Beijing, as usual, and Don decided to walk from the Da Du to the college. It was a pleasant hour's walk. The streets were alive with people and bicycles, but all was very quiet. Beijing is an extremely peaceful city, most of the time. Over the four years he had been with the Dinosaur Project, he had fallen in love with China. He studied its language, read its history, and respected its people. As he walked to Peng Jianghua's, he stopped at a small shop and bought four bamboo place mats as a gift for Xiao Ma, bartering with the owner in Chinese, and at the Friendship Hotel he bought six cans of Five Star beer to take as well. Then he crossed the street and passed through the gates of the agricultural college compound.

The college grounds were so filled with gardens that he felt he had stepped into the countryside. After the quiet of the street, the college seemed like a rural oasis. Students stood on stairways chatting, or walked in pairs along the garden paths. The air smelled of fresh earth and luxuriant growth, with a faint whiff of poultry in the background. Peng Jianghua and Xiao Ma's single room, which Don approached through a darkened grape arbor, was small but brightly lit and very neat. Like many Beijingers, Peng Jianghua and his wife owned a color television, but they also had a refrigerator and a microwave oven, two almost unbelievable luxuries. Peng Jianghua's salary at the IVPP was less than 100 yuan a month, about $20, but there were travel allowances and food bonuses, and as long as Xiao Ma was a student they paid no rent for the room. Yes, their names were still on the waiting list for an apartment in the city, they told Don, but the normal waiting period was two or three years.

Peng Jianghua poured beer and sweet Chinese wine while Xiao Ma served the meal: five cold plates followed by rice and whole cooked crabs. "They are less expensive this year," she told Don, "since the export markets have dried up. Tienanmen Square has been good for the Chinese people."

WHEN THE PROJECT RESUMED IN 1990 AFTER THE SETBACK CAUSED BY TIENANMEN Square, the Canadian and Chinese scientists were equally relieved. The IVPP needed Ex Terra's support. "We were short of money," Chang Meeman says with her usual candor. "The IVPP could never have mounted such a large-scale expedition alone, even into our own country, without the aid of Ex Terra." Neither could any single Canadian institution have afforded such an enterprise on its own. The cost of sending fifty scientists and technicians into the field — any field — for two months is staggering, and Ex Terra's ability to initiate, concentrate, and coordinate the necessary fiscal resources had resulted in a major contribution to international science.

"As every explorer knows," wrote Roy Chapman Andrews, "the effort and nerve strain involved in financing a large expedition far surpasses the difficulties of actual field work." Even so, in 1920, Andrews walked into J. Pierpont Morgan's library on Thirty-third Street in New York City, explained what he wanted to do in Asia, told him how much it would cost, and fifteen minutes later walked out with a check in his pocket. Those days are long gone. Over the five years of the Dinosaur Project, Ex Terra, the museums, the federal and provincial governments, the Donner Foundation, and Canadian Airlines contributed to the work of the scien-

Peng Jianghua and Don Brinkman work on a turtle specimen in Don's laboratory in the Royal Tyrrell Museum. Peng and other Chinese scientists make frequent trips to Canada to study Canadian dinosaur localities, collecting methods and preparation techniques.

tists in the field. Each year, apart from the cost of getting the Canadians to China and the Chinese to Canada, Ex Terra handed the IVPP a check for $100,000 — more than ¥400,000 to an organization whose normal annual research budget for each of its scientists is ¥600.

But the direct benefits of the Dinosaur Project to Chinese paleontology go well beyond the merely fiscal. On this, Chang Meeman is again typically frank. For her, the primary importance of the IVPP's association with the Project has been the opportunity it gave young Chinese students to work with seasoned Western scientists. "I should tell you the truth," she says. "My colleagues are not as strong as the Canadian scientists are. That was of course another reason I wanted to have this joint project, that our colleagues could learn from others. Probably some people will not be happy to hear me say that, but I must tell you what I think."

In January 1991, Qiu Zhanxiang became Chang Meeman's successor as director of the IVPP. A soft-spoken, intelligent man in his early sixties, with a quick, open smile and an aura of patience and wisdom, Qiu is extremely popular with the younger IVPP scientists, all of whom jostle for a chance to work with him. He began his career studying mammal biogeography during the Paleocene, became director of a group of eight IVPP mammal specialists known as the Neogene Group, and in 1989 was asked by Chang Meeman to shift his interest and leadership abilities to Mesozoic mammals. "He is an excellent scientist," says Chang Meeman.

"Having a long history can be a real burden," Qiu said one rainy afternoon in Linhe. "It means there has been time to develop some bad habits and harmful traditions. Like Confucianism, for example." Confucianism is the Doctrine of the

Mean, the concept that order — in the individual, the family, the state, and the universe — is the supreme good. The word for Confucianism in Chinese is *Ju*, which also means "weaklings," referring to specialists in the arts of ceremony, music, archery, charioteering, history, and mathematics, and since Confucianism was adopted as the state cult in 136 B.C. until it was officially set aside in 1911, all government officials in China were chosen on the basis of their knowledge of *Ju*. It is one of the many profound ironies of Chinese politics in this century that the chief tenet of the May Fourth Movement of 1919, the intellectual revolution that paved the way for Mao Zedong's triumphant declaration of the People's Republic thirty years later, was a rejection of Confucianism as the state doctrine in favor of reforms encouraging Western-style science and democracy — the same demands made by the students in Tienanmen Square in 1989.

Anti-Confucianism is thus a deliciously ambiguous position, since it can indicate sympathy with the pro-Maoist reformers of the 1930s and 1940s, the students of Tienanmen Square, and the Communist Party leaders who ordered them shot. "Confucianism has its good side," said Qiu. "It has taught us to be polite and kind — but it has also taught us to choose the Middle Way in all things, to always be passive, never to excel at anything. As a consequence, the Chinese are a very inefficient people. This must change. And I think it will change fastest with the help of outside influences."

During the Cultural Revolution — referred to in China as "the Ten Years" — a million people with "outside influences" were killed, 30 million more were tortured, humiliated, imprisoned, or transported to work camps, and uncounted thousands of students escaped the reign of terror by fleeing the country, ostensibly to attend foreign universities. Through execution, imprisonment, exile, and fear, the Cultural Revolution silenced an entire generation of Chinese intellectuals, creating a huge gap in its schools and scientific institutions. "We call them the Third Generation," said Qiu, "the generation of students lost during the Cultural Revolution. We have good students of the ages twenty-five to thirty, and good teachers in their fifties and early sixties, but we have no one in between, no one from thirty-five to fifty who can take over from us and train the younger generation. They are either more or less permanently living outside China, or else they were lost to us in some other way...."

This generation gap is particularly acute in the physical sciences, such as geology and biology and paleontology, in which direct, practical field experience is essential. Reading about rock formations in a textbook is no substitute for walking an outcrop; a photograph of an ankylosaur tooth will not go very far toward helping a student find one in the Gobi Desert. "The older generation is tired and ready to retire," Qiu said, "and the younger students do not have enough field experience to take our place."

The Dinosaur Project, he added, has helped to fill that gap; the opportunity it gave to young Chinese scientists to work in the field with seasoned scientists — both Canadian and Chinese — has gone a long way to making up for the loss of China's Third Generation.

WHAT HAS THE DINOSAUR PROJECT MEANT TO THE CANADIANS WHO PARTICIPATED in it? To all members of the Project, the personal rewards have been immeasurable. Phil Currie, who moved into the new Tyrrell Museum building in Drumheller the same year he first went to China with the Dinosaur Project, says he "had two dreams come true at the same time." He followed in the footsteps of his boyhood hero, Roy Chapman Andrews, and brought home specimens that were new to science — opening new windows in that dark building of paleontology. And unlike Andrews, he established personal links with Chinese scientists that will long outlast the more tangible treasures of the Project. There is also the sheer excitement of discovery that never leaves the true scientist. For Phil, one of the greatest thrills in paleontology "is in taking off that last layer of sandstone, seeing the bones of a creature that died a hundred million years ago, and knowing that you are the first human being to lay eyes on them." When that creature turns out to be an entirely unknown specimen, the thrill is even greater.

For Dale, who had studied dinosaurs on every continent except Asia, the Dinosaur Project provided him with first-hand knowledge of Chinese paleontology and geology, which he can now fit into an overall picture of the planet as it was 100 million years ago. Like Phil, Dale sees the Dinosaur Project as a continuation of the work done by the American Museum expeditions of the 1920s. "We had the opportunity," he says, "to chart the Cretaceous history of Asia, just as the American Museum team charted the Cenozoic. Other groups have helped — the Sino-Soviet

Expedition, the Polish-Mongolian Expedition — but we have the ability now to
pull it all together."

Dale, too, shares the sense of wonder that comes with penetrating the
mystery of time. "When you examine
the fossil record," he says, "the tremendous distance in time is just blown
away. Just think: We are the world's first
sentient beings since the dinosaurs; we
can hold a piece of bone in our hands
and, looking back 75 million years, say,
'I think I understand....'"

For the other members of the
Dinosaur Project, the rewards have been
equally great. The chance to go to Asia
provided Dave Eberth, for example, with
an appreciation of the physical dimensions of science. "When I was at gradu-

Darren Tanke preparing the skull of a
Pachyrhinosaurus, **one of the most comon
ceratopsians found in Dinosaur Provincial
Park. Skeletons have also been found seven
hundred kilometers north of Edmonton
and on Alaska's North Slope: their graves
could mark a dinosaur migration route.**

ate school," he says, "it was pretty much taken for granted that all the major discoveries had been made, all the big theories about dinosaur evolution had been
postulated, and all that was left was to fill in the blanks, to add little pieces of evidence that would support or question the major hypotheses. Then, when China
opened up to me," he continues, "it was suddenly all there to be done. A whole
new field of investigation, untouched, untrammeled, unknown. It was just like
Alberta and Montana must have been to paleontologists a hundred years ago."

And finally, what has the Dinosaur Project contributed to science? Over the
five years that the Project was in the field, hundreds of new specimens were collected. These fall into four main categories of scientific discovery: new specimens
of known animals; new parts of partially known animals; known animals found
in new areas; and entirely new animals.

Most of the finds belonged to the first category: animals already known to
paleontologists. By far the most common dinosaur collected during the five-year

program was *Protoceratops*. Discovered by the American Museum Expedition in the early 1920s, it was known by specimens that were all from the same locality (the Flaming Cliffs in Outer Mongolia). The Dinosaur Project added nearly two hundred new specimens of *Protoceratops* — and one new species — all from sites in Inner Mongolia, providing an almost complete record of growth from hatchling to adult (minus embryo) and extending the animals' range over a much wider territory. Such data, when prepared in the laboratories of the three institutions and analyzed over the next few years by the top paleontologists of two continents, will be of inestimable value in determining the relationship of *Protoceratops* to its environment and its place in dinosaurian evolution.

The second category — new parts of incompletely known dinosaurs — is of obvious importance to those working in dinosaur anatomy. Few dinosaurs are known to science from complete skeletons; many are known by only a few bones. *Troodon formosus*, for example, the first small theropod known to science, was named after the discovery of a single tooth in 1856. Dale Russell's ground-breaking paper on *Stenonychosaurus*, published in 1969 after he discovered a new skeleton in the Oldman Formation in southern Alberta, was a major stepping stone in Phil Currie's eventual synonymization of *Troodon, Stenonychosaurus*, and possibly *Saurornithoides*. Dale's discovery consisted of the back of a skull, a few ribs and gastralia, and "appendicular elements" scattered over a few square meters of sediments. Not until he and Clayton uncovered the specimen Dale and Dong Zhiming have tentatively named *Sinornithoides* from the redbeds of the Ordos Basin has there been a virtually complete troodontid skeleton to work with. Charles Darwin complained of the paucity of the fossil record when it came to supplying evidence for his theories on evolution; the Dinosaur Project has done more to fill in the blanks than any other expedition in paleontological history. Other important pieces of the Troodontidae puzzle contributed by members of the Dinosaur Project include the *Troodon* braincase found by Tang Zhilu in Dinosaur Provincial Park in 1986 and the *Saurornithoides* hind foot and fibula found by Hou in Bayan Mandahu.

The two pinacosaur "nests" discovered in the North Canyon at Bayan Mandahu also fill out our knowledge of a known species. Their contribution to new theories of dinosaur behavior is extremely important; we now have a better idea of how the large herbivores lived. It is likely that they traveled in herds, that they nur-

A resin model of the troodontid *Sinornithoides*, created on the basis
of the specimen found in the Ordos Basin. Small, swift predators, the
troodontids were probably warm-blooded and highly intelligent, and
aspects of their anatomies suggest strong affinities with modern birds.

tured their young in nests — or at least that the young stayed together after they
hatched — and we know something about the kind of environment they preferred.

One of the most sensational finds of the Project also falls into this category:
the partial *Mamenchisaurus* skull that was finally discovered at the end of the
sauropod quarry in Xinjiang. Although the genus *Mamenchisaurus* was almost
completely known from other parts of China, the absence of a skull was a serious
handicap when scientists tried to relate the animal to other sauropods in Asia and
North America. With the jaw fragments and teeth from Xinjiang, lines of descent
can now be drawn with some confidence, and more is known about the early evolution of the huge long-necked dinosaurs and their world than ever before.

The third category, that of known animals found in new places, has made it
possible to work out the movement and diversity of dinosaurs and other animals
during the Jurassic and Cretaceous periods. Again, finding *Mamenchisaurus* in

Xinjiang improves our knowledge of sauropod dispersal and diversity. Evidence of hadrosaurs on Bylot Island in the Canadian Arctic, for example, has corroborated guesses Dale and Phil had been making about the mass migration of other types of dinosaurs from the lush grasslands in the south to summer feeding grounds in the north and helped to substantiate the suggestions of many paleontologists that dinosaurs traveled in huge herds. Similarly, the discovery of theropod footprints in Grand Cache, Alberta, identical to those found earlier in the Peace River Valley of British Columbia, and possibly to those found by Li Rong in the Ordos Basin, have extended our knowledge of dinosaur movements.

It is now possible to say that nearly every family of North American Late Cretaceous dinosaurs is also found in Asia. The troodontids of Alberta are very nearly identical to those from Erenhot; both Alberta and Bayan Mandahu have ankylosaurs that differ in size and bone structure, but that are remarkably similar; both Dinosaur Park and Iren Dabasu have segnosaurs. And a type of small varanid lizard found in Bayan Mandahu for the first time in 1990 was previously known only in the Judith River Formation. These correlations and many others are now possible because of finds made by the Dinosaur Project.

Finally, the Dinosaur Project has contributed at least sixteen entirely new species to the very small list of Mesozoic animals previously known to science. Some of the more significant finds include the two new Jurassic theropods from Xinjiang, one tentatively called *Jiangjunmiaosaurus* (its official name is now *Monolophosaurus dongi*, which means "single ridged lizard found by Dong Zhiming") and the other referred to simply as the Jiangjunmiao theropod, whose official name is now *Sinraptor dongi*. A new species of *Avimimus* from Erenhot will tell much about the relationship of that little-known theropod to its more familiar cousins. And there are two new genera of lizards — one each of the Iguanidae and Agaminidae families; two species of turtles — *Sinemys gamera* and *Ordosemys leios* — and an entirely new species of trionychid turtle based on the beautiful skull found in Erenhot. That specimen, says Don, has a "fundamentally different construction from other trionychids in the way the stresses were distributed throughout the skull," suggesting that the animal had adapted to different food — possibly small dinosaur eggs — from other turtles of the same family. Whether or not it is a new species depends on the age of the bed in which it was found; its features seem primitive, but the animal may have retained primitive characteristics into the Late Cretaceous. There have also been new species of stegosaurs, psittacosaurs, segnosaurs, protoceratops, lizards, crocodiles, champsosaurs, mammals, and trace fossils.

The Dinosaur Project has provided new evidence for almost every new theory of dinosaur anatomy and behavior except extinction (there are no Cretaceous-Tertiary boundary sites in northern China). As the traveling exhibition of the major Dinosaur Project finds will show, theories of dinosaur herding, migration, dispersal, and locomotion, and the ancient links between Asia and North America, will be either substantiated or debunked with evidence turned up by the Dinosaur Project scientists.

THE THIRD AND FINAL PHASE OF THE TIPI-YURT EXCHANGE TOOK PLACE AT HEAD-Smashed-in-Buffalo Jump, in southern Alberta, during the third week of July 1990, almost three years after the first ceremony was held in the Tien Shan Mountains of Xinjiang. Ex Terra brought four people to Alberta from Xinjiang and four from Inner Mongolia — including Kazakh elder Erdowlet Slabek, physicist Teng Tingkang, Wang Shoulian from Academia Sinica, and ethnologist Jige Jide. There they presented two furnished yurts to Ex Terra and to the Elders Council of the six tribes of the Blackfoot Nation — the Northern and Southern Peigan, the Blackfoot, the Blood, the Stoney, and the Sarcee. A small tipi camp had been set up in the Old Man River Valley for their annual powwow. There were native dances, horse races, a rodeo, and traditional feather and hand games. The event, according to the *Lethbridge Herald*, "symbolically links the indigenous people of Asia and North America."

Ten days later, in Beijing, Xiao Ma presented Don Brinkman with a chocolate birthday cake. She had never made a cake before and had to ask other members of the Dinosaur Project what it was and how it was made. There were candles on it, and "Happy Birthday, Don" written in white icing across the top. Peng Jianghua and Xiao Ma sang "Happy Birthday to You" as they set the cake down on the table. The three friends ate pieces of cake and drank cups of green tea together. Afterward, they watched the English newscast on television, which comes on every night at ten o'clock. Nothing else that had happened that day seemed important.

ILLUSTRATION SOURCES

From the collection of the Ex Terra Foundation:

Brenda Belokrinicev: *pages 5 (top right), 17 (right), 170; color section II, page 1 (top).*

R. L. Christie: *page 35.*

Stephen Godfrey: *page 138.*

Brian Noble: *pages vi (middle), viii (middle and bottom), 4, 9 (right), 26, 91, 106, 110, 144 (left), 147, 149, 153, 154, 158; color section I, pages 1 (bottom left and right), 2, 3, 4; color section II, page 1 (middle left).*

Photographer unknown: *pages 71, 74.*

Mike Todor: *pages vi (bottom), viii (top), 5 (bottom right), 9 (left), 17 (left), 31, 119, 137, 144 (right), 155, 177, 182, 183, 192, 194, 197, 198, 206, 208, 215, 216, 221, 222, 226, 228, 231, 237, 240, 242, 248, 251; color section II, pages 1 (bottom left and right), 2-3, 4 (top right and bottom); color section III, pages 1, 3, 4 (top).*

Linda Strong-Watson: *pages 189, 253.*

The publishers gratefully acknowledge the following for permission to reprint their photographs.

Alan Bibby: *pages 88, 93, 109.*

American Museum of Natural History, Department Library Services: *pages 68 (Neg. No. 411044, Shackelford), 73 (Neg. No. 410952, Shackelford), 125 (Neg. No. 410748, Shackelford).*

Canadian Museum of Nature, Ottawa, Canada: *pages 48, 51.*

E. H. Colbert: *page 47.*

Wayne Grady: *pages 232; color section III, page 2 (bottom), 4 (bottom).*

Mark Hallett: *page 139: "Dawn at the Rookery," © 1993 Mark Hallett, all rights reserved.*

J.B. Tyrrell Papers, Thomas Fisher Rare Book Library, University of Toronto: *page 52.*

Clayton C. Kennedy/Canadian Museum of Nature: *pages vi (top), 87, 98, 112, 173.*

Vladimir Krb: *color section II, page 4 (top left), detail.*

Kate Kunz/courtesy of Greey de Pencier Books: *page 121.*

Royal Tyrrell Museum/Alberta Community Development: *pages 5 (left), 19, 49, 132.*

Smithsonian Institution: *page 44 (Photo No. 856814).*

Tom Walker: *page 127.*

Cliff Wallis: *page 14; color section I, page 1 (top).*

INDEX

Page references in italics represent illustrations

This book was designed by Peter Enneson under the creative direction of James Ireland, set into type by Peter Enneson for James Ireland Design Inc., Toronto, and printed and bound by D. W. Freisen, Altona, Manitoba.

The text face is Scala, designed by Martin Majoor and issued by FontShop International, Berlin, in 1991. Captions, chapter headings, and running heads are set in Frutiger, designed by Adrian Frutiger in 1975 and originally issued by Mergenthaler. Frutiger was issued in digital form by Adobe Systems Inc.

Maps by James Loates

Line drawing of *Tyrannosaurus rex* by Linda Strong-Watson; all other line drawings by Stephen Godfrey

Dinosaur means "terrible lizard," and the Chinese word for dinosaur, *kong long,* means "monstrous dragon." One of the most monstrous was *Velociraptor,* a man-sized carnivore with slashing claws on its hind feet. *Velociraptor* lived in Asia about 80 million years ago and was remarkably similar to its North American relatives.